To Pretty Wyrrell – Great Warren
You are a lovely lady –

"Rudy's Time was our Time"
And Now

"My Time is Your Time"

Goo Bless!

Eleanor Vallée

My Vagabond Lover

My Vagabond Lover

An Intimate Biography of Rudy Vallée

Eleanor Vallée
with Jill Amadio

TAYLOR PUBLISHING COMPANY
Dallas, Texas

Published by Taylor Publishing Company
        1550 West Mockingbird Lane
        Dallas, Texas 75235

Library of Congress Cataloging-in-Publication Data

Vallée, Eleanor.
    My vagabond lover : an intimate biography of Rudy Vallée / Eleanor
Vallée, with Jill Amadio.
        p.   cm.
    ISBN 0-87833-918-3
    1. Vallée, Rudy, 1901–   . 2. Singers—United States—Biography.
I. Amadio, Jill. II. Title.
ML419.V2V35   1996
782.42164'092—dc20
    [B]   96-2899
                                                              CIP
                                                              MN

Printed in the United States of America

10   9   8   7   6   5   4   3   2   1

This book has been printed on acid-free recycled paper.

RUDY

He led the parade when the streets were unpaved,
And brought the embryos out of their cells;
He taught them and paced them, instructed and placed them—
This man of the "Heigh-ho!" yells.

His time was your time all through the years,
And his Westbrook dreams came true;
His Connecticut Yanks deserve a million thanks
For the pleasures they gave me and you.

This saxophone king of the "Wiedoeft" days
Made radio a lasting and living art
With the song of the stein, from Broadway to Hollywood's Vine,
He sang to America with all of his heart.

When history tells the saga of music on the air
These words will appear on the cover:
"Here is the story of the greatest of the greats,
The inimitable Vallée, the Vagabond Lover."

DAVID RANDOLPH MILSTEN

$\mathcal{C}$ontents

Acknowledgments

I wish to thank the many friends and families who have generously given of their time and reminiscences for this biography.

Special gratitude goes to Stella Atkinson, Frank Bresee, my sister Betty Bruce and her husband Gil, Michael Bruce, Paul Caruso, Phyllis Diller, Alice Faye, Valerie Florman, Marilyn and Alex Grasshoff, Chris Harris, Paul Henning, Vic Hyde, Dr. Marvin Jensen, Mary and Bill Keller, Pat Karch, Elaine and Jack LaLanne, David Randolph Milsten, my stepmother Irene Norris, Norm and Rose Ostrowski, Bert Pratt, Buddy Rogers, Paul Ross, Jane Russell, Walter Scharf, Joy Claussen Scully, Helen Steward, Bill Vallée, and Jonathan Winters.

I also thank Jill Amadio, my friend and collaborator; and Brad Miller, librarian in charge of Special Collections, and Martin Getzler, the archivist for the Rudy Vallée Collection, at the Thousand Oaks Library, Thousand Oaks, California, who spent many hours helping with our research.

I would also like to thank my dearest friend and helpmate Byron Clark for his unwavering support and utmost encouragement.

Introduction

Rudy Vallée, one of the greatest names in the history of broadcasting, was my husband.

In this intimate biography devoted to telling you of our life together, I am realizing a dream I've had since the day he died: to pay tribute to a radio pioneer, Broadway star, musician, and world famous singer and to honor my husband, lover, friend, and companion.

Although this book does not attempt to cover the entire complex life and career of Rudy Vallée, my tale reveals the private life we shared.

Rudy loved people, parties, and performing. Some say he was not an easy person to know, and many did not take the time to understand him.

In my opinion he was too often judged superficially; within these pages I am making the effort to dispel many of the myths associated with Rudy's character.

My husband's entire life centered around entertaining people. Whether it was in a 25,000-seat hall or to an audience of two or three, Rudy could never resist being "on stage." Driven by a healthy ego that he attributed to a God-given talent, Rudy continued singing, playing the sax, and performing skits well into his eighties and giving free performances at hospitals, orphanages, senior centers, and civic clubs. His sense of value was payment enough.

Our home, Silver Tip, in the Hollywood hills, was arranged for the pleasure not only of ourselves but of others, from all walks of life. We held parties at our pool and tennis court, put on plays and screened movies in our little private theater, and maintained an open-door hospitality policy for friends, family, and even strangers who stayed with us, sometimes sharing our home for weeks at a time.

My role was that of a traditional wife who gave up any thoughts of career to be with her man. I make no apology for accepting this role. Rudy was my full-time career and I never wanted to change a moment of it. Once I had fallen in love with him, I put all thoughts of a separate career behind me. I adored Rudy and everyone knew it. I admit perhaps I am old-fashioned. I wanted to be with my husband at all times, and I never tried to change him—not that anyone ever could. I felt it a duty, a loving duty, to conform to his lifestyle. This isn't armchair philosophy on my part. I made my life over to suit his, and I haven't a single regret.

"Ellie was Rudy's angel, sent down from heaven to take care of him," was one of the beautiful thoughts expressed by our housekeeper, Fumi Ito, who spent five years with us in Hollywood. "No matter how many times she listened to his jokes, she would laugh as if it were the first time she's ever heard them."

It was easy to laugh when you were with Rudy. He was witty, kind, generous, fair-minded, highly principled, intelligent, and very, very loving. Was he perfect? Of course not. He had a temper. He was compulsive. He was opinionated. But he didn't have a mean bone in his body. He helped dozens of stars on their way to the top, and so many people when they were in need.

Rudy and I were a unit. While we both kept our individuality, we were life partners. I miss my Vagabond Lover.

Eleanor Vallée
Los Angeles, 1996

A Look at
a Legend

"You were a vision of Venus walking out of the water. I wanted you immediately."

As my dying husband, slumped in his wheelchair, whispered those words, the memories flooded back again: Rudy and me in Hollywood, New York, Paris, London, on film sets, in nightclubs, jumping in and out of limousines, rushing past the paparazzi, appearing on Broadway, radio, television . . . and the summer alpine coldness of the water of Lake Tahoe where it all began.

When I stepped onto the sand after a swim at King's Beach that hot Fourth of July weekend and into the whirlwind life of Rudy Vallée, he was already a legend. He had become a show business success long before I was born.

"Without a doubt Rudy Vallée was the Elvis Presley, the Glenn Miller, the Frank Sinatra, and the Michael Jackson of the 1930s all rolled into one," was the candid opinion of composer Walter Scharf in his 1995 memoir. The *Boston Globe* once called my husband "the most important name in American entertainment."

But as a young girl in my early teens when our paths first crossed at Lake Tahoe, I knew nothing of Rudy Vallée. I was completely ignorant of this man whose name had blazed over Broadway, sparkled in lights worldwide, starred in forty-four movies, and changed the sound of radio forever. My idol was current movie heartthrob Ronald Reagan, and my friends and I jived to the hot brass of Stan Kenton's band. Rudy Vallée? Never heard of him.

As I came to know later, Rudy's sensational fame as an orchestra leader, singer, actor, songwriter, film star, comedian, impresario, and host of the most successful radio show in the country was unequaled. He was America's original entertainment megastar. Rudy Vallée, I learned, was the first coast-to-coast live radio broadcaster, the top recording artist for ten solid years, and the first to "chat" with a radio audience. His broadcasts heralded the arrival of the Golden Age of Radio.

"He's so different!" marveled the men. "He's so sexy," gushed the women. Being the hard-working and enthusiastic trouper he was, it's no surprise his show business career spanned seven decades. He even formed his own music publishing company, affiliated with ASCAP. Rudy's first two records were "A Dream" and "Nola," for Columbia in 1921. Rudy made his final recordings in 1973, narrating Grimm's fairy tales.

Along with popularizing the style of singing that came to be known as "crooning," Rudy Vallée pioneered broadcasts of variety radio shows that glued men and women to their boxy, wooden radio sets every Thursday night at 8:00 P.M. With the help of J. Walter Thompson Advertising Agency executives who represented Rudy's sponsor, Fleischmann's Yeast, Rudy left the simple radio shows of the era in the dust.

Instead of a violin solo, an operatic star, cooking recipes, and poems typified early radio shows, Rudy spiced up the airwaves with comedians Milton Berle, Red Skelton, Eddie Cantor, George Burns, and Gracie Allen. Cantor is reported as saying his career began in earnest on Rudy's show. Other guests included Tallulah Bankhead, George Gershwin, Boris Karloff, Peter Lorre, Ethel Merman, Sophie Tucker, Ethel Waters, and Fay Wray. The format for "The

Fleischmann Hour" which is how the Rudy Vallée Hour was billed, was a live variety revue. Rudy's guests were a mixture of the famous and the unknown.

When radio was in its infancy, Rudy was the first to invite black musicians to guest on his show and in appreciation, Josephine Baker, Louis Armstrong, and other African-American entertainers invited Rudy to their clubs in Harlem. After Rudy and I were married, he took me to Harlem frequently and was still remembered and loved there. During those early years, few of these superstars had yet made a name for themselves, but many gained instant fame after appearing on Rudy's radio show.

"I can spot talent," Rudy told me years later. "I've discovered many stars who have gone on to become huge successes. But among my blunders was turning down three young women called The Andrews Sisters, and believing that Barbra Streisand had no chance."

One person Rudy believed in was Kirk Douglas. Rudy met him through a friend when Kirk was a struggling young actor in New York. Rudy found a spot for him on his radio show, where Kirk did a scene called "The But and the Button" about a man in prison whose only diversion is a button.

As his fame grew, Rudy was occasionally invited to lecture on the psychology of musical talent. At one point he wrote to Professor Carl Seashore at the University of Iowa, describing an idea to travel throughout the country "weeding out children with talent from those who have it not." Another of Rudy's ideas was to run a talent agency when he retired, to help young performers get ahead in their careers. I don't know when he meant to fit this work in because he refused to retire and was seeking out bookings until the day he died.

Trailblazing broadcasts on radio, he strove for something different. Rudy originated radio theater by presenting scenes from Broadway shows with the original cast members, comedy sketches, and patter. When he suggested having then little-known ventriloquist Edgar Bergen as a guest, Rudy's producers thought he was crazy. How could listeners relate to an unseen dummy? Rudy insisted, and Bergen became a smash hit on the show.

Soon the Rudy Vallée programs became the benchmark for every celebrity-hosted radio and television show that followed, including Bing Crosby's and Ed Sullivan's. Standard Brands signed Rudy to an unprecedented ten-year contract for a show that completely dominated the airwaves.

Always careful not to upstage his own guests, Rudy often played the straight man to visiting comedians. But it was the romantic, intimate way Rudy sang a song—softly, caressingly, without histrionics—that accounted for the mesmerizing effect he had on his audiences. Music critics pointed out that Rudy controlled his voice by not straining for notes out of his natural vocal range and sang better than anyone else the difficult musical trick of rubato, dwelling on certain phrases longer than others, alternately lagging behind and then catching up with the accompaniment. He was also praised for his accuracy of tone: true to pitch, not even a half-tone off.

From February 6, 1928, millions of people tuned in to the weekly Rudy Vallée radio show. Thousands wrote fan letters every day, forming one of the first-ever fan clubs. One lady in Ohio was so devoted to his show, reported *The New York Times*, she shot her jealous husband with his own rifle when he tried to turn the radio off.

Men, too, admired the singer. Norman Ostrowski, a Detroit autoworker back in 1930, became Rudy's most loyal fan, following his idol by bus, train, and tram as Rudy entertained at concerts, nightclubs, shows, and eventually as a star on Broadway. "When Rudy performed with his band each night at New York's Paramount Theater, mounted police had to hold back the crowds," Norman said proudly.

Tales of Rudy's talents, life, and loves appeared almost daily in the newspaper columns of Earl Wilson, Hedda Hopper, Louella Parsons, Walter Winchell, Ed Sullivan, and other top entertainment writers of the day. So many stories were printed about him, Rudy eventually filled 251 huge scrapbooks with clippings.

His biggest regret was that none of the networks ever offered to broadcast a "special" on him as they did for Bing Crosby, who Rudy first introduced to New York audiences at the Paramount Theater, and many others Rudy helped make their way to stardom.

Sadly, my husband was unable to comprehend why he received so little recognition for many of his "firsts." A case in point is the haunting song "As Time Goes By." Widely recognized as the theme song from the classic movie *Casablanca*, the composition caught Rudy's attention when he was at a baseball game. He was seated next to Herman Huppfield, who wrote it and asked Rudy if he thought it was any good. Rudy fell in love with the melody and lyrics and recorded it in 1930 for RCA Victor, thirteen years before the film was made. But by the time *Casablanca* debuted, Jack Warner owned the song. Several different artists recorded "As Time Goes By," and its revival made it a bestseller on the music charts, but it seems that no one remembers that Rudy recorded it first. It really infuriated him, and he never failed to complain about it to anyone who'd listen. Sometimes he'd get so angry I'd have to walk away.

But I shared that hurt as well as many other disappointments. I understood his moods, especially when he flailed away at people he believed—sometimes mistakenly—had wronged him.

I never stopped loving Rudy Vallée. To this day I carry in my heart an unswerving devotion to my controversial, world-famous husband. I shared a tumultuous life with him that few women will ever have the good fortune to experience.

Yes, I knew of his mistresses and girlfriends before we were married. I knew he'd had affairs with dozens of glamorous stars, had bedded exotic dancers and beauty queens, and had earned a reputation as one of America's most insatiable womanizers—before we met. After he died I read the diaries in which he wrote about his relationships with friends and lovers like Ginger Rogers, Hedy Lamarr, Dorothy Lamour, and over a hundred other women.

Looking back, I now realize our successful life together was remarkable. With three short-lived, marriages to beautiful, talented women behind him, what chance would anyone have given a teenager like me? The truth is, no one knew the real Rudy Vallée as I knew him.

Ronald Reagan called him "an American institution." The National Museum of American History described Rudy as "a major figure during this century . . . with international influence." The public saw a sophisticated, confident, practiced performer, a fair-haired, blue-eyed, all-American college boy who swept across the musical landscape of America, conquering women's hearts and thrilling audiences. Fellow entertainers, agents, and colleagues saw the perfectionist, the workaholic, the disciplinarian.

But only I knew of his insecurities when he had business failures and rejections, and only I shared his heartache. I wiped away his tears when critics attacked his performances in later years, and I sprang to his defense against those who insulted him or called him a pennypincher. It's true that Rudy was reported as "something of a tightwad" and typecast as having a parsimonious personality. This was a myth. In fact his charitable gestures were a well-kept secret. He gave hundreds of free benefit shows, donating his time and talents to philanthropic causes. It's true he often carried his own baggage in and out of airports and hotels, but that was his preference. He didn't begrudge the tip, he simply preferred to handle his bags himself.

As a celebrity, Rudy was also concerned about being "taken for a ride," as he called it. Hundreds of people were after a piece of his action, always trying to sell him something, get him to invest in a business deal, or ask for a loan. It was a natural reaction for him to view such offerings with suspicion, yet all his life he was naive, gullible, and trusting.

When it came to helping others, Rudy believed generosity to be strictly a private matter in order to avoid embarrassing the recipient. Rudy rarely spoke of the musicians and performers he helped when they could no longer work due to illness or hard times. He kept Vic Hyde, Ed Howell, Mannie Lowy, and many other ailing musicians on his payroll, some until they died. Rudy wrote to his pianist Cliff Burwell, stricken with an illness, that he would send him a weekly salary. "If you need more at any time, let me know," his letter said.

A movie director Rudy helped financially in his later, nonworking years was Preston Sturges, who directed Rudy in his best film role, in *The Palm Beach Story*.

Rudy once paid for someone's funeral he barely knew; his friend, attorney Paul Caruso, told me the story. Cyril Smith, an ex-British Marine captain and vaudevillian, hung out with Cully Richards, who was seeing movie star Ann Sheridan. When Cyril died penniless, Rudy footed the bill for his burial. Musical director Walter Scharf wasn't surprised. "Rudy supported plenty of people when they got sick, and he paid us double the money other orchestra leaders paid their musicians back in the early 1930s. At his peak, Rudy carried forty-one people in his company, which was unheard of at that time. He had twenty-eight musicians and thirteen entertainers," Walter told me. "Rudy may have been frugal about some things, but salary wasn't one of them."

Walter was hired by Rudy after Alice Faye recommended him; he was Helen Morgan's accompanist at the Embassy Club at that time. Walter, who said he reached the top of the tree with Rudy, had proposed marriage to Betty King, Alice Faye's stand-in. When Alice's movie offers increased, she moved permanently to Hollywood and Betty went too. At that point, Walter followed his fiancée to Los Angeles, accepting an offer from Warner Brothers to join their film music department. Walter went on to become one of the most renowned film composers in Hollywood, and I often lunch with him and Betty at his yacht club.

Rudy's incredible career was chronicled all over the world in his heyday, and his later tussles with everyone from presidents on down are matters of record, yet to me he was the most caring, kind, and romantic lover of all time. Nothing will ever dim the passion I still feel for him.

A few people think Rudy Vallée's life became a Greek tragedy. They perceive a fatal flaw in his personality that they claim led to his own destruction in middle age and destroyed his place in history. To them he turned into a bitter, bad-tempered man who swore like a trooper and wrote shockingly crude and critical letters whenever he felt an injustice was being perpetrated—a far cry from the cultured young Yalie whose love songs thrilled a nation. They said his ego was too big, his attitude arrogant.

To me, and to his real friends and fans, Rudy was always an

articulate man of high principles, integrity, and honesty who felt a desperate need to set the world right as he saw it. He saw everything in black and white, unflinchingly presenting an opinion or piece of advice. It galled him when neither was appreciated.

Rudy could be tactless, blunt, and outspoken. He fired off furious letters to newspaper editors and politicians all over the country if he disagreed with them. With an intense interest in a wide range of subjects from animal rights to semantics, Rudy kept up a correspondence with all manner of people. And he never forgot a slight.

In 1961, just before he starred in *How to Succeed in Business without Really Trying*, a Broadway musical satire about executive life, Rudy admitted to New York columnist Hy Gardner that he held a grudge against NBC. "I'm bitter about NBC's Artists Bureau selling me down the river to RKO for a picture in 1929. They really gave me a royal double-crossing," Rudy told Hy about the thirty-year-old incident.

TWO

Falling in Love

A chance encounter in my early teens changed not just my life dramatically but Rudy's as well. In retrospect, I realize I played Galatea to his Pygmalion. On our fourth wedding anniversary Rudy told me, "I've looked for my ideal woman all my life. She must have class, brains, beauty, vitality, and a wonderful heart. And you are that person."

Indeed, I was. Young, impressionable, eager to learn, I embraced Rudy's attitudes and lifestyle, from the passionate way he wanted me to make love to him to the slinky satin dresses and four-inch heels I wore. I did indeed become the lifelong companion and lover he had long sought. It took a few years to fully understand how to cope with this complex, secretly insecure man I married. But my strong family background stood me in good stead and I resolved from the first day of our marriage we would have a true partnership.

My youthful vivaciousness matched his dynamic energy, and he liked the fact I'd attended both the University of California at Berkeley and the University of Nevada, where I studied psychology and drama. Both disciplines were to prove crucial in my life with Rudy Vallée.

Rudy credited the driving ambition that took him to stardom in his twenties for his lifelong self-sufficiency. He was proud of the fact he'd reached the top on his own, and he expected others to show the same idealism. When he learned that human nature gave more motivation to some and less to others, he became frustrated and no longer trusted other people to carry out his requests.

On the other hand, I was an impetuous, carefree young Californian who practically lived at the country club and the swimming pool. Outside of school, I rarely took time to schedule anything. At the drop of a hat I'd go to a party, play tennis, shop, watch a movie, or visit friends. I experienced no anger growing up, neither at home nor among my friends and dates. I lived, I suppose, an idyllic life.

Born in San Francisco and raised in the East Bay area, I was spending the summer vacation with my parents and friends at a Lake Tahoe cottage. King's Beach, with its backdrop of towering pine trees, was my favorite spot.

On Friday of that holiday weekend I took a morning swim with my neighbor's nine-year-old son, Buddy. We were frolicking in the frigid but calm water not far from shore and I was well aware that the new white satin two-piece bathing suit I wore clung to my figure. "Hey, Eleanor," whispered Buddy, dog-paddling as he bent his head towards me, "who's that guy behind you? He's been staring at you forever."

Turning lazily onto my back I glanced towards the other side of the lake as if searching for sailboats. A few yards to my left was a man who looked to be at least thirty years old—middle-aged to me— swimming in circles. He caught my eye and smiled.

I immediately flipped onto my stomach and swam hastily away, Buddy trailing along behind me. "Probably a new summer tenant," I said to Buddy as he swam alongside. "I've never seen him before."

I looked back and watched the man swim to shore and join two other men, whom I later knew as Charlie Wick and Jack Bates. Charlie was a pianist from Cleveland, Ohio, who lived at Rudy's home for a while. Charlie studied law and eventually became head of the U.S. Information Service in Europe. Later, he was a member of President Reagan's Cabinet.

Men thought I looked a lot older than I was. I was tall for my age, almost 5-foot-8, and my body had matured early. Although I modeled as a size eight for I. Magnin and other department stores in San Francisco and at the Claremont Hotel in Berkeley, I was neither skinny nor flat-chested. I had curves. The attention was flattering and I had learned how to handle men like this persistent swimmer.

"Let's go in. I'm hungry," said young Buddy.

"Right. Race you to the beach." Reaching the shore first, I walked onto the sand, only to find myself face to face with the stranger.

"May I invite you to dinner tonight at the Cal-Neva Club?" he asked, his blue eyes twinkling and his manner polite. My, he really was handsome. Athletic looking too. Still, even though he had a boyish charm, I thought perhaps he was too old for me.

"I really don't go out with strangers," I said, tossing my long red hair, "but thank you."

"Have you ever been to Hollywood?"

"Yes," I said. As a child I'd watched Alice Faye, a friend of my family's, and other stars on film sets. At one point I'd had a screen test myself as a five year old when my father worked in Los Angeles, but before my career could begin, my father became co-owner of the Hotel Alameda near San Francisco, and we moved back north.

"Some day I want to entertain you in Hollywood."

"Thank you." I left him standing there but I could feel his gaze on my figure as I walked away.

Well, I thought, at least he had the good taste to invite me to the best place in Lake Tahoe, where everyone summering at the lake could be found most evenings.

Located literally on the California-Nevada border, Cal-Neva's main dining room floor was painted with a wide black band running across it, indicating the actual state line. Gambling was allowed only on the Nevada side of the stripe.

"Mother, I met a man from Hollywood on the beach today. He wanted to take me to dinner," I said arriving home.

"You mustn't talk to people like that, Eleanor. You stay away from those Hollywood characters."

"But he seemed very nice."

"No, Eleanor. Please be very careful."

Intrigued with this attractive man whose charm and charisma somehow drew me to him, I made a point of going back to King's Beach a couple of hours later on my bicycle to see if he was still there. He was sitting with friends but jumped up when he spotted me. Approaching hesitantly, he looked at me so admiringly I couldn't help smiling at him.

"Have you changed your mind about dinner?"

"No," I replied. "Thank you for the invitation but I'm having dinner with my parents tonight. My father is down for the holiday weekend."

"Could I ask your name?"

"Eleanor."

"And may I ask where you live?" asked Rudy.

"Berkeley."

"Would you tell me your father's name?" My father's name? Why would he want to know that?

"Harlie Norris."

"Next time you come down to Hollywood, I'd like you to be my guest at Don the Beachcomber. It's one of my favorite restaurants."

"I'll have to ask my parents," I said followed by a quick goodbye. I jumped back on my bicycle and rode off. Rudy later told me that he was too apprehensive to tell me his name in case I said, "So what? I've never heard of you!"

This was a clue to Rudy's character, although I didn't realize it at the time. Onstage he was completely self-confident. Offstage he was bashful and sensitive. He was hesitant to introduce himself by name because he didn't want to be hurt.

My parents planned to go to the Cal-Neva Club after we had dinner at an Italian restaurant that same evening, so off we went, taking Buddy along with us. Because of my age, I wasn't allowed to gamble. While my mother and father spent time in the casino, Buddy and I ran over to the nightclub. We knew a place backstage where we could peek through the heavy curtains to watch the show.

"If you see that Hollywood character," I told Buddy, "tell me so I can hide. Mother says I must stay away from people like that."

In the meantime, Rudy told me later, he scoured Cal-Neva's dining room and casino, then drove down to the movie theater, over to the bowling alley, and to another small club called Cal-Vada, searching for me and hoping he wouldn't find me in someone's arms.

As Rudy related it, he finally caught sight of me behind the curtains. As a paying guest, Rudy had no plans to perform that night, but he begged the club manager to let him sing so I would realize he was a bona fide entertainer and not just some jerk I'd met on the beach.

"I even offered to sing for free, which is unprecedented for me because I only do that for friends and for charity!" he said.

As Buddy and I watched through the curtains, a man sang some romantic love songs, but because he had his back to me and was wearing a white Coast Guard uniform I didn't recognize him. Soon after, my parents came along to collect Buddy and me and we went home to bed.

The next morning, Rudy later told me, he rushed out to King's Beach hoping to see me again, but it was a cloudy day and I had stayed home.

I thought nothing more of the incident with the stranger at the beach. It would soon be time to go back to school. We returned to Berkeley. Three weeks later I was swimming at the Orinda Country Club when my mother called. "Come home quickly, Eleanor! There's a letter here for you from Rudy Vallée! Oh, I'm so excited I can't breathe!" she said.

"Who?"

"Rudy Vallée, Eleanor. Rudy Vallée!"

"I've never heard of him," I said. "Why would he be writing to me?"

"I don't know, dear, but he's so famous. He's a big star. Please come home now, I can't stand the suspense! "

Mother was at the front door when I got home. "Here's the letter, Eleanor! Open it! Open it!"

I studied the handwriting with interest. Written in the bold, tall, distinctive script Rudy developed in first grade and never changed, the letter was addressed to Miss Norris. Pinned to the back of the envelope was something I'd never seen before: two inches of copper wire shaped to form the name RUDY.

"How on earth did this get through the mail?"

"For Heaven's sake, Eleanor, stop admiring the pin and tell me what's going on!"

The short note read: "My dear Miss Norris, I hope to come up your way in the next two weeks. May I have the pleasure of entertaining you and your father and mother at Omar Kayyam for dinner some evening, and dancing at the Mark Hopkins Hotel? I would appreciate a reply from you and a snapshot of yourself if you have one. Sincerely, Rudy Vallée."

"I have no idea what this is all about, Mother. What does he look like? I may have met him somewhere but that name doesn't ring a bell."

My mother, one of the most elegant women in Berkeley, leafed quickly through her glossy fashion magazines. Nothing. I found one of my sister's movie magazines.

"There, Eleanor. That's him. That's Rudy Vallée!" I peered at the photo with curiosity. He was wearing old-fashioned pince-nez perched on the end of his nose.

"That looks something like the man I met at King's Beach. That's the Hollywood character you warned me against."

My mother's mouth fell open.

"I don't want to meet him. He doesn't look so handsome now," I said. The guy on the beach was so gorgeous, how could it be the same person?

"We can't turn down an invitation from Rudy Vallée, Eleanor. It's such an honor. Give me the phone. I'm going to accept."

My mother called the number in Rudy's letter and left a message.

He showed up at our house with a limo. I sat in front with Rudy and the chauffeur in my bouffant dress.

After dinner, Rudy took us to the Mark Hopkins' supper club. Guiding me expertly around the floor, his arm firmly in the small of my back, Rudy pressed me to him. There was no doubt about it. I felt intense sexual vibrations passing between us like electric pulses. I was now highly attracted to him.

"Look at that girl to your right, in the tight, black satin," Rudy said softly into my ear, nudging me out of my daydream. "One day you'll wear a dress just like it for me." I glanced over and admired the woman's slinky, form-fitting gown, but I was more worried about my fingernails. Like many teenagers, I picked them.

"You can't go to dinner with Rudy Vallée with those terrible nails," my sister Betty said earlier at home as I was getting dressed.

"But I've just polished them," I said.

"I'm going to run to the store and get you some false ones."

"I'm not putting on any cheap fakes from the five-and-dime store." Mother, one of the most elegant and style-conscious women in town, had taught me to cherish quality.

"No one will know. You've got to do something." So Betty bought the nails and glued them over my ragged ones. Unused to such long talons and afraid one would pop off onto my dinner plate or into Rudy's hand as we danced, I spent most of the evening protecting my hands.

As we said our goodbyes, Rudy spoke to my mother.

"I'd like to invite you to see my show tomorrow night. All of you. How about it?"

Mother's eyes lit up, "We'd love to."

The next evening I eagerly waited to hear Rudy sing. When the band started playing my parents looked at each other fondly. Then mother turned to me.

"Eleanor, that song is called 'My Time Is Your Time.' It's the Rudy Vallée signature tune."

I watched the self-assured man in the blue tuxedo with satin lapels walk briskly onto the stage as the audience broke into noisy applause. He looked even more handsome than last night. My heart started to flutter, and again I experienced a thrill running through me. I decided I was definitely interested in this man, even though he was a lot older than anyone I'd dated.

Rudy's eyes searched the room, obviously looking for our table. When he spotted us he raised a hand in salute as he started to sing.

Suddenly shy, I hid my face behind my Dad's broad back, then I nudged my mother. I was still unsure of the great interest my parents showed in him.

"What's so special about Rudy Vallée, anyway?" As I peeked at him from behind my father's shoulder, Rudy gave me a broad smile. "Who is he?"

"Only the heartthrob of the century, that's who," said my dad, laughing. "Only the guy who was the biggest name in radio, America's first crooner, that's who."

"But I've never heard of him!"

"Well, he was before your time, honey," said Mother. "The whole country used to stop everything they were doing every Thursday night to listen to his radio show back in the thirties. As soon as the first bars of that song came over the airwaves, I always got goose bumps." Mother sighed.

"He used to have the most well-known orchestra in the country, too," said Dad. "First it was called the Yale Collegians, because he went to Yale, then the Connecticut Yankees, and finally the Rudy Vallée Orchestra. He was a fabulous success. After conquering New York, he went to Hollywood and made movies."

"He's a Yalie?" I asked, my interest piqued. I was wondering if he'd played football for Yale because I had a crush on a linebacker at Berkeley.

"Sure. He's the guy who made the raccoon coat famous at those college games. He led the college band there," said my mother. "My oh my! Rudy Vallée. This is one of the greatest thrills of my life."

I still couldn't understand what all the fuss was about, but I knew I wanted to spend more time getting to know him.

A few days later, Rudy called and once more asked us out to dinner and, this time, to the theater. Aunt Kate was visiting, and he invited her along, too. My aunt and mother were godmothers to the Gale quadruplets, June, Jean, Jane, and Joan, who were in show business. June married composer and pianist Oscar Levant; another quadruplet married Barry Wood, who was with the top radio show, "Hit Parade"; and another married Lou Shreiber of 20th Century Fox. The Gales were really two sets of twins; they appeared in *George White's Scandals* and other musicals.

This time Rudy had tickets to the comedy *Harvey*, in which he played the lead.

After dinner at Trader Vic's, Rudy said to my father, "Harlie, why not let Eleanor drive back with me in my car?"

I tried to signal to my father to say no. For some reason I was scared to be alone with Rudy, and up until then, except when we were on the dance floor, my parents were around the whole time.

"Sure, Rudy, fine with us," said my father, ignoring my frantic eye-rolling. Rudy so charmed my parents they couldn't refuse him anything. I reluctantly climbed into the back seat of the limousine with Rudy, who immediately took me in his arms and tried to kiss me. Afraid of the new emotions that suddenly enveloped me, I fought him off.

"No! No!"

He released me instantly. I could see he was furious but, gentleman that he was, he got out of the car and called over to my parents as they were beginning to drive off.

"I think Eleanor had better go with you after all," he said, sending me home in disgrace. He was upset because he'd spent so much time with me and was not rewarded with so much as a kiss. That was a first for Rudy! I heard no more for several months. Finally, Rudy began writing again. We exchanged a few letters and phone calls. Then he invited me for a visit to his home in Hollywood.

"He's nearly as old as I am!" My father's face was purple with indignation.

"Dad, he looks so much younger."

"Maybe he does but he was born in 1901, the very same year Queen Victoria died." Those words gave me pause. My, talking about Queen Victoria made Rudy sound pretty ancient.

"Calm down, Harlie," said my mother. "You know very well Rudy's a very nice man. As far as I'm concerned he's a real gentleman. There's no reason Eleanor and Roberta can't visit him." My Kappa Alpha Theta sorority sister, Robbie Whitney, had invited me to Los Angeles for a visit, and Rudy learned of it when he called to talk to my mother. "Stop fussing and listen to the news," mother went on. "I want to see what Tom Dewey has to say about Harry Truman beating him out for the presidency yesterday."

By the time I met Rudy, he'd divorced three wives after brief marriages, loved being around the opposite sex, and always had a girl on his arm.

Yet at forty-seven years old, this suave charmer began his first full-length letter to me formally: "Dear Miss Norris . . . " and in stilted prose asked me for a photo of myself. The note, on pale blue paper, was short and to the point. I was invited to visit Rudy in Los Angeles, take a tour of the various film studios, dine at his home off Mulholland Drive, and dance at the Cocoanut Grove, where he was performing.

"There's no reason not to accept his offer to spend the day together. Roberta will be with her," my mother said in that firm tone she used to indicate further argument was useless. I took a train to Los Angeles, and Rudy met me at the station and drove me to Silver Tip, where he proudly gave me the grand tour of his Spanish-style "castle," as he called it. When we reached the bedroom, he wasted no time in throwing me on the bed and lavishing me with hot, sensual kisses.

Silver Tip was named after a small pine tree with a white tip growing just below the patio. The mountaintop property off Mulholland Drive in the Hollywood Hills housed a music room; a theater with a stage at one end and a projection area at the other; a game room with a twenty-foot bar, four pool tables, slot and pinball machines, shelves filled with memorabilia, and two picture galleries lined on both sides with hundreds of framed photos of Rudy with friends, celebrities, and businesspeople; six bedrooms; several baths; and servants quarters.

Brought up near metropolitan San Francisco and having worked as a model, I was prepared for a lavish lifestyle. But I gasped when I first saw the fortress-like stucco walls and soaring red tile roofs of Rudy's estate. The surprise started at the bottom of the driveway when we passed through the tall stone pillars and gatehouse that marked the entrance.

Already wide eyed at the huge mansions I'd seen on our drive along Sunset Boulevard, I was tongue-tied when we got to the top of the small mountain where Rudy's immense main house, painted pink, pierced the sky. A separate lower building measuring thirty thousand square feet held a rooftop tennis court, a pool, a spa, a theater, and a playroom.

The hill up the mountain was so steep and the driveway so narrow a turntable was installed so that cars could be turned around for the trip back down.

At 1,500 feet above sea level the 360-degree view from Rudy's courtyard was breathtaking.

"On a clear day," said Rudy, "you can see the island of Catalina twenty-five miles offshore. At night, with the entire city of Los Angeles spread at your feet, millions of lights twinkle like a distant fairyland."

As my host guided me through the heavy, carved oak front doors with Spanish-style iron grilles, he pushed the doorbell. Chimes tinkled out the tune "My Time Is Your Time." Rudy chuckled.

"Your mother knows that tune, but you probably don't," he said. "Do you like my house? What do you think? Is it how you imagined me living? Do you like the furniture? Isn't this fireplace wonderful?" Rudy peppered me with questions, seeking my approval.

Inside Silver Tip, the crimson tile floors and Spanish tiled dining table, the spiral stairs, the circular terraces that could accommodate entire orchestras, and the glamour and opulence of it all so stunned me I could only nod in disbelief.

The pleasure he took in showing me the oak-beamed sunken living room, the secret staircase that led to a private sun porch, and the formal dining room that seated twenty, was that of a happy child. This quality of Rudy's—to enjoy his fame with a sense of wonder, joy, and innocence—was one that endeared him to me throughout his life. Although he may have taken his stardom for granted as a result of what he called his natural-born talent, Rudy never failed to appreciate the celebrity status it brought him, as if it were a surprise, a gift.

"There is nothing worse than a gifted person being acutely aware that he possesses this gift," Rudy said, "because it means we must strive to fulfill its potential."

Although he was not shy about touting his own talents and scolded those he believed wasted theirs, my husband always tried to help others achieve their dreams if he believed they were destined to become a great star.

Rudy had an uncanny knack for foreseeing success, whether it was a new restaurant, a play, a singer, or a comedian. The first time he heard Bing Crosby sing, Rudy remarked: "I am the first of the legends but that's the guy who's going to topple me off my throne." Bing was singing with the Paul Whiteman band at the time, but Rudy was the bigger name. Later, of course, Rudy's prediction came true.

As we continued our tour of Silver Tip, I admired the immense glass-domed rotunda; the long, completely stocked bar, and the two small dressing rooms behind Rudy's private, 150-seat theater in a separate lower building. Little did I imagine I was to perform on its stage myself one day in Bernard Slade's *Tribute*, and other plays.

Rudy even had a *"Christmas Room,"* which was decorated with large red wall panels filled with Christmas cards from show business pals. In the lower building's cellars, called "B Deck," over one hundred feet of wine racks stacked with bottles from all over the world stretched out. Dozens of cabinets held shellac records of bands and artists of by-gone days, including every recording Rudy made from

1922. "I was paid fifty dollars for each saxophone solo back then," Rudy remarked, leading me up to the rooftop tennis court.

"Can you believe the Hardings played tennis on top of a wooden surface covered in canvas before I moved in?" Rudy exclaimed. "I had the court resurfaced, of course."

I particularly liked a tall grandfather clock in Rudy's living room. Today, the beautiful old timepiece stands in my living room, along with many of my husband's favorite pieces of furniture he brought back from England, France, and Italy.

Rudy showed me the master bedroom, which he called the Princess Suite, with its seven foot square bed, then we went out to the pool and tennis court.

He bought the home in 1941 from silent screen star Ann Harding, who had it built in 1930. When Rudy died and I decided to sell my Silver Tip I received a wonderful letter from her daughter, Grace, asking if she could revisit her childhood home one more time.

"Is the original turnstile still there in the driveway?" she wrote, "Also the tennis court where so many of the greats used to play on a Sunday morning? I have vowed never to return to former homes, and never will to our beautiful Connecticut Estate, but somehow this home, I would like to see once again . . . Sincerely, Grace Kaye (Harding)."

Rudy was so proud of the home, he printed up maps and full-color brochures describing Silver Tip's amenities to give to friends. He took people on tours at the drop of a hat. Even after we were married and in residence, I'd sometimes find Rudy showing visitors around while I was still in my bathrobe. As I left Silver Tip that first time, on our way to the Whitney's home, I never dreamed I would one day be its mistress.

For the next two summers when he was performing in the San Francisco area, Rudy invited my family to dinner or a show. It was just casual dating because he was always traveling, but I hoped our relationship would become more serious. It did. Our first significant date was during the time I was pinned to Ted Gramko, a really good-looking college boy I met when we were both students at the

University of Nevada. Coincidentally, he belonged to Rudy's fraternity, Sigma Alpha Epsilon.

Ted had taken a job as a construction worker in Guam during the summer vacation, with the intention of making enough money for us to get married. To me, being pinned wasn't really *serious*-serious, we were so young, and I certainly had not led Ted to believe I would marry him. However, I soon learned that he felt differently.

It was a few weeks before Easter. Rudy called my parents early one morning to ask if I could go to Marin County to play tennis with him, then go out to dinner.

"We don't allow Eleanor to drive across the Bay Bridge by herself," Mother told Rudy.

"I'll meet her there, in my car."

So I got my tennis gear together and a little blue dress to change into later and jumped in the family Buick convertible. Rudy met me at the car ferry and drove my car across the bridge and to the club, where we played a few sets of tennis. He favored a big wooden racquet that he wielded with both hands.

A southpaw, Rudy was ambidextrous on the tennis court, using his left hand for backhands and his right for forehands. Rudy's sister, Kay, noticed his versatility when she tried to teach him the piano, "but he played backwards," she said. "The melody with the left hand, and the accompaniment with his right!"

After the tennis game, we changed our clothes and Rudy took me to some friends in Mill Valley for cocktails.

As I walked into the home of Parker Pen Company's Carl Priest and his beautiful wife Nan, I felt very shy. Although they were very kind and welcomed me, the guests were older than I expected and I could see they were business tycoons; one man, Henry Fennenbock, owned most of the concessions at Disneyland, and he and the others spent the entire time discussing marketing and sales. I didn't understand a word they were saying.

Even worse, the zipper on the back of my dress broke apart from top to bottom. I could feel its metal teeth slowly separating one by one all the way to my waist as I bent to sit down. Seeing how uncomfortable I looked, Nan came over.

"My zipper's come apart," I whispered, red-faced. She took me into her bedroom and sewed me into the dress.

Rudy and I thanked our hosts and left for dinner at the St. Francis Hotel in San Francisco. As we were sitting in the lobby afterwards, I looked up and saw a very angry Ted standing at the reception desk, glaring at me.

"Rudy, there's Ted, the boy I'm supposed to be engaged to," I said, mystified at his sudden appearance. "He's back from Guam!"

"You'd better go over and talk to him," Rudy suggested quietly.

Ted, looking tanned and gorgeous, lashed right into me: "Why weren't you at the airport tonight to meet me? I sent you a wire!"

"I never got it." Of course I didn't. I'd been with Rudy all day.

"And what are you doing with this guy?"

"He's a friend of mine."

"You're coming with me. I'm going to drive you home. I'm calling your parents right now and tell them so."

"Okay, calm down. I'll tell Rudy."

"Make sure you do. Meet me in the bar in half an hour," said Ted, now a little calmer.

I went back to Rudy.

"You don't have to drive back with me across the Bay Bridge, Ted's taking me. I have to say goodnight to you and meet Ted in the bar." I didn't want to leave Rudy, of course, but here was Ted, all the way from Guam.

"Fine." Rudy was the perfect gentleman. "Let's go down and get your car so we can park it in front of the hotel ready to go."

As we walked into the parking structure, Rudy grabbed my arm, wheeled me around and kissed me. And kissed me. And kissed me.

I came unglued.

"Oh my God," I whispered. I couldn't believe it. Rudy's sexual energy was so passionate it was like electricity. I always suspected such strong feelings existed but I was stunned by their intensity and stood there trembling.

"That was fantastic!" I said, catching my breath. Rudy held me tight. This was the first time he had really kissed me, and we were hot. Rudy now knew how much I desired him. Trying to play it cool, Rudy said goodnight and went upstairs to his hotel room.

I walked in to the St. Francis lobby and found the bar. This was the first time I had ever entered a bar alone. I felt so naive. I looked around. Oh, no, there's no Ted. Where was he? What should I do? I decided to go outside, jump into the car, and head for home.

I must have had an angel on my shoulder because not only did I not know how to get to the Bay Bridge, I didn't know what to do about paying the toll. Yet I drove unerringly in the right direction and managed just fine. All the way back I knew my parents would have a fit when they found out I drove alone across the bridge.

As I approached my driveway, around 3:00 A.M., the whole house was ablaze, lights on in every room. Ted had called my Dad from San Francisco, saying he couldn't find me and didn't know where I was. My father was a complete wreck. But everyone was so happy to see me, they all went crazy; and I was forgiven. Then Ted called. He was still in San Francisco. Dad advised him to take the last train home to Berkeley, where we picked him up. Two days later I gave Ted back his pin. I felt terrible about the situation, but I couldn't get Rudy's kiss out of my mind.

My third serious date with Rudy was in Palm Springs, and that's where I fell in love.

My father invited his secretary, Marge, to spend Easter vacation with mother and me to cheer her up because her husband had just died.

"Where would you like to go?" Dad asked at breakfast a few days before the holiday.

"Palm Springs," I said. I'd never been there, and it sounded like a fun place.

"That's a terrific idea," said my mother. "Maybe Rudy can get us some passes for the racquet club." The Charlie Farrell Racquet Club was the most exclusive club in Palm Springs with stiff restrictions on guest passes.

I wrote to Rudy that the family would be spending Easter in Palm Springs, although my father ended up not being able to get away. Rudy suggested we stop in Los Angeles and have dinner, then see his show at the Cocoanut Grove. We were thrilled.

Most of the women at the Cococanut Grove were in satins and sequins. I wore my new outfit, a demure navy-and-white linen sailor suit with a short, pleated skirt, and a white Panama straw hat with a blue ribbon and turned-up brim.

As we sat watching, Mother and I were distracted by a loud conversation at the table behind us between a florid-faced man and a flashy-looking brunette in a sexy dress.

"Betty Sue, if you can get Rudy to New York, I'll make sure he marries you." The speaker, I later discovered, was an agent friend of Rudy's, and the girl was Betty Sue Otto, who handled some clerical work for Rudy.

"Mother," I said, horrified, "did you hear that?" If this was one of Rudy's girlfriends, I thought, what must he think of me in my little sailor suit? Mother and I were shocked at what we'd just heard. We didn't say anything to Rudy at the time but after we began dating I asked him about Betty Sue Otto.

"She's a lovely girl and takes care of my scrapbooks. She's just a loyal friend," he said. I let it go.

As Rudy began his performance, I sat there enthralled. He told me later that when he saw me in my cute Easter outfit and the smile on my face, he decided there and then to spend Easter in Palm Springs too. During our entire Easter vacation, Rudy entertained Mother, Marge, and me almost every evening. During the afternoons—he never rose till noon—we played tennis.

Early one morning, however, there was a knock at our door. I was sunbathing at the swimming pool. Expecting no friends, I'd washed my hair and tied it up into strips of fabric we called "rags" to curl the ends. You tied the rag into a knot and let the ends dangle down. The result wasn't pretty but it did the trick.

As Rudy walked out to the pool with mother, I jumped up and dashed inside. I could hear his laughter follow me in. Rudy had come to invite us to dinner and asked if he could take me to a nightclub afterward.

My mother was reluctant to allow me out without a chaperone because I was still so young. But she finally agreed—if I was home by midnight. I was tremendously excited and felt very grown-up even though my protective parents imposed a curfew.

That evening at the nightclub, Rudy and I danced so close you couldn't fit a single sheet of paper between us.

We got back to my hotel around 11:30 P.M., but Rudy had yet another request. He asked Mother if I could go swimming with him.

"Now? No, I don't think that's a good idea," she said.

"Aw, Nell, it should be OK," Marge said. "Just for an hour." I didn't wait to hear any more. I dashed madly inside and changed into my black bikini.

As we splashed in the warm water under a new moon slicing through the deep black of the starlit sky, Rudy slid his arms around me. His sensual lips brushed my wet cheek, then covered my mouth. The urgency of Rudy's emotions was as insistent as ever. It was our second real kiss and sent shudders of desire through me. It was even more compelling than our first in San Francisco.

"I'd better take you home," he said. We were both shaking with desire. As I put on my white terry-cloth robe, I looked at my watch.

"Oh Rudy, Mother'll kill me. It's 2:00 A.M.!" We scrambled into his Chrysler station wagon and set out for my hotel. As we pulled up to the entrance, mother passed us in our Buick convertible on her way to bring me home. She came back, parked, and approached us, obviously apprehensive.

"Mrs. Norris, have no fear," Rudy said in his most soothing voice. "I have brought your daughter back to you in exactly the same condition you gave her to me earlier this evening." Relief washed over her face, and all three of us broke into laughter.

As I lay in bed that night, thinking about this man whose

romantic singing made women swoon when I was just an infant, I knew he would be my first lover.

Throughout the next few weeks Rudy continued to court me with all the gallantry of a true gentleman. He showered me with bouquets of red roses, amusing love notes, champagne, and pages of sheet music where he altered the words to fit our relationship. Although I refused to allow anything further than heavy petting—I was determined to remain a virgin until my wedding night—there was no denying we were both consumed with passion for each other and Rudy, in particular, had a difficult time concealing it. Sophisticated, debonair, and dignified in public, he was a seething mass of sexuality in private.

"We could get married right now! Today!" he'd plead. "I can't stand it. I want to wrap your flame-red hair around my chest, feel your long, slender legs under mine. Oh God, Eleanor, you have such a sensuous body. Everything about you is perfect. Let's elope."

He loved to touch, to feel, to explore with his slim, manicured fingers and that searching mouth. His caresses set me on fire, but I was committed to remain chaste.

Since I was ten years old my dream of a storybook wedding was to wear a pearl-encrusted satin gown with a long train, have a traditional marriage ceremony at Corpus Christi Catholic Church in Piedmont, a huge reception at the Orinda Country Club with hundreds of guests, and admire my father in a black silk top hat. Elope? Never!

I was, and still am, a romantic. My scrapbooks are overflowing with treasured mementos of my childhood: festive birthday cards, gilt-edged invitations to parties and dances, Christmas photos with family and friends. Even the dried and pressed pink orchids from my senior prom corsage still crackle on those pages.

I wanted a wedding with all the bells and whistles. The honeymoon, too, was on my mind. I couldn't wait to get into bed with Rudy, and I wanted it to be exciting and glamorous at a beautiful resort. My heart was set on spending a lengthy honeymoon in Hawaii but Rudy had engagements to fulfill, so we discussed alternatives.

I'd visited The Lodge at Pebble Beach in Carmel, California, and its fabulous setting on the Pacific ocean. "Can we have our honeymoon there?" I asked Rudy.

"Sure, sweetheart, since it's on our way to Los Angeles." As Rudy's pre-nuptial lovemaking became more and more heated, I became as highly aroused as Rudy.

"Eleanor, I sense a river of lust under that schoolgirl smile of yours, and I'm going to be the one to unleash it," he said the night we became engaged. He was right. Nothing is more thrilling to me than to be in love. I like men, and enjoy passionate relationships.

When I was in the fourth grade I was expelled from Catholic school because I kept kissing all the boys. As a teenager I couldn't wait to start dating and had fantasies about every male student in high school.

Throughout my marriage to Rudy I was to find that sex played an extremely important part in our lives. Rudy always wanted to make love to me, and I to him. He'd come home unexpectedly in the middle of the morning, mid-afternoon, anytime, and we'd go upstairs. I knew he loved me with every fiber of his being throughout his many moods, and to Rudy, the best way to show that love was to hold me, to make love to me. For my part, I adored Rudy. To me, he could do no wrong.

Ours wasn't the violent lovemaking seen in the movies today but a gentle, caring, almost spiritual experience, tempestuous and tender with lots of laughter. The foundation of our marriage and the secret of our relationship, until the day Rudy died, was both the physical desire we felt for each other and the deep, nurturing love that bound us together. Our mutual love was as solid as a rock and nothing throughout the long marriage made me love Rudy any less, whatever stresses and strains we experienced.

Friends and relatives often told me that I was the strong one, able to keep Rudy in balance when needed. Indeed, I was no pushover. A year into our marriage I needed to have my tonsils removed. Rudy, taking charge as usual, took me to the best doctor he could find.

"Well, young lady, you're going to have to spend several days in the hospital, and your throat is going to hurt a lot," said the doctor brusquely.

"Thank you so much, but I don't think so," I said, giving him my most dazzling smile. "Come along, Rudy," and I turned on my heel and walked out of the clinic. I was damned if I was going to let this ghoul work on me. Rudy was flabbergasted.

"Wow, Ellie, what was that all about?" I could see he was secretly delighted I'd turned down the highly recommended surgeon.

"I'm going to my family doctor in Berkeley, and that's that."

A ready sense of humor played a large part in the success of our marriage. We both inherited that famous Irish humor from our parents, so we looked at life from the same perspective. In addition, I studied psychology in college, and Rudy studied philosophy, so we each had some idea how to handle the other's idiosyncrasies: I analyzed, he reasoned. It didn't always work.

We loved to laugh, tease, surprise each other. Rudy's wit was quick, pointed and very, very funny. Interviewed on our fifteenth wedding anniversary, Rudy was asked how he and I spent our time. "We make love and drink champagne. This keeps us very busy," he replied, straight-faced. We always had fun together, joking about everything. Sometimes the road was rocky but we always made the effort to cheer each other up. That was the magic of our marriage.

THREE

A Crooner Is Born

My husband's childhood was simple but not humble. He was born Hubert Prior Vallée on July 28, 1901, in the small town of Island Pond, Vermont, near the French Canadian border where his father, Charles Alphonse Vallée, was also born.

Rudy came from a long line of wealthy French gentlemen farmers on his father's side, and prominent Irish merchants and shipbuilders on his mother's, Katherine Agnes Lynch.

Rudy's grandfather wrote to Rudy that the first Vallée came to America with Lafayette to fight in the Revolutionary War, then worked for the Hudson Bay Company in Canada. Charles Vallée, whom Rudy called Pop, was the first Vallée to settle in America. An aunt was a nun at the Hospital of the Grey Nuns in Montreal.

By the time he was four, Rudy's family had moved to the mill town of Westbrook, west of Portland, Maine, where his father ran a pharmacy.

Charles and Katherine Vallée bore five children, but two died before their third birthday. Rudy was the middle child, with an older sister and a younger brother. Rudy told me that his musical talent was inherited. His mother, a gifted violinist, mimic, and singer, encouraged Rudy to learn the snare drums at the age of four, partly at the doctor's suggestion to relieve a severe earache. His sister, Kathleen, played the piano. Rudy's kid brother, Bill, became an artist and a brilliant illustrator.

Later, the snare drums gave way to a full drum outfit. Rudy played with the junior high school band and at the local Star Theater as accompanist to silent movies. He also began playing with small area orchestras, earning money to supplement his job as a stock clerk in his father's drugstore.

Rudy admits he always had a difficult time reading sheet music. Instead he would simply listen to a song a few times, and then he could play it perfectly on his sax or clarinet.

School bored Rudy. While he excelled at English, earning As, his scores in science and mathematics were Cs and Ds. At fifteen he decided to join the Navy and see the world.

"I needed to expand my horizons," he told me, chuckling as he related the caper that ended up in the U.S. Senate and nearly required an Act of Congress to get him released. Accepted at the U.S. Navy recruitment center in Portland, Maine, without revealing his true age, Rudy spent several months as a lowly apprentice seaman, shoveling coal into furnaces and performing other menial chores. One night he fell out of the hammock he slept in, breaking his nose.

Finally fed up with scrubbing down the barracks floors, he asked when he could expect to be promoted to ensign. "Never," replied his Chief Petty Officer.

"Why not?" asked Rudy.

"You haven't been to college."

As the realization sank in that a lack of education meant he had to spend four more years swabbing the decks of old side-wheelers like the *Calvin Austin*, Rudy wrote home to Dad. Both Katherine and Charles Vallée appealed to their friend and state senator, Frederick Hale, seeking their son's release from the Navy, revealing that he was under age.

The senator replied, asking for a copy of "Hubert Vallée's birth certificate" and warning that such a release would "leave a blot on the character of the boy discharged." However, Hale wrote that an "immediate discharge for fraudulent enlistment" could be arranged.

Curiously, the Navy wrote separate letters to each parent. Mrs. Vallée subsequently received a letter from the Lieutenant-

Commander at the Navy Training Station, Newport, Rhode Island, informing her that Rudy would be discharged May 17, 1917. She was instructed to send her son his fare home "as he is in debt to the government and will therefore have nothing due him upon discharge."

The letter to Vallée *père* was shorter, addressed to the pharmacy on Main Street in Westbrook, signed by the Commander at the training station, with no request for funds. Charles was told that his son would be discharged "by Special Order of the Secretary of the Navy, on the seventeenth instant."

Rudy was elated but a hitch soon developed. The discharge was held up because the U.S. Navy Department mistakenly believed that Rudy's father had consented to the enlistment. Senator Hale again successfully intervened, and Rudy was finally released. Once safely back home again, Charles Vallée offered his son a deal.

"Hubert, I'll buy you that $200 motorbike you've been asking for if you'll promise to work part-time behind the counter at the soda fountain." Rudy readily agreed but discovered he still hated working in his father's drugstore. To relieve his boredom, he played records on the store's phonograph and listened to music all day.

We often laughed over Rudy's favorite story of his short career as a soda jerk. His father's head clerk mixed up the syrups at the soda fountain. When Rudy picked up the chocolate syrup jug to refill the receptacle, lime juice poured out instead. Rudy's famous French-Irish temper exploded. "I blew my top. I called the head clerk an idiot. Dad took his side, so I quit."

At this point in the story, Rudy never failed to remind me that we'd never have met if it hadn't been for the chocolate syrup fiasco. The incident set his life upon another path.

Rudy found a job setting pins at the local bowling alley. His pay was three and a half cents a string. Word quickly got back to Mr. Vallée, however, who told the owner to fire Rudy because he didn't deserve a job. Determined not to be outsmarted, Rudy tried another bowling alley, where he met Fred Girard who had just quit as projectionist at the local Star Theater. Rudy rushed off to apply for the position. He was hired to hand-crank the movie projector for the royal sum of seven dollars a week. But it was neither the show business environment nor his newfound rebellious independence that sealed sixteen-year-old Rudy's future fate.

"Between school and working part-time, I was still studying music and by now I'd taken up the clarinet," Rudy told me. "Then I was offered a job as chief usher at the Strand Theater in Portland. The chief electrician knew I was a musician and asked if I'd take over the payments on a saxophone he was renting and could no longer afford. He knew I was a southpaw, and this was a left-handed sax." The rest, as they say in Hollywood, is show business history.

Rudy undertook the study of music as he did all his projects: with total concentration and an insatiable search for knowledge about the subject. He never left a stone unturned in his quest for answers to his questions.

"Shortly after trying to master the sax I heard a recording of the most pure, soul-penetrating musical tones I ever imagined existed. I knew I had to learn to play like that," Rudy later told a journalist.

The recording that caught Rudy's attention was "Valse Erica," on Victor Records, played by Rudy Wiedoeft, who was considered by my husband as well as others to be the most remarkable saxophonist of his time. Wiedoeft became Rudy's idol.

"I bought every Wiedoeft record," Rudy said. "I ate, drank, and talked Rudy Wiedoeft so much, it earned me the nickname "Rudy" by my Sigma Alpha Epsilon fraternity brothers at the University of Maine." Eventually, Hubert Prior Vallée decided to formally change his name to Rudy Vallée in homage to his hero. Rudy later developed a penchant for changing other people's names, too, among them his piano player, Clyde Zulch, who Rudy rechristened Clyde Dupont, and Sam Narefsky, who he renamed Sam Narvo.

"I was determined to play as heavenly as Wiedoeft did. His clean-cut expression and the terrific speed of his tonguing on the instrument hit me like a thunderclap. I practiced five hours a day to capture the same quality," Rudy said. "I got to be such a pain in the ass at home with the noise, I had to find a field far away from everyone!"

Anxious to improve his sax playing, Rudy tried to contact Wiedoeft, seeking his advice in several letters, but there was no reply. Finally, felled by an appendectomy when he was nineteen years old, young Rudy penned a plaintive plea from his hospital bed. This time he was rewarded with a reply from his idol, who invited him to visit next time he was in New York.

"Back home in Westbrook I celebrated with a brand new French saxophone," Rudy recounted. "But I still couldn't get that emotional vibrato quality in my playing that Wiedoeft did. I sounded more like the bleat of a nanny goat."

The hours of practice, however, paid off, especially after writing Wiedoeft for advice. He replied: "The staccato I used in making the record "Crocodile" is what I would term 'slap tongue.' This peculiar type of tonguing is used in comedy and oriental effects . . . and can be used to produce the very low notes. As an example, when you are playing in the upper register on a rapid passage and instantly you have to jump to a low B flat, B natural or C, then to attack this low note and be sure of getting it, you would necessarily have to use slap tongue." Wiedoeft noted in a postscript to the letter: "Your G sharp and G natural should play just as clear as any other note. I use a mouthpiece of American Rod Rubber of my own make, which I expect to put on the market."

Rudy tried hard to copy his master until, "I accidentally stumbled upon the secret at the end of a particularly grueling four-hour practice session when I was really tired," he told me. "I'd play a few bars, then relax, then play again. Suddenly, I realized this action achieved the vibrato I was searching for. All I had to do was alternately relax and tighten the lower jaw on my reed. Incredible! I was so happy I could have cried!"

With his gift now in full bloom, Rudy became one of the youngest and most sought after saxophonists on the East Coast, playing at theaters all over New England.

"Dad was so proud, he gave up all thought of my becoming a priest," said Rudy.

"A priest?" I exclaimed the first time I heard the story.

"As you know, my family were strict Catholics, and my parents decided that if I didn't become a druggist, then the priesthood was a good way for me to go. Can you imagine, Buttercup, me as a priest?"

I laughed at the thought. Joining the church to become a priest would certainly have deprived millions of women of the man who became known as the Vagabond Lover and me of a wonderful husband. Rudy earned the Vagabond Lover nickname after he recorded one of his bestselling songs, "I'm Just a Vagabond Lover" and starred in the film *The Vagabond Lover*.

He was once asked by a newspaper reporter in Los Angeles if he was ever embarrassed by it.

"No, I didn't resent it. Besides it's a very lovely song," he said.

A mutual respect and friendship blossomed between the two Rudys to such an extent that Wiedoeft became a visitor to the Vallées' Westbrook home, and, towards the end of his life when my husband's career was at its zenith, he stayed at Rudy's Manhattan apartment overlooking the East River.

"Wiedoeft was only forty-six when he died from a stomach ailment," Rudy told me. "It was as if my own father had passed away. I was devastated. Maybe he had a drinking problem, but I'm not sure."

As a young man, Rudy didn't approve of drinking, except for the wine his French father loved. Rudy had an aversion to alcohol that was part of the strict, health-oriented lifestyle he mapped out for himself as his career began to take shape: early to bed, no smoking, no liquor, nutritious meals, few dates, lots of music practice. I must confess that attitude didn't last all his life, at least as far as alcohol and women.

Rudy's disciplined New England childhood—with loving parents who enjoyed a good marriage—gave him a solid foundation for the ethical and moral values he held. Sometimes those beliefs got him into trouble with friends and colleagues when he insisted on imposing them on others, yet he was always well meaning when he did so. It wasn't until Rudy reached the top of his profession and owned The Pirate's Den nightclub that he allowed himself to indulge in his favorite rum drinks. Later in life alcohol flowed freely at our parties. Yet I never saw him falling-down drunk as I did so many other famous singers. I firmly believe Rudy's healthy lifestyle was one of the reasons he had no serious illnesses until his fatal throat operation when he was in his early eighties.

When it came time for Rudy to attend college, his natural choice was his home state university. Rudy's paternal ancestry went back to 1645 when Pierre La Vallée of Normandy emigrated to Quebec, and his maternal ancestry to Cork, Ireland. His mother's family educated their daughters by governesses and private tutors before sailing for America. So it's not surprising that Rudy later chose an Ivy League school.

Initially, he decided to stay close to home and was accepted at the University of Maine.

A few months later, following his mother's and Wiedoeft's advice that transferring to Yale would offer him more music courses and greater career opportunities, Rudy applied and was accepted. Harvard was willing to admit Rudy as a provisional sophomore, and Bowdoin as a full sophomore but he chose Yale where he was admitted as a freshman.

Finances were a problem for Rudy. Although his family helped out with tuition fees, he needed outside playing engagements for rent, meals, books, and other expenses. In addition to classes, he had a hectic schedule of leading the Yale football band and playing at prep schools, country clubs, and a few hotels in the area.

For two weeks Rudy was engaged to play saxophone solos at the Strand Theater in New Haven as an added attraction to Gloria Swanson's starring role in the play, *Under the Lash*. A few weeks later Rudy played, billed as Hubert Vallée, saxophone soloist with the Strand Symphony Orchestra for Mary Pickford, starring in *Rosita*.

Rudy admired educators and loved the collegiate life. Languages came naturally to him; he studied French and Spanish. In fact, he liked Spanish so much he considered moving to South

America. In 1927 Rudy wrote to an American company that was planning to open a large manufacturing plant in Buenos Aires, asking for a job as a salesman. "And tell me very frankly just what hopes I may have to find work on the saxophone." Fortunately for me, Rudy received no reply. He and I toured Central America together after we married.

Rudy's diction in any language was excellent, and he became incensed if anyone "murdered English grammar," as he put it. "It was two Yale professors who really schooled me in the art of reeling off words fluently and easily," Rudy wrote to a friend, "and to make the subject, no matter how mundane or uninteresting, glow with life and interest. Chauncy B. Tinker and William Phelps taught me to treat every word with respect. That's my goal when I sing."

With every word he spoke, Rudy made a conscious effort to pronounce it with great clarity. When he sang, you could understand the lyrics. Charles Laughton praised Rudy as having the finest diction and speech of any American. He told Rudy he once sneaked into a vaudeville theater in London, where Rudy was performing during King George's coronation in 1937, to listen to him.

Correcting a person's pronunciation became a crusade throughout his life. Rudy wrote vitriolic letters to all and sundry when he claimed they stumbled. Sometimes when we were watching television, he'd start yelling at the newscaster, berating him or her for poor diction.

When Rudy left the University of Maine, he took an enduring memento with him. Known as the Maine Stein Song, it was based on "Opie," a march by U.S. Army bandmaster Emil Fenstad, and became sacred to the 103rd Infantry during World War I. A later version with lyrics by Lincoln Colcord and a musical arrangement by Adelbert Sprague became the school's upbeat drinking song, roared out by a thousand voices on campus.

Rudy introduced the song in a slightly faster version on his "Fleischmann's Hour" radio broadcast in 1930. No sooner had the program ended than he received hundreds of phone calls, telegrams, and letters, and he knew he had stumbled upon an instant hit. Rudy later recorded "The Stein Song" for Victor Records, performing a new orchestration by the Carl Fischer Music Company. It became the fastest selling piece of sheet music on the market, with millions of copies sold. It was translated into several foreign languages, including Chinese and Norwegian.

Rudy said that "The Stein Song" records sold about twenty million worldwide and was the only college song to be on the national Hit Parade of popular tunes. In fact, *The New York Times* wrote an editorial on April 18, 1930, focusing on the power of a new medium called radio, crediting Rudy Vallée's continual broadcasting of the song for its worldwide popularity. This editorial—and mention of Rudy's phenomenal success with the song—found its way into the *Congressional Record* on April 21, 1930.

For years, fan mail about Rudy and "The Stein Song" poured in from all four corners of the globe. Fred M. Wren with the American Consular Service in Holland wrote that he was a fellow graduate of Maine, and when Rudy's recording of "The Stein Song" was played in a Rotterdam restaurant, he was choked with emotion. "My only recollection of you is that of a lonesome-looking bird in a Freshman cap [but] thank you for the biggest thrill I've had in years," wrote Wren.

Not everyone was thrilled with the broadcast of "The Stein Song." Mrs. Louisiana Kennicott, of Bala, Pennsylvania, wrote in outrage to her local newspaper, protesting against the song and threatening to ask her congressman to pass a national law banning it for promoting beer. In 1933 *The New York Sun* editorialized on October 9 that Rudy Vallée's version "loses much of its roistering swagger and Bacchanalian abandon when crooned throatily over the ether waves."

In 1961 Mitch Miller ruffled a few Maine students' feathers by singing his own version of the song on his NBC television broadcast "Sing along with Mitch."

While a junior at Yale, another song took Rudy's fancy, "The Whiffenpoof Song." The chorus was based on a poem by Rudyard Kipling, according to Rudy, although copies of the sheet music give credit to Lincoln Colcord for the lyrics and Emil Fenstad for the music. Rudy composed a new piano arrangement, and it became a classic. Yalies from all over the world wrote with appreciation.

However, this recording embroiled Rudy in one of the most painful experiences of his life that lasted many, many years. He was accused by the elite group of Yale glee club singers called "The Whiffenpoofs" of commercializing their college ditty and making a fortune off it on Victor's Bluebird label. In response, Rudy offered to turn over his royalties to the Yale alumni fund and sent a check for $2,000. Two years later he sent another large check. But the offerings were rebuffed and the bitter feud continued. Letters flew back and forth until finally they reached an impasse. Rudy then published his own arrangement of the song. As it turned out, whenever the Whiffenpoof song was to be used in a motion picture or stage production, Rudy's permission had to be secured, as it was for the film, "Winged Victory."

Several years later, Rudy was bewildered but delighted to find himself invited, he said, to a Yale reunion where he was to be made an honorary member of The Whiffenpoofs. He accepted with great excitement. Recognition and forgiveness at last! Rudy then received a second letter, withdrawing the invitation "in case of embarrassment."

The University of Maine, whose former assistant director of admissions Bert Pratt is still a dear friend of mine, was not as upset as Yale about Rudy recording their school song. After all, Rudy's popularizing of "The Stein Song" put the small New England college on the world map and, he said, helped increase student attendance ten percent.

Although Rudy only spent one year at Maine, there was a special place in his heart for his first college. I often accompanied him as he returned time and time again as a volunteer orchestra leader and fund-raiser.

After a busy junior year at Yale, Rudy decided to take a sabbatical and travel to England.

He had received a twelve-month offer from the Savoy Hotel in London to join their dance orchestra, "The Havana Band." It was an exceptional opportunity, and Rudy jumped at it. He also contemplated studying at London University but, as it turned out, my husband told me he was far too busy performing to complete his education there.

Sailing on the S.S. *Olympic* with two other American musicians engaged to perform in England, Rudy tooted his sax in the ship's nightclub, playing hit tunes from the current musicals: "No, No, Nanette," "Tea for Two," and "Hard-Hearted Hannah, the Vamp of Savannah."

In England Rudy discovered many Brits wanted to learn the saxophone. His days were crowded with teaching, recording for Victor and Columbia, and playing and broadcasting from the Savoy's ballroom.

After a few months at the Savoy Hotel, Rudy was approached by aides to the Prince of Wales, later known as the Duke of Windsor, who abdicated his throne when his admiration for a certain American lady became an embarrassment. His Royal Highness was interested in learning the saxophone. However, Rudy returned to the U.S. before lessons for the then-Prince could be set up.

The Savoy's afternoon tea dances were famous for their elegance and were broadcast over the air. Rudy played tangos, waltzes, fox trots, and other popular dances of the day.

"My favorite recollection," Rudy related, "was when a party of people at one of the front tables was making an awful racket stirring their tea. The ladies kept tapping their teaspoons on the sides of the cups. It irritated me to no end. I didn't know whether to throw down my baton, chastise these gossipers, or ignore them. Finally, in the middle of a song, I abruptly stopped the orchestra. Walking over to the offending table, I told them to stop drinking tea and listen to the music." Rudy and I laughed at his insistence that people at tea dances shouldn't drink tea.

A more sinister interruption came a few years later when I found a press clipping about an incident with the Italian Mafia at the Bellevue Stratford Hotel in Chicago. Here's what the reporter wrote: "Rudy Vallée was doing his radio show from a Chicago night-club when Al Capone suddenly jumped up in the middle of Rudy's song and said 'Here's a toast to dis guy, folks. He got sumpin' in the way of talent!'

"'Mr. Capone,' replied Rudy, 'while I have a performer's vanity for praise, I don't like to receive it during the course of my perfor-mance. And, er, I have a preference for it to be couched in slightly more elegant language than is at your disposal.'

"Capone gave Rudy his full attention, his face flushed red with anger, while Capone's flunkies stared at Rudy in disbelief. Then Capone grinned.

'You got some nerve, kid,' he shouted, 'But you're right. Al Capone says he's sorry.'"

The Savoy Hotel offered a Rudy a six-month extension of his contract but Rudy, remembering his mother's and Wiedoeft's admoni-tion to get a degree, wanted to return to Yale. Rudy's final recording as a musician in England was for His Master's Voice, a popular record company, titled "Broadway Melodies," sung by Gertrude Lawrence and Bea Lillie. Bea was married to Sir Robert Peel, head of London's police force and the reason cops are called Bobbies in England.

Rudy also discovered a song that became his signature tune for the rest of his life, "My Time Is Your Time." Another favorite he packed into his music case was a waltz destined for acclaim called "If You Were the Only Girl in the World."

Back at Yale he continued playing to help pay tuition. But his living arrangements improved. With savings from his Savoy Hotel earnings, he was able to stay on campus at the upscale Harkness Memorial Quadrangle instead of the poky little rooming houses he occupied in his freshman year.

A little more money also meant Rudy could realize one of his fantasies: owning a raccoon coat. While some collegians wore them around campus, Rudy is credited with popularizing it as a "must" at Yalie football games. The truth is, he confided to me, he loved it so much he never took it off. He treasured that coat. It was the warmest piece of clothing he owned, and he used its deep pockets to hide a flask of whiskey—never opened—but a grand gesture to flourish.

"A few years later," Rudy said, "I wore the coat one night when I was getting mobbed by fans every night in New York. They tore the thing to shreds!"

Rudy developed his love of elegant clothes in London. He bought yards and yards of England's famous tweed fabrics to have suits made and started his lifelong collection of ties and cufflinks. Until the day he died, Rudy wore velvet smoking jackets and silk cravats. Most of his American wardrobe was tailored by one of his fraternity brothers, Al Heimann, in Cincinnati.

After Rudy died, his publicist, Christopher Harris, and I discovered a huge cache of cufflinks and ties in the attic. In green silk, red brocade, blue damask, yellow satin, every color and fabric, the five hundred ties were matched by the two hundred silver, gold, and platinum pairs of cufflinks that sparkled in their boxes.

Rudy gifted friends everywhere from his "secret stash." In 1955, an ailing President Dwight Eisenhower wrote to Rudy thanking him for "the cuff links and a tie clasp. They are truly designed to spur my recovery forward."

Rudy loved being meticulously groomed. "I cut such a dashing figure at Yale," he said years later as we pored over yellowed photos of him in the raccoon coat. "I finally felt I would be a real Yalie and attract all the girls!" He also set a fashion trend in the 1920s with his Yale sweater; the sweater and other Rudy Vallée memorabilia were once exhibited by the Smithsonian Institution.

Rudy's taste in women at that time was far more exotic than his wardrobe. He leaned towards sultry brunettes. It was not until three wives later that he turned completely around and fell for the typical all-American girl—fortunately for me!

Leading the school band, the Yale Collegians, playing at swanky country clubs and snazzy hotels like the Westchester Biltmore, New York's Rendez-vous Room, and dozens of other dates, Rudy's junior and senior years at Yale were filled to the brim with music. He managed to study, too, and left the university with a bachelor's degree in philosophy.

By now magazine critics were describing him "in music, a natural pioneer. Rudy's performances are notable for imaginative and poetic power and beauty, and in plasticity of pose and mobility of expression he is so attractive that the dancers always keep their eyes on him."

Convinced he could take New York by storm as his reputation as a fine saxophonist gained momentum, he headed for Manhattan. Rudy was on a roll even though he was practically penniless. Nothing could stop this ambitious young man. He knew he'd be famous, knew he had talent and could parlay it into becoming a sensation. With energy, ambition, desire, and youth, how could he fail?

At this stage in a show business career, fate often forces a star's fortunes to plummet, but Rudy seemed to live a charmed life. In fact, he often told me that his early successes came too easily. Perhaps that's why, many years later during the downside, he became frustrated and occasionally bitter. He expected his popularity to last forever.

But New York in 1927 glittered with stars in smash-hit shows like *Funny Face, Hit the Deck*, and *Show Boat* on Broadway. The flapper era was in full swing; Al Jolson sang in the first talking movie, *The Jazz Singer*, and Charles Lindbergh became the first man to fly nonstop across the Atlantic. It was a golden time and Rudy, stardust in his eyes, plunged right in. He contacted musician friends, seeking work as he carried around his baritone sax, an alto sax, and a clarinet.

Although Rudy was not considered a jazz musician, he's credited by a handful of jazz greats as their inspiration for entering the music field. Charlie "Bird" Parker told *Downbeat* magazine that Rudy was his first musical idol and that at eleven years old he was so moved by listening to Rudy on the radio his parents bought him a saxophone.

In 1936 Louis Armstrong asked Rudy to write the introduction to his autobiography, *Swing That Music*, a book that was later rereleased in paperback in 1993; and Arnold Shaw mentions Rudy several times in his 1989 book *The Jazz Age*.

A 1956 documentary film, a compilation of songs and performances by the jazz greats of the thirties and forties included Rudy, along with Louis Armstrong, Cab Calloway, Duke Ellington, Betty Hutton, Gene Kruppa, Peggy Lee, the Mills Brothers, Red Nichols, Buddy Rich, and Artie Shaw.

Rudy told a newsman in 1929 that he wanted to have his own jazz band one day, but it would be, in effect, a dance band like Paul Whiteman's. "There's no such thing as jazz. It's really dance music," Rudy claimed.

In many of his broadcasts Rudy played a few nonvocal instrumental tunes, the closest he came to Paul Whiteman's style of dance music termed, at the time, "symphonized syncopation."

In Armstrong's book, Rudy commented on the fact that "Armstrong's delightful, delicious sense of distortion of lyrics and melody has made its influence felt upon popular singers of our day cannot be denied. Mr. Bing Crosby, the late Russ Colombo, Mildred Bailey, and others have adopted, perhaps unconsciously, the style of Louis Armstrong, [who] antedated them all [with] his ideas of 'swinging.'"

Abe Burrows, whom Rudy had hired in 1940 to write for his "Sealtest Hour" broadcast, sent a letter to Rudy in 1977 saying, among other things: "You gave us a sound and a beat that one hardly hears any more. It stirred up a lot of romantic feelings."

Several orchestra leaders hired Rudy to play in their bands in New York and surrounding states because of his "different" sound, resulting in a grueling schedule of seven-day weeks, dashing madly from one dance engagement to another.

It was an education that stood him in good stead when we spent the first seven years of our marriage on the road. I was always amazed at Rudy's unflagging vitality, his meticulous organization of our travel routes, and the detail with which he planned each performance.

Learning at an early age how to preserve his strength when he traveled, the best time to nap, the most judicious time to eat, Rudy set himself up at a young age for a lifetime of performing.

Towards the end of 1927 Rudy formed his own band, The Yale Collegians, and began auditioning. They were an instant sensation labeled "soothing" because there was no brass in the band. "We couldn't afford a brass section," Rudy told me, "so here we were with two strings, two saxes, and a lot of piano."

Booking agents, club managers, and vaudeville theater owners agreed the band's sound was different; the Yale Collegians found themselves in great demand. Rudy explained in one of his books how this "difference" came about: "I was one of the first to split choruses up into phrases. Most other orchestras played songs in a style that made them sound all the same, with the result that the audience's attention was inclined to wander. So I developed a way of weaving in and out of melodies and obbligatos." He also discovered that changing the musical key each time he changed a group of songs jolted the listeners to attention.

One friend, pianist Don Dickerman, was about to open a supper club on East 53rd Street called The Heigh-Ho Club. He told Rudy to bring his Yale Collegians along and see how it sounded at the new, exclusive but smallish Heigh-Ho Club.

Rudy asked one of his violinists, Jules de Vorzon, a formally trained singer, to be the orchestra's soloist for the audition. Don listened to Jules, Rudy said, then made a face. Don didn't like Jules's style, this was an intimate nightclub and it needed a different type of singing.

Fearful of losing the engagement for the New Year's Eve opening of the club, Rudy hastily offered to handle all the vocals himself. He'd sung before, but mostly as a teenager at home and a couple of times at Yale.

Rudy knew his voice was not robust. He felt he needed some help. Although microphones to boost singers' voices were introduced in the mid-1920s, they were rarely used in intimate nightclubs at that time. What to do? Rudy grabbed the cut-off megaphone he used with his baritone sax to amplify the sound and started to sing softly through it. The song was "Rain," and not until it was ended did Rudy dare to look at Don's face.

"*You* do the singing," pronounced Don.

"We were thrilled," Rudy told me. They had a steady job, no

more one-nighters! And little did Rudy know, he was about to launch a new style of singing called "crooning." Soon Rudy exchanged the standard Spaulding Fibre Company megaphone he'd been using and had the company design a shorter, wider, new one.

"Crosby and Sinatra would have been laughed out of the studios if I hadn't led the way for singers to drop the formal operatic style of singers such as Nelson Eddy," Rudy wrote in his autobiography. "I was the first to sing in a natural, soft, untrained style, and it came to be called crooning. Since my voice didn't have a lot of power, I had to find a different approach so I just sang without forcing my voice. Then I discovered that by using a megaphone the way musicians did to amplify their instruments, it worked just as well for a voice. If I hadn't broken ground for them as the first crooner, Bing and Frank, well, who knows?"

The Heigh-Ho Club soon became known nationwide when WABC broadcast its first live program from the club. Because of budget restrictions, the station couldn't afford to hire an announcer so WABC asked Rudy to do the introductions himself for the broadcast. With typical Vallée aplomb, he instantly agreed even though he'd never announced over the air before.

Looking for something different—Rudy always claimed a unique approach to anything that attracted attention—he used the name of the club as a salutation: "Heigh-Ho everyone! This is Rudy Vallée announcing and directing the Yale Collegians from the Heigh-Ho Club in New York City." He also chatted with his radio guests, becoming the first talk show host. He included comedians and excerpts from Broadway shows by the original cast.

"I wanted the radio show to be informal, friendly and low-key, just like me, Buttercup," he told me.

"Low-key? You?" Rudy shrugged. We both laughed.

The response to this new type of variety show was so overwhelming, WABC decided to broadcast with Rudy every night; soon he was doing twenty radio shows a week. Three weeks later WOR also asked Rudy to do a radio show, and he began using the new microphones. Unlike the hand-held, cordless models of today, early microphones were free-standing, attached to a tall steel column on a circular steel base. They were perfect foils for entertainers to use as a stage prop.

The young singer became immortalized in cartoons depicting him wrapped around his microphone. One drawing by Fred Morgan in the *New York American* was captioned "Maestro of the Microphone." Another by Covarrubias was exhibited in the Library of Congress.

Rudy used his microphone as something to make love to. As dance audiences watched and radio fans listened, Rudy's entire body engaged in a sensuous dance with the mike, his fingers sliding up and down the slender column. He stroked, caressed, whispered, brushing his full lips against the cold metal, electrifying listeners and setting millions of feminine hearts fluttering with desire. Rudy well knew the effect his style of singing had on his audiences and he played directly to it.

At this time Rudy decided to change the name of his band. The "boys," as he called them, were no longer students. A successful Broadway play at the time was titled *A Yank in King Arthur's Court*. Rudy changed his orchestra name to "Connecticut Yankees." Soon the name was changed again, to the Rudy Vallée Orchestra, and Rudy formed second, third, and fourth units of his original band in order to satisfy the huge demand for appearances.

Hospital patients wrote to Rudy, saying how restful it was to listen to his soothing voice; other notes came from six- and ten-year-olds asking for photos and sax students seeking his advice. One fan wrote at great length; her final letter to Rudy was forty-eight pages long. One young teenager said she owned 279 photos of Rudy and could she form a fan club?

Buried under a mountain of mail, Rudy hired one of his most loyal fans, Marjorie Diven, to handle the sacks of letters and to paste up press clippings in scrapbooks. Much of the fan mail was requests for songs, and I was surprised when I read the letters many years later to discover how many men wrote in.

Rudy met Marjorie when she came to the Hotel Lombardy's

daily tea dances to listen to his smaller eight-piece orchestra and hear him sing. She always sat alone because her husband worked long hours. Rudy got to know her and often stopped by her table. Sometimes Marjorie brought in newspaper clippings she'd collected about her idol and gave them to him.

After a few weeks Rudy opened a small office in Steinway Hall, near Central Park in New York, and installed Marjorie as his secretary. Four years later they moved to a larger office complete with a music library filled with thousands of copies of sheet music, a baby grand piano, a bar and icebox, and a recording studio.

Many of Rudy's highly emotional fans came up with innovative gimmicks to grab his attention, signing themselves "Purple Pansy Petals," "The Shorn Lamb," "The Red-Headed Snorer," "To Adonis from Psyche," using steamy language. Some sent rose-scented love notes, poems they composed, and cartoons they'd drawn or found in magazines. Mrs. Diven said that one fan cut photos of herself into several pieces, sending Rudy one part at a time to whet his appetite.

Marjorie stayed with Rudy for thirteen years, then went to work in the same capacity for Frank Sinatra. I considered her a dear, long-time friend until her death in 1970, and I still miss our telephone talks.

With the Heigh-Ho Club's broadcasts launching Rudy and his Connecticut Yankees on their way to stardom, Rudy's radio fame grew. "He was the first to have screaming teenagers surround the stage door," Marjorie Diven said, "long before Frank Sinatra."

Although the stock market crash was looming in 1929, it was a landmark year for my husband. In April Rudy played his first engagement at the New York Paramount Theater, breaking the house record. Then the Brooklyn Paramount was added to his schedule.

"We did five shows a day at each theater," he told me.

"How did you manage that?"

"We'd finish at the New York Paramount on Broadway, run

down into the Times Square subway loaded down with our instruments, and come up near the stage door of the Brooklyn Paramount just in time to go on stage."

When he had to drive his car and was caught in a traffic jam, he'd pull an old envelope and a pencil from his pocket and write another verse for one of his songs.

Rudy signed a contract with RCA Victor to record albums, producing hundreds of records that sold in the millions. Although electricity had sent the wind-up gramophone into obsolescence, there was a huge market for Rudy's sheet music; his likeness was on almost every front cover sold in the country.

A reporter for the *Newark Evening News* called Rudy the successor to Rudolph Valentino with a Charles Lindbergh profile: "He has the quality that Valentino had, that makes the young ones see dreams and the older ones dream. Its possession has made Rudy Vallée the toast and enigma of Broadway."

Another journalist also concluded that Rudy was an enigma after a lengthy four-part series in *The Saturday Evening Post* was unable to define him.

Now a national treasure, it was not surprising that the *New York Daily Mirror* reported Rudy was kidnapped and the soles of his feet burned by his abductors.

"No such event ever occurred," Rudy assured me. "The police examined my feet and certified there were no burns. So I sued the *Mirror* for a million dollars to secure a retraction." I never learned how the case was resolved.

Now at the heart of the pop music scene, Rudy launched the most remarkable career of its era. NBC's "Fleischmann Hour" radio program, commonly known as "The Vallée Hour," reflected Rudy's great popularity.

His image was on five thousand billboards in the five boroughs of New York City, showing Rudy smoking Old Gold cigarettes and enjoying candy bars. Parents named their newborn sons after him and men began wearing the dapper, deep blue serge suits and dark ties Rudy Vallée favored.

Young, fresh, energetic, well-educated, smiling, he captured the heart of the nation.

Herbert Hoover decided that if anyone could resurrect the spirit of the country, it was Rudy Vallée, and he invited him to breakfast at the White House where he met congressmen and senators. The toast of Washington, Rudy was even asked by Hoover to write a new song to help America out of its depressive malaise. But Rudy declined. He composed very few songs, although he orchestrated many of his own arrangements. Among the most popular lyrics he wrote were for "Deep Night," recorded in 1929 for Victor with music by Charlie Henderson. He is also credited with writing "I'm Still Caring" and "A Little Kiss Each Morning."

Merely by introducing a new song on his radio show, Rudy ensured its national and international success.

By now his fame was not only national but celebrated throughout the western world, thanks to international sales of his recordings and music.

At this point, at the age of twenty-eight and with his name on the lips of practically everyone in the country, Rudy decided it was high time to write his autobiography, *Vagabond Dreams Come True* (published in 1930).

Credited by the sheet music industry for saving its life during the Great Depression when sales of everything except Rudy Vallée's music went down to zero, Rudy also embarked on appearances for charity organizations, whatever their cause, race, or denomination. He'd take his orchestra along to churches, temples, hospitals, orphanages, and hotels. His free performances in Brooklyn in particular, and other concerts raised hundreds of thousands of dollars for the less fortunate.

Rudy's fame was greater than ever, and he was making a fortune. Several newspapers reported he was making two million dollars a year. The new singing sensation also became somewhat of an impresario and agent, searching for and auditioning new talent introduced on his radio show. Rudy represented established stars, too, including Faye Emerson, Victor Borge, and Slapsy Maxie Rosenbloom.

As soon as he heard their acts, he signed on future stars Larry

Adler, Alice Faye, Fred Astaire, Ginger Rogers, Billie Burke, and violinist Richard Himber, who became the director of Rudy's national tours and later conductor of his own band, the Ritz-Carlton Orchestra. Rudy also had ventriloquist Edgar Bergen and his dummy, Charlie McCarthy, as radio guests. He'd first heard Bergen at the Chez Paree club. Rudy was always willing to listen to young, aspiring newcomers, too.

"Rudy was kind enough to give me my first professional audition, " June Haver told me. "I didn't know if I had the talent to make it in show business, so when Rudy Vallée and his band came through Rock Island, Illinois, to perform at the local armory, I had the chance to sing with his band. You can't imagine the thrill it was, singing with the most famous band in the country. The song was 'Daddy, I Want a Diamond Ring,' and with Rudy's enthusiastic encouragement, my show business career took off from there."

June and her husband Fred MacMurray were dear friends of ours. June starred in many movies including *I'll Get By*, *The Dolly Sisters*, and *Irish Eyes Are Smiling*.

Rudy also extended both professional help and friendship to the brilliant violinist David Rubinoff, whose wife Mertice, a poet, became a second mother to me when I first met Rudy.

Dorothy Lamour was another of Rudy's finds, and he immediately booked her into New York's chic El Morroco. In 1974 she wrote us a letter about a book she was writing: "Naturally," the letter said, "the book could not be complete without something from you, because I still remember all that you did, and tried to do, for me in those very early days." Dorothy was thoughtful enough to add a final paragraph asking Rudy to give her love to "your little bride."

Not all of Rudy's star discoveries were accepted by his radio bosses, and he was forced to turn down what he called "a brilliant find," Arthur Godfrey, who became the first television host of America's hottest morning magazine show, *The Arthur Godfrey Hour*.

One talented musician Rudy helped is Vic Hyde, who to this day is fiercely loyal to Rudy's memory. "I met Rudy in 1935 in Washington D.C.," Vic told me, "when I had a not-too-successful

A young but determined
Rudy at age six.

Musical talent ran in the Vallée
family, and Rudy got an early start
on the snare drums at age four. By
the time he was twenty, he had
purchased his first saxophone.

Charles and Katherine Vallée had five
children, two of which died before
they reached the age of three. Here
they are pictured with Rudy and his
younger brother, Bill; older sister
Kathleen is not pictured.

The Heigh-Ho Club is where it all started for Rudy Vallée and His Connecticut Yankees. They began performing there in January 1928, began broadcasting their performances a month later, and were soon local favorites.

Rudy (front row, fourth from left) met *Alice Faye (second row, fourth from left) in 1931 when they costarred in* George White's Scandals *on Broadway. Alice went on to join Rudy's band as its first female singer.*

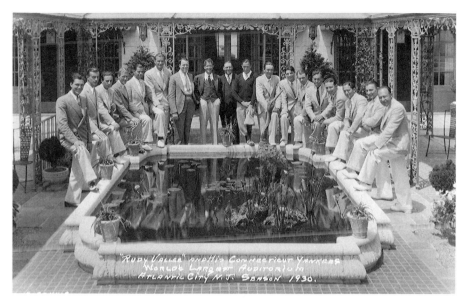

Rudy Vallée and His Connecticut Yankees, shown here in Atlantic City in 1930, were better known in later years as The Rudy Vallée Orchestra.

The Lodge, a 365-acre lakeside resort in the pine woods of Maine, was Rudy's favorite getaway, and his friends were always welcome.

Rudy called the fifty-two piece Coast Guard Band he led during World War II "the best I ever directed."

While in Paris filming Gentlemen Marry Brunettes, Rudy perfected his imitation of French actor and singer Maurice Chevalier, which he often did in local clubs to the amusement of the other patrons.

Rudy made history by hosting the first ever talk show, NBC Radio's "The Fleischmann Hour."

World famous for his mastery of the saxophone, Rudy considered playing more a science than an art.

When the Rudy Vallée Orchestra performed in New York, they overshadowed all other bands and performers.

May 22, 1936.

Dear Rudy Vallee,

Although this letter is extremely belated, yet the wish to write it will not let me alone.

I want particularly to share with you the pleasure I have had in the appreciation shown by many who listened to our broadcast on February 27th. Since that evening people without number have praised the charm with which you conducted the programme to help the "Better Vision Institute," and I have received many pleasant letters expressing interest in the blind and the work of keeping the light in human eyes. The tenderness of your voice and the competent, happy way you presented a subject beset by peculiar difficulties brought this outpouring of good-will. I bless you for so generously putting your personality and art into an objective for which I have striven, prayed and labored during almost a lifetime. Once you said your art was somewhat like that of a physician, and now I realize how true that is, such a multitude calls upon you for the cheer or your songs and the healing balm of your sympathy.

With cordial greetings and all good wishes for your continued health and success, I am,

Sincerely yours,

Helen Keller

Rudy's friends and colleagues often commented on the amazing resemblance between myself and Mary McBride (pictured here with pianist Walter Gross and his wife, Rudy, Walter Scharf, and Alice Faye). Those who don't know better often think it's me seated next to Rudy in this picture.

MARY MACK SEPT. 20TH/81

    I WILL NEVER QUITE BE ABLE TO COMPLETELY SHUT MARY MACK OUT OF MY MEMORY!
WHEN A GIRL CAN ALMOST MAKE ME WISH TO END MY LIFE, SHE OBVIOUSLY HAD A VERY
STRONG GRIP ON MY BEING, AND THAT WOULD HAVE HAPPENED THE NIGHT I WATCHED HER DANCI
ON THE FLOOR OF THE COCONUT GROVE WHERE I HAD PLAYED FOR TWENTY WEEKS IN 1938 AND
1930. I WATCHED FROM THE BOOTH WHERE THE SPOTLIGHT HAD SHOWN ON ME AND MY COM-
PANY OF PERFORMERS SO MANY TIMES, AS SHE PRESSED AGAINST A YOUNG, TALL GOOD LOOKIN
OFFICER OF THE MERCHANT MARINE WHILE THE ORCHESTRA PLAYED THE RODGERS & HART SONG,
" FALLING IN LOVE WITH LOVE " I HAVE NEVER FELT SO LOW AND UNHAPPY IN ALL THE
YEARS OF MY ASSOCIATION WITH WOMEN.

    BUT FOR THIS GIRL, I WOULD NEVER HAVE MARRIED MY PRESENT WIFE, WITH WHOM I
HAVE ENJOYED THIRTY TWO YEARS OF MARRIED LIFE, BECAUSE PRIOR TO MY MEETING MARY
MACK, I HAD ALWAYS, BUT ALWAYS, GIVEN ALL MY ATTENTION AND AFFECTION TO WOMEN OF
ONE TYPE, AND IT WAS MARY WHO WAS TO COMPLETELY REVOLUTIONIZE MY TASTE IN THE
FAIR SEX.

    I FIRST SAW MARY ONE NIGHT IN 1941, WHEN THE UNITED STATES HAD NOT YET EN-
TERED THE WAR, BUT WAS GETTING VERY CLOSE TO IT.
    JUDY STEWART, A PETITE BRUNETTE WHO I WOULD HAVE MARRIED, EXCEPT THAT I
HAD BEEN FORCED TO REALIZE THAT ALTHO SHE HAD GIVEN HERSELF TO ME, AND HAD MADE
MANY HOURS WITH HER, MOMENTS OF SEXUAL AND AMOROUS DELIGHT, BUT I CANNOT RECALL
HER EVER UTTERING THE WORDS THAT ANY MAN WANTS TO HEAR, THE SIMPLE BREATHLESS AD-
MISSION, THAT SHE CARED.
    JUDY HAD COME OUT TO PERFORM WITH A DANCE TROUP, WORKING IN A SMALL NIGHT
CLUB THAT GEORGE RAFT HOSTED ON VINE STREET, IN HOLLYWOOD.

    SHE WAS FREE THE NIGHT I TOOK HER TO THE BEVERLY HILLS HIGH SCHOOL TO SEE
A MUSICAL REVUE PUT ON BY SOME OF THE BRITISH COLONY TO RAISE MONEY FOR BUNDLES
FOR BRITAIN, WHO WAS NOW CATCHING HELL FROM THE NAZIS.

    AS WE APPROACHED THE ENTRANCE, WE WERE HANDED PROGRAMS FOR THE AFFAIR BY
A VISION OF LOVLINESS, IN A WHITE GOWN THAT SOUTHERN BELLES MIGHT HAVE WORN. BUT
IT WAS HER SMILE, SHOWING THROUGH A WIDE, GENEROUS MOUTH WITH BEAUTIFUL WHITE
TEETH AS SHE DELIBERATELY CAUGHT MY EYE AND PRESSED THE PROGRAMS INTO MY HAND.

    AFTER THE SHOW, I TOOK JUDY TO THE PIRATES DEN, A NIGHT CLUB I HAD PUT TO-
GETHER FOR A MAN WHO HAD, ON OUR OPENING NIGHT AT THE HEIGH HO CLUB IN NEW YORK
CITY, WHEN AFTER LISTENING TO MY SINGING OF SEVERAL SONGS (HE HAD COMPLAINED
THAT HE DIDN'T LIKE THE MEMBER OF OUR ORCHESTRA WHO WAS SUPPOSED TO DO THE SINGING
AND ON HEARING HIS COMPLAINT, SEEING THE JOB GOING OUT THE WINDOW, I HAD TAKEN A
SMALL MEGAPHONE OUT OF MY BARITONE SAXOPHONE CASE, AND SAID TO OUR PIANIST, WHOM
I HAD BROUGHT UP FROM NEW HAVEN, " RAIN " IN THE KEY OF " C ".) AS I APPROACHED
THE OWNER OF THE SWANK ROOM, HAD SIMPLY SAID, " YOU!!! DO THE SINGING!!! "
HAD COME OUT TO HOLLYWOOD, AND SUGGESTED THAT WE DUPLICATE ONE OF HIS
THREE SMALL CLUBS IN GREENWICH VILLAGE IN NEW YORK CITY. I PERSUADED FOUR-
TEEN BIG NAMES, CROSBY, HOPE, TONY MARTIN, KEN MURRAY, FRED MC MURRAY, JIMMIE
FIDLER, VIC ERWIN, AND SEVERAL OTHER MEN IN AND OUT OF SHOW BUSINESS, TO INVEST IN
THIS UNUSUAL SUPPER CLUB AND OUR OPENING HAD ALL THE REAL TOP ÉLITE OF HOLLYWOOD
WHICH I HAVE ON A PATHE NEWS REEL. HAD INVESTED OVER ONE HUNDRED THOUSAND
DOLLARS IN A FOURTH CLUB IN GREENWICH VILLAGE, LOSING EVERY PENNY OF IT, BUT NEVER
FORGETTING THAT ON OPENING NIGHT, HE HAD CHANGED THE WHOLE COURSE OF MY LIFE BY
SIMPLY SAYING, " YOU! DO THE SINGING!!! "
    THE PIRATE'S DEN, LIKE THE ONE IN NEW YORK CITY, HAD TWO " BRIGS " OR SMALL
PRISONS INTO WHICH SOME OF OUR GUESTS, PARTICULARLY WOMEN WERE THROWN SOMETIMES,

Despite my veil catching on fire at the reception, our wedding was as perfect as I had imagined it would be.

Our wedding in Oakland, California, made papers around the world.

Our pink stucco "castle," as Rudy called it, was nestled on a mountaintop in the Hollywood Hills. At 1,500 feet above sea level, it featured breathtaking views in every direction.

Rudy hung this picture of me as a child in his office and taped the label on it, "The Most Beautiful Girl in the World."

This picture of me was taken during a visit to Silver Tip before Rudy and I were married. When Rudy saw me in this Ceil Chapman dress, he handed me a roll of money and told me to buy a dozen more just like it. Of course I didn't take the money, but I did learn quickly that he loved seeing me in satin dresses and high heels.

Rudy and me goofing off in Nassau in 1951.

Our dear friends Cliff and Helen Steward, shown here dining with us at the El Morocco night club in New York, had a spur-of-the-moment wedding in our hotel suite in New York—which Rudy gave me less than a day's notice to plan!

The gang at Glenn McCarthy's ranch outside of Houston. Glenn, shown here on Rudy's left, spent the weekend in the company of Swedish beauty Ilsa Bay, who is standing to my right.

Gary Cooper and a publicist joined Rudy and me for a stroll at the Boca Raton Beach Club.

Jane Russell and I enjoyed exploring Paris and shopping at the designer boutiques when she could get away from the Gentlemen Marry Brunettes *set.*

Rudy took me on my first trip to Europe when he filmed Gentlemen Marry Brunettes *in Paris with Jane Russell and Jeanne Crain. We had a ball dining at out-of-the way restaurants and visiting every music store in the city!*

Rudy and me enjoying an afternoon with William Holden and Alice Bernstein in 1956.

Just two days after our wedding, Rudy and I hit the road, doing shows all across the country.

Marty Allen was one of the more unusual people I met through Rudy's show business career.

Rudy was always prepared to make his favorite frozen drinks in the Waring blender he never left home without.

Zsa Zsa Gabor was just one of the many glamorous people we socialized with in the Hollywood set

We couldn't resist getting Rudy's picture at Al Hill's club in Colorado Springs, The Garden of the Gods, where the watch-covered wallpaper was the perfect backdrop for the man whose theme song was "My Time Is Your Time."

one-man band act playing four trumpets at once. Rudy gave me his card, told me how to change my act, and said to look him up in New York. After I arrived, Rudy wanted to send me out on auditions, but I didn't have the right clothes. Rudy gave me $100—a lot of money back then—and sent me shopping. I spent $28 on a suit and gave Rudy the change. He nearly fainted with surprise that I'd given him back some money. He thought it was funny and told me to include it in my act. It made all the newspapers and made me famous." Years later Rudy picked up all the medical bills for Vic, who was in an iron lung with tuberculosis, and paid him $350 a week, even though he could no longer perform.

"He's my God, he set up my life," Vic told me feelingly.

As millions more people began listening to his show on Thursday nights, Rudy became a legend within the first nine months of his arrival in New York. His name appeared in all the gossip columns, and he joined the New York social whirl full time. He was invited to the best nightclubs, first-night openings, and to exclusive, glamorous parties.

Rudy also found himself invited to speakeasies, where Prohibition gin flowed freely. Although he occasionally agreed to play an engagement at a couple of them, socially he shunned these flapper hang-outs because of his busy work schedule and because of his New England prudishness.

Amid this hectic whirl, Rudy somehow found time to take the train to Hollywood and star in his first film, *The Vagabond Lover*. Other movie roles followed, starring Rudy with dancer Ann Miller in *Time Out for Rhythm* and with ice skating champion Sonja Henie in *Second Fiddle*. Rudy made another movie with Sonja and Gene Nelson, who later became our tennis partners.

Rudy also made *International House* with Cab Calloway and W.C. Fields; *Palm Beach Story* with Claudette Colbert; *Happy Go Lucky* with Betty Hutton; *The Bachelor and the Bobbysoxer* with Cary Grant, Myrna Loy, and Shirley Temple; *Father Was a Fullback* with Maureen O'Hara and Fred MacMurray; and *Mother is a Freshman* with Loretta Young and Van Johnson.

Rudy's arrival in the film capital of the world was heralded by eight motorcycle patrolmen who met Rudy and his parents when the train rolled into Los Angeles from the East Coast. "We were packed into a huge white Rolls Royce," Rudy wrote in a memoir, "and escorted down Sunset Boulevard, over to Hollywood Boulevard, and into the Roosevelt Hotel. You'd have thought royalty was arriving. We were greeted by Aaronsen's Commanders, a popular band at the time, who started playing, 'I'm Just a Vagabond Lover.' Flash bulbs popped from every direction. It was grand."

Ironically, although Rudy was to make a total of forty-four movies, he never had a role as a leading man again. In fact, he was most often cast as a frumpy, pompous tightwad wearing a pince-nez, which added weight to the myth that Rudy never gave tips to people.

"Why am I called a tightwad just because I can't stand waste?" Rudy would ask me. "I'm frugal, not stingy."

Another myth was that Rudy had a pay phone at his home, Silver Tip. "I had slot machines, Ellie, not a pay phone," a fact I confirmed when I went to live there.

People also said that Rudy smoked five-cent cigars and bought cheap ties.

"If I see an inexpensive tie I like, I buy it," he said when we went on our first shopping spree as a married couple.

Stingy? Not my Rudy. When we went out to restaurants, Don the Beachcomber or Trader Vic's, Rudy always sent tips back to the chef and the bartenders, sometimes more than the drinks or meals cost. He also gave them pens inscribed "Gratefully, Rudy Vallée" and other small gifts he carried around.

During stays at hotels, Rudy handed out pens to bellhops, redcaps, maids, switchboard operators, and kitchen help in addition to gratuities.

However, to my mind, Rudy must take some of the blame for his reputation as a tightwad. He loved to imitate one of his broadcasting rivals, Jack Benny. Admiring Benny's hilarious performances as a stingy man, Rudy sought the same reaction, but instead of laughing at Rudy's antics audiences took him seriously.

During the 1930s, with his financial security assured for at least several months, Rudy found time to enjoy his second love: women. He intended to make up for lost time.

Although he told me he never saw himself as attractive, my blue-eyed, curly-haired, clean-cut, all-American, witty Yalie did understand that, by the standard of the day, he was a "good catch." Most women considered him one of the handsomest men of his day.

"To a certain extent, audiences were bored with dark, Latin bandleaders and the Rudolph Valentino look. They wanted something fresh, different," he told me.

Press agent Paul Ross knew Rudy from his early days in radio. He told me, "Rudy could've had an affair with any woman he wanted. He was good-looking and so famous that everyone in the country knew him. He was better educated than most entertainers back then, he was in a different dimension. It took Frank Sinatra twenty years to develop, Rudy only about eight months. But then Rudy was a real workaholic. He needed a strong wife like you, Eleanor, to calm him down. Good thing you finally showed up and married him!"

To tell the truth, I was certainly not a starry-eyed fan when I met him. I didn't know he was a singer. I found him irresistible with his classic features and aristocratic bearing. But I didn't have a clue who he was. But when I began traveling with Rudy, I realized as soon as the media showed up in full force and fans came out of the woodwork that my husband was indeed a legend.

Rudy's preference in women back in the 1930s was dark-haired beauties with ruby-red lipstick. He loved girls in really high heels, long, slinky satin dresses, with two-inch long painted fingernails. He told me he couldn't keep his eyes off women as they slithered around the dance floor at the Heigh-Ho Club, looking, as he put it, "Sexy as hell!"

I could well imagine the scene because Rudy's libido was always in overdrive. He bought me dozens of satin gowns after we were married, in many different colors, from designers like Ceil Chapman and Helen Glickstein. In three-inch heels, I'm just an inch under six feet.

But Rudy loved it and was proud of me on his arm. I still like satin dresses—my favorite is a strapless version in midnight blue.

In 1982, when he was eighty-one years old, Rudy wrote a letter to Raquel Welch, who was starring in *Woman of the Year* on Broadway.

"Dear Luscious Woman: You were always one of the women I wish I had met, because when you put on those tight-fitting gowns with *Sheen* and five-inch *Heels*, I could climb the wall!!! But many years ago I met a gal on the beach at Lake Tahoe, who had never heard of me! She had a crush on Ronald Reagan! And turned me down for dinner, but relented to marry me later and with whom I have had twenty-five years of fabulous love-making. She puts on a tight-fitting thing in black satin and high heels and drives me absolutely *Wild*! We are still deeply in love."

Besieged by the beauties of the day when America was carefree, long before World War II, Rudy fell in love with one woman after another. None of the relationships lasted long, and Rudy once settled out of court for alienation of affections in a suit brought by Julie Stewart, a Ziegfield chorus girl.

Rudy was young, handsome, famous, and now wealthy. His affairs—real and imagined—were topics of the day, often national headlines. Howard Hughes is rumored to have asked, "How does Rudy Vallée get all his girls?"

Had I been around then, I could easily have answered that question. A suave, chivalrous gentleman, my husband treated women as if they were fragile orchids. He had great respect for the ladies, lavishing attention on them. Rudy knew how to romance a girl and whisper sweet nothings in her ear, and his soft, murmuring style of singing plus an intimate way of speaking made women melt in his arms.

After we had been married several years, Rudy told one newspaper reporter during an interview, "My red-haired wife here is a real beauty, not only physically but with beauty of loyalty and passion, very human, very real." He was always quick to compliment me and rarely failed to tell the media how much he loved me. That was one of the many reasons for our wonderful marriage—his constant out-pouring of love.

Frankly, I believe he used to date so many women before he married me because he was seeking something special, his one "true love," but he didn't yet know the qualities such a woman should possess. With his passionate nature, Rudy realized he needed matching sexuality in a mate, but he also needed someone who understood his personality with all its complex, conflicting philosophies. He'd been a womanizer but was chivalrous; he was overly generous and occasionally too frugal; politically, Rudy supported conservatives yet his views on certain issues were activist and liberal; he was the most romantic singer of his day yet agreed to play stuffed-shirt roles in movies.

Often called arrogant, egotistical, and stubborn, Rudy always seemed to know where he was going, and I think people envied him for that. He had an unshakable sense of purpose that never deserted him, striking out on his own against agents' advice if he felt it was the right direction. Rarely deviating from his vision of a lifetime devoted to show business, he always told me he intended to contribute his talents for as long as he possibly could, offering to entertain for free if it was for a good cause.

The fact that success and idolatry were offered to him so easily allowed Rudy to believe this state of affairs could go on forever. Perhaps that was behind his allegedly cocky demeanor. Even later, when some people thought he was all washed up, he doggedly pursued his dream, starring again on Broadway in a hit show at the age of sixty-one.

Like all men in their twenties, especially during the flapper era, Rudy played the field. His opportunities to meet dazzling young starlets, models, and debutantes were unlimited, especially in Hollywood. Moving from one girlfriend to the next like a bee flitting from flower to flower, Rudy soon gained a reputation as a charming womanizer.

Rudy loved to make love and he'd take advantage of every opportunity wherever he was, whether in the back seat of a limousine, on his boat, at a party. He confided to a friend, however, that he probably came to orgasm most frequently on a dance floor and usually the one at Ciro's supper club.

Living up to his star billing as America's most romantic singer during his heyday, he considered himself an accomplished lover.

"One of my greatest disappointments was breaking into the apartment of a girl who planned to dump me and finding she'd failed to mention both my musicianship and my prowess as a lover in her diary!" he complained.

In the waning years of his life, well into his seventies, Rudy reminisced about the young ladies he dated, as we watched the sunset from our patio. Just before bedtime he liked a glass of his favorite rum-and-pineapple, and we'd sit, just the two of us, talking about his early days in show business. "I remember the name of every girl I knew," he told me, "even what they were wearing on our first date."

In Rudy's archives I found an old phone book. It had an orange cover patterned with telephone cords. Many of the names on its yellow pages were followed by cryptic jottings, I assume in order for him to remember who the women were; other names were crossed out in thick, red pencil.

Although I don't know if they were friends or lovers, the names included Gail Patrick, who later produced the enormously successful Perry Mason series and whose husband was Ed Cobb, owner of the Brown Derby restaurant and creator of the Cobb Salad; Polly Adler; Joan Blondell; Linda Christian; Celeste Holm; Carole Landis; Virginia Mayo; and Janice Paige.

One entry read: "Service elevator, Hotel Senator, Sacramento." Another: "Scotch hat, Pickfair." And one "Texas Doug's home, blonde." Only Rudy knew what they meant.

FOUR

Friends, Lovers, and Good Times at the Lodge

ven more revealing than Rudy's private phone book were his secret diaries. They provided great insight into his early search for happiness. As he looked back on his life in his late seventies, Rudy planned to write a book called *Dolls of the Vallée*, enumerating the various amours he enjoyed. I am only mentioning a few here—the entire account would fill a book of its own!

Only I and a few close friends knew of this project. Rudy had an office on the lower floor in our house where he'd spend hours alone each day. After breakfast he'd retreat down the stairs, close the door, and pound away on his typewriter.

I'd forgotten all about the idea until I was sorting through Rudy's files after he died and found the intimate memoirs in a locked drawer. They were filled with more than fifty legendary star names: Hedy Lamarr, Linda Darnell, Ann Southern, Judy Canova, Wendy Barrie, Gene Tierney, Yvonne de Carlo, Joan Crawford, Alice Faye, Jane Wyman, Jean Harlow, and Betty Grable were just a few.

Some names merited several pages of notes, others only a line or two. Describing relationships, some obviously entirely innocent, the notes stated they were merely business or "convenience" dates while on location, and a few were romantic dates that went nowhere. After Jane Wyman's name, Rudy noted: "It was a quiet, relaxed dinner. I don't remember if we kissed."

However, a great deal of my husband's writings were devoted to describing racy sexual exploits, especially his remembrances of a Latin movie star, Lupe Velez, who was described as "a wild, Mexican spitfire with silky black hair and flashing dark eyes." She was dating Gary Cooper, who brought her to a Hollywood party in 1929.

"I was filming *Vagabond Lover* and the party was at the Blossom Room, in the Roosevelt Hotel on Hollywood Boulevard. The film colony elite met here for Monday night soirees and she caught my eye immediately," wrote Rudy. Lupe later married Johnny Weissmuller, the legendary Olympic swimmer who won five gold medals and starred in nineteen Tarzan movies. Rudy appeared in two or three movies with Weissmuller, including *Glorifying the American Girl* and *Phynx*. Sadly, Lupe Velez committed suicide soon after their marriage.

Writing about Betty Grable, Rudy commented: "Just one date and I chastised her for divorcing Jackie Coogan."

About Susan Hayward Rudy wrote: "She drove me up the wall as I saw her in a film but she was so different on our one date."

Here are some of the other comments:

Wendy Barrie: "A wonderful, crazy, darling girl who desired me very much but we were only friends."

Joan Caulfield's: "A delightful armful."

Madame Ouspenskya: "She tried hard to seduce me."

Jean Harlow: "RKO suggested I bring her to Villa Vallée. Instead, I put her in a cab and sent her home."

Ginger Rogers: "She proposed to me in a New York taxicab." (For years Ginger was a guest of ours at Silver Tip, and she always denied this story. But when she and I met in Palm Springs at the International Film Festival in 1995, two months before her death, she admitted that the story was true.)

In contrast to these brief notes, Rudy wrote a full six pages about singer Frances Langford, including: "She looked like nothing at all, as she had very plain features and with her flat heels, simple dress and hairdo, you would have said, 'A star? Never!' But when she stepped up to the microphone that afternoon [to audition for Rudy at the Olympia Theater in Miami] I realized how generous yet cruel fate can be to a human being. She had a vocal quality that was just pure, sheer, beauty of voice, with a natural gift for phrasing, breathing, and all that goes into perfection in the art of delivering a melody and lyric."

Some entries were extremely intimate. About his first date with Hedy Lamarr, Austrian-born star of the erotic film *Ecstasy* made in Europe, Rudy wrote that even the Vagabond Lover was shocked: "She invited me back to her apartment, which she shared with Ilona Massey, who was also at MGM Studios. After a few drinks Hedy suddenly stood up and took off her dress. As she saw the expression on my face she said, 'Yes! Just like a boy!' Then she declared that we must enjoy each other the Viennese way. She proceeded to lie face down on the floor."

Another slender, raven-haired beauty was Marie Windsor, who, Rudy noted, "had the largest and most awesome eyes I'd ever seen" and was another statuesque beauty. She later married Jack Hupp, a handsome ex-college basketball player. Rudy, myself, and the Hupps later became close friends and tennis partners.

Rudy met Linda Darnell, he recounts, when he was in Hollywood to make *Goldiggers in Paris* at Warner Brothers. "I had seen Linda in New York in a light play called *The Male Animal* and was captivated by her, in spite of a slight overbite of the two upper front teeth!"

Always dear and close friends since the day they met, Rudy and Alice Faye were linked romantically many times in the media, and she credits him with helping her get her dazzling career off to an early start. Rudy always said she was so great, she'd have made it on her own in any event. Alice sometimes substituted for Helen Morgan at New York's Embassy Club.

Devoting ten pages to his platonic relationship with Alice, whom I later met and became good friends with along with her husband Phil Harris, Rudy recounts how he met Alice in 1931: "A top producer and a real bastard louse of a man, George White, had put out feelers for me to star in the eleventh edition of his *Scandals* show on Broadway. As I was introduced to the cast, which included Ethel Merman and Ray Bolger," his diary continues, "one very, very young sweet little face stood out from all the rest. I learned her name was Alice Faye and she was only fifteen years old. A few years later I managed to persuade her to sing with my band. We shared a few kisses but Walter Winchell somehow got hold of us as an item, so we cooled it."

Since Rudy's marriage to his second wife, Fay Webb, was on the rocks at the time, I'm not surprised. Fay's father, Clarence, was Chief of Police in Santa Monica.

Alice still bears a small V-shaped scar over her left eye, however, as a souvenir of her performances with Rudy. "In 1933, Alice was my girl band singer," he wrote, "and we were playing the Steel Pier, Atlantic City. Alice, two Yale classmates, and myself got into one of my Cadillac 16's to head for Virginia Beach. Driving in heavy rain, around 2:00 A.M., I lost control and slid right off the highway. The car turned over twice, landing upright! To my horror I saw that the right front door was open and Alice had been thrown out into a field. I rushed over and saw a pool of blood in her left eye. Cleaning it out, I was overjoyed to see it was just a cut near her eyebrow."

Rudy eventually starred with Alice Faye in the 1933 film version of George White's *Scandals* in which they had several love scenes.

When I first met Alice in 1966 at Charlie Farrell's racquet club in Palm Springs, I'll never forget that the moment she saw me, this gracious lady took my hands and said, "I'm happy that you have made him happy. He needed someone like you." Alice went on to marry Tony Martin, and later, Phil Harris.

As I read Rudy's diaries I alternately experienced surprise, amusement, and compassion for this wonderful young man who went through so much turmoil with women. I also found it embarrassing to read these diaries, and I prefer to keep most of the memoir unpublished even though Rudy completed a few chapters.

When Rudy fell for someone, he fell all the way—and hard. However, the biggest surprise of all was when I came across my own name. It seems that Cora Canning, a young, attractive, redheaded debutante, was a great fan of Rudy's in 1934 and she chased him all over the country. She faithfully showed up at all his performances, whether it was a New York nightclub, a Los Angeles hotel ballroom, or a Florida theater. The pursuit continued for years.

"In 1937," writes Rudy, "Cora flew on the *Hindenburg* airship to see me play in London." Two years later she arrived on Rudy's doorstep in Hollywood, where he had just bought a home. Although not attracted to her at first—since his focus was on exotic brunettes—he nevertheless found her Irish looks quite appealing. Suddenly, he found himself desperately in love with her. At the same time, Cora's love for him appeared to be waning.

Rudy ended the account: "You might wonder why I chose my present wife who was a *Real Redhead* when I first saw her at Lake Tahoe. Eleanor was lucky that I had met a girl, called Mary McBride, whose features resembled hers. She devastated me so completely that when I realized that she could never return the great feeling I had for her, I began a search for another girl who resembled Mary and Cora physically, sexually, and in honest emotion. In Eleanor Norris I finally found my mate."

I laughed when I read that passage because after we were married I had fun wearing all different kinds of wigs depending on the gown I wore or the occasion, and I'd switch from brunette to blonde and everything in between. But it was as a redhead, my own natural color, that Rudy liked me best. Many years later I decided to go blond.

Rudy first saw Mary McBride when she was dancing with a naval officer at the Cocoanut Grove: "But for this girl, I would never have married my present wife, Eleanor, with whom I have enjoyed so many years of married life. Prior to my meeting Mary, I had always given all my attention and affection to women of one type. It was

Mary who was to revolutionize my taste in the fair sex. A beautiful wide smile, a generous mouth with beautiful white teeth, and light brown hair made her a vision of loveliness. A girl of class and quality, she had spent two years at the University of California, Los Angeles."

However, the romance with Mary died when Rudy recorded in his diary that he found a love letter she had written but not mailed to a serviceman in the South Pacific. Rudy's response was to go into the bathroom, tear off four feet of purple toilet paper, fold it up, and include it with Mary's letter, which he promptly posted to the poor man.

When Rudy first met Mary McBride, he broadcast a radio program called "The Sealtest Hour." The show enjoyed top billing, thanks to great writers like Abe Burrows, who later directed *How to Succeed in Business without Really Trying*; Paul Henning, who created *The Beverly Hillbillies*, *Green Acres*, and *Petticoat Junction*; Mel Frank; Norman Panama; Jess Oppenheimer, who created *I Love Lucy*; Charlie Isaacs; and Frank Galen.

Burrows' first comedy material appeared in 1937 in a sketch he and Frank Galen wrote for mimic Eddie Garr who was a guest on Rudy's show. "[With it performed] on the Rudy Vallée Hour, we felt as though we had been invited to Buckingham Palace," Abe said.

Katharine Hepburn was similarly grateful after appearing on Rudy's radio show. In a note written with a quill pen, she commented, "How nice you were to me at my first radio effort."

Rudy's show featured the top stars of the day including Phil Silvers, Gabby Hays, Dinah Shore, Burns and Allen, Lionel Barrymore, Henny Youngman, Orson Welles, Billie Burke, Charles Laughton, and, in his declining years, the legendary John Barrymore, whose gallant fight with alcoholism was eventually lost.

Rudy enlisted in the Coast Guard at the beginning of America's entry into World War II but continued his broadcasts. He led the fifty-two-piece Coast Guard Band complete with fifteen in the brass section, eight trumpets, and seven trombones. "That was the best band I ever directed," Rudy told me.

In great demand at military events, Rudy's schedule was frantic. He and Mary McBride drifted apart. The resemblance between Mary and myself was startling. She was tall, well-shaped, with long auburn hair and blue-green eyes. We both have a healthy, outdoors, athletic look and could be taken for sisters. More than a few people told me of the similarities we shared, and when I finally met Mary after Rudy and I were married, she and I giggled about it and became very good friends.

"Mary was a typical American beauty," I read in Rudy's diaries. But it appeared that she didn't reciprocate the passion Rudy felt for her. Once when I was at the Cal-Neva Hotel swimming pool, a good-looking man approached

"I'm sorry to keep staring at you, but you look just like a girl I know. You laugh like her, you even dive and swim like her. It's uncanny," he said.

"You must mean Mary McBride," I said, laughing. His eyes widened.

"How on earth did you know?"

"My husband dated her."

In spite of Rudy maintaining that he had vowed to go out with a different girl every night when he reached fame and fortune, he was, in fact, a great romantic and longed to settle down with his ideal woman.

In his book, *Vagabond Dreams Come True*, Rudy talks about women and refers to his mother, who died a year after the book was published: "A woman's physical charm is the thing that first attracts me, but unless she has many other wonderful qualities that my mother has, I am afraid we could never be happy. I love an industrious woman who enjoys housework, taking care of a thousand and one household things, and likes to cook."

Although accused by husbands and lovers that he somehow seduced their women over the radio, Rudy wrote: "Buddy Rogers does more damage to female hearts in one embrace with his heroine than I do in twenty broadcasts." Buddy starred with Rudy at the Paramount Theater in 1929.

When I told my parents Rudy had proposed to me, I wasn't surprised when my father protested because of Rudy's three previous wives. "With me, he's going to stay married, and we'll be lovers forever!" I said firmly.

What did surprise me was all three of his marriages were so short-lived. Rudy's first betrothal was to a young divorced New York singer, Leonie Cauchois. He met and married her while he was still a student at Yale and performing in Manhattan. She had a two-year-old child, and her father was a wealthy property owner and coffee merchant. After a whirlwind engagement, Rudy and Leonie were quickly married in Manhattan's City Hall. After just three months, the couple realized they'd made a mistake and mutually agreed to an annulment.

Rudy's marriage to his second wife, Fay Webb, was his longest, until our own, and kicked off a raucous four years of acrimonious accusations and distressing fights, culminating in a highly publicized divorce case. His courtship of Fay was a little rocky, too. In January 1930, Rudy felt compelled to write an apologetic letter to her father, Santa Monica Police Chief Clarence E. Webb, explaining away a newspaper account of his engagement to another girl, Agnes O'Laughlin, as a hoax. She was a chorus girl in Ziegfield's show *Whoopee* with Eddie Cantor. Seeing Agnes at his club, Villa Vallée, Rudy sent a waiter over with a note.

"The waiter came back white-faced," Rudy recounted. "It turned out that Agnes was with Larry Fay, a top gangster. The waiter dropped the note on the table and fled. Larry picked up the note and read it. Ellie, I was scared stiff! But he saw me watching him and smiled, waving me over to the table. He said, 'Rudy, she's all yours!'"

After a brief relationship, Rudy ended the affair and left for Hollywood, where he met Fay. Agnes sued Rudy for breach of promise and Rudy's attorney, Hymie Bushell, settled the case out of court for $1,000—after Hymie found out Agnes was a friend of mobster Legs Diamond's girlfriend, Kiki Roberts.

Writing about Fay in his 1962 book *My Time Is Your Time*, Rudy devotes an entire chapter to what he called this disastrous part of my life. "Fay Webb," Rudy said, reading to me from the book during one of our long evening conversations, "was the epitome of my type of woman at that time: sultry, dark-haired, long dark lashes, and dark eyes." She was under contract to MGM. Rudy met Fay through Marie Dressler when he was in Hollywood to star in *The Vagabond Lover* in 1929.

"A passionate love affair began, and she came to see me in New York a few times," Rudy went on. "Finally, she claimed that her father, the chief of police, said if I wanted to see her again, marriage would be necessary."

It was now 1931 and Rudy continued to enjoy the fruits of a fabulous career. At the Brooklyn Paramount, where he often did eight one-hour shows a day, he was pulling in $40,000 a week; he was starring in *Scandals* on Broadway; and although Rudy had left Don Dickerman's Heigh-Ho Club, he began playing at the Versailles on 60th Street in New York. Although it was later to become the Copacabana, during Rudy's engagement there its name was changed from Versailles to Villa Vallée because it was Rudy who was packing in sell-out crowds. It was reported in the press that by now Rudy Vallée was a millionaire.

Fay and Rudy were married by a justice of the peace in New Jersey, but their honeymoon in Atlantic City was cut short when Rudy was summoned to his mother's side. Near death, Katherine Vallée lingered a few more weeks before she was laid to rest in St. Hyacinth's Cemetery just outside Westbrook, Maine.

Returning to New York, Rudy told me that his grueling schedule—what a workaholic my husband was!—meant leaving Fay alone much of the day and evenings. Rehearsals for *George White's Scandals* often lasted from 10:00 A.M. until 10:00 P.M. then Rudy went to Villa Vallée for his regular performances. Fay became restless. He suggested she pay her parents a visit in Santa Monica. Once there, however, he said she refused to return. Soon, gossipy items appeared in the newspapers linking her with handsome men-around-town in Hollywood. Rudy flew out to the West Coast, and the couple began househunting, but the search ceased immediately when Rudy said he found her in the arms of his NBC agent on New Year's Eve.

They returned to their New York apartment, where Rudy, still suspicious, set up a tape machine to record Fay's phone conversations. Armed with evidence, Rudy confronted her. After a two-day silence, they made up.

"But I tell you, Ellie, my heart was no longer in my marriage," Rudy said. "She also had a terrible drinking problem."

After three more years of unceasing fights, Fay filed for divorce and the legal battle began in New York, just after Rudy finished filming *Scandals* in California. During the court proceedings, Rudy controlled his Irish temper until Ben Hartstein, Fay's attorney, insulted Rudy's best friend and lawyer, Hymie Bushell. Rudy glared at Hartstein with what Rudy called "malevolence."

"Then Hartstein said to me, "Stop acting! You're not in the movies now!," and I let fly with a right that just missed him." Rudy recounted. I can imagine what an uproar that caused in court. Flashbulbs popped everywhere and the next day every newspaper in the country ran a photo. On top of that, Fay demanded $90,000 a year. In 1935! The case was eventually settled out of court for a lump sum of $25,000. Fay stayed in Santa Monica but contracted tuberculosis and died just six months after the divorce.

Rudy's next marriage was much happier. At least, at first. While a Chief Petty Officer in the Coast Guard during World War II and stationed in Los Angeles, Rudy still managed to fit in radio broadcasts every day from the NBC studios at Sunset and Vine in Hollywood. As he left the backstage door one night, a group of fans clustered around. Signing autographs left and right, he heard what he called a lovely, fluid voice speaking to him.

"I looked up, Ellie, and there was this vision of loveliness in a flowered dress, with a little black velvet bellboy cap on her head. Her eyes were very slightly slanted, with a Chinese touch to them I found intriguing." She told him she was Bettejane Greer (later known in films as Jane Greer) and reminded him they'd met in Washington. In a flash, Rudy asked for her phone number, as he was due to play with his Coast Guard band at a war bonds benefit concert in Alhambra, California.

"When I called her later that night and invited her to dinner," Rudy said, "she first said yes, then no. It turned out that Howard Hughes had heard her sing at the Shoreham Hotel in Washington and sent her out to Hollywood. Hughes had proposed to her several times, but she always turned him down so she thought she'd better not come over to the house."

Did I get jealous when Rudy told me about his love affairs and described his wives and marriage in such detail? Did I wonder if every woman friend he introduced me to had slept with Rudy? In a word, no. I knew these women were before my time, so there was no reason to be jealous. Besides, I knew Rudy was completely faithful to me, as I was to him, from the day we married. All his old friends were amazed at this, having known Rudy in his bachelor days. They said he used to be a terrible flirt. Yet he never was in my presence, and I never felt threatened.

Rudy began to court Bettejane Greer. "Invariably," Rudy said, "when we were at the movies an usher would come down the aisle around 10:00 P.M. and lead her to a phone. I would have to drive her to Howard Hughes's offices just off La Brea Avenue. He'd grab her hand, she told me, look to see if there was an engagement ring on it, then tell her to leave."

Bettejane and Rudy were married in a military-style wedding under swords at Westwood Community Methodist Church, a small church on Wilshire Boulevard. U.S. Navy Captain John E. Johnson was the chaplain. Rudy was resplendent in his uniform, but Bettejane didn't wear white. Nor did she have a veil. Her dress was of silk, V-necked, and long-sleeved. Just seven months later, the pair were granted a divorce in Los Angeles. Bettejane, realizing Rudy's heart belonged to someone else, offered him his freedom. It was a friendly, mutual parting, and they remained good friends. Jane Greer later married Ed Lasker.

"I just couldn't get Mary McBride out of my system," Rudy told me. "Everywhere my wife and I went, there she was, dancing with some handsome military officer."

I met Jane myself many years later, after Rudy and I were married. We were invited by Tony Hulman to his Indy 500, where Rudy was to be one of the guests of honor. Tony was a fraternity brother of Rudy's, and we were treated like royalty at this famous race. I remember months later carefully pasting in a scrapbook every single one of the thirteen different pit, press, paddock, observation deck, gate, race day pass, staff sticker, and parking pass Tony gave us. Rudy loved collecting these mementos, however ordinary they were. Jane, as she was now called, was at a prerace party. I thought her extremely beautiful, and I could see why Rudy had fallen for her.

Rudy's favorite relaxation spot during the height of his fame was the 365-acre lakeside resort he built in the fall of 1930, hidden away in the pine woods of Maine. It symbolized his success.

Situated south of the White Mountain National Forest and close to the New Hampshire state line, Rudy's resort was on Lake Kezar. *National Geographic* magazine described Lake Kezar as one of the three most beautiful lakes in the world for its ideal size, beauty of surrounding trees, foliage, and sweep of mountains. Rudy's nearest neighbor was Don Dickerman, owner of the Heigh-Ho Club.

"I escaped to my retreat whenever my terrific road manager, Sam Narefsky, gave me a break!" Rudy said, showing me photos of the red mini-piano that Edgar Bergen and Charlie McCarthy presented him with on their first visit to The Lodge.

I saw from the photo albums there were plenty of other musical instruments on hand that, Rudy told me, were put to good use during weekends, including a pipe organ. After mice finally ate the chamois leather off the organ's pipes, Rudy replaced it with a Hammond Novacord.

There were several phonographs, of course, and record albums ranging from hit tunes of the day to the classical *Sheherezade*, Rudy's favorite. All day long music filled the air, the greater number of songs sung by Bing Crosby. Bing became Rudy's favorite vocalist. My husband snapped up just about every album Bing made.

In return, in December 1931 Crosby wrote to the Elks Home, in Portland, Maine, which was honoring Rudy with a testimonial dinner: "I want to join Portland in paying tribute to the man who has labored earnestly and effectively for the elevation of the popular American song; who is outstanding and pre-eminent in the radio world and enjoys the whole-hearted respect and admiration of all his contemporaries."

One of Rudy's dear friends at the time, Adela Rogers St. John, wrote to him from Hollywood in the early 1930s: "I have been seeing something of your friend Mr. Bing Crosby. He's working at the studio and I have decided to do a one-part yarn on him for *Liberty* [magazine]. He wouldn't be worth any more than that. I'm glad I've gotten to know him slightly, for there is the King of Nuts."

Generous in his praise and suggestions to promote his discoveries, Rudy would nevertheless let loose a tirade of abuse on the unfortunate people he felt were ungrateful for his efforts on their behalf.

Victor Borge probably felt the most heat from this trait. Until the day he died, Rudy never forgave Victor for what he perceived as the renowned pianist's refusal to thank Rudy for giving him his start in show business. I sat through many an hour's ranting as Rudy vented about the way he felt Borge treated him—sixty years ago!

"That damned man," Rudy's usual preamble began. "Borge is without question one of the most brilliant creative comedic minds performing today. But back then no one would hire him. When I first auditioned him, he was down and out. His wife and kids had no food. But I flipped over Borge's act, he performed "Phonetic Punctuation," and it sent me into hysterics. He was fantastic. I wanted to use him on my Sealtest radio show but the timing wasn't right—it would have meant dumping John Barrymore. But I was so impressed with Borge I told him to call Bing Crosby to see if he could get on his radio show. The rest is entertainment history. Did Borge ever thank me? No! Never! Not once! He made millions because of me."

"I know, Rudy dear. Calm down. Forget it," I'd say soothingly.

"Ellie, you're an angel. You never hold a grudge against anyone. But I do. How can I forget it? It's the most outrageous ungratefulness in show business! I won't calm down." And Rudy would stomp off down to his office and fire off another angry letter to some poor soul currently in the news Rudy disagreed with.

Although I was surprised that my articulate Yalie couldn't come up with a better name for his rural refuge than "The Lodge," the sprawling complex of luxurious rustic cottages was a magnificent hideaway. Oriental carpets covered the floors, specially made log chandeliers hung from the beamed ceilings, and the exquisite furnishings—Irish linens, Italian and French pottery, and other fabulous accessories—were custom ordered from New York's most exclusive stores.

Rudy loved to shop, especially when we were in a foreign country. I can just picture him back then going from store to store on Fifth Avenue picking out made-to-order tablecloths, goosedown pillows, and the little bar and chromium chairs for the Clubhouse, as he called the building near the tennis court he built in 1938.

"I imported lead glass windows from England," he said proudly, "and had shelves of bestsellers in every bedroom."

Rudy was constantly remodeling and adding to the seven buildings as his guest list grew. He filled the multitude of rooms with musicians, movie stars, performers, showgirls, and anyone else he took a fancy to. He usually invited his entire band and their wives up for a weekend, when an average crowd ranged from fifty to one hundred people, bringing them in by train or limo. Other times he'd have the band spend a week's vacation at The Lodge with full pay.

After Rudy's father Charles became a widower in 1931, he was a regular guest. There are photos of this friendly little Frenchman in a formal suit and grey spats, lounging on a velvet sofa. His Gaelic charm attracted the ladies in spite of his short, rotund shape and the perennial cigar in his left hand. Rudy adored his father.

"Dad loved pretty women," Rudy told me. "When he came on tour with me, he'd tip his hat to all the chorus girls. After he taught them the French greeting of a peck on both cheeks, his face was always covered with lipstick." I'm sure Rudy inherited his own gallantry and charm from the paternal side of his family, along with his love for the company of women. Unfortunately, I never had the pleasure of meeting my father-in-law. He died several months before our wedding, but Rudy told me many wonderful stories about him and of Charles's pride in his son's ownership of The Lodge.

Rudy loved huge, stone, log-burning fireplaces—there were several at our Hollywood home—and before guests arrived, he requested the staff to light roaring fires in each cottage.

Concerned about hygiene, a trait that continued during our marriage when he launched public campaigns for awareness, Rudy paid particular attention to The Lodge's fixtures, especially in the many bathrooms. He imported inlaid colored tile, unheard of in such a rustic setting in 1930, and decorated each bathroom with a specific color scheme, matching faucets, fixtures, sinks, and bathtubs in ebony black, sky blue, and pale green. Everything in the Pink Lady bathroom was pink including the tissues, soap, towels, floor, fixtures, and walls.

"I stocked The Lodge's several bars with every kind of liquor available," he told me once as he mixed us one of his favorite drinks, "and I made thousands of daiquiris on the Waring blender."

Rudy was the first to own the mechanized drink mixer, courtesy of our friend Fred Waring, its inventor. For years Rudy and I carried the blender in our luggage everywhere as we fulfilled nightclub, film, radio, and television dates. On the train, in hotels, at the pool, in the backstage dressing room, Rudy kept the machine at his side to make rum drinks.

"Rudy made something called a frozen daiquiri, which I'd never heard of back then," Paul Henning told me. "It was the best thing I ever tasted. When Paul and his wife Ruth got back home from the lodge, there was a box awaiting them, with all the necessary ingredients to make daiquiris and a Waring blender, courtesy of Rudy.

Never doing anything in a small way, Rudy kept The Lodge's tennis court supplied with one hundred cans of balls at all times and dozens of tennis racquets. There were also boxes and boxes of shuttlecocks for the badminton court. The game room closet held eighty-five board games; the larder, hundreds of cases of canned food; and the lakeside cabin was filled with every kind of float and raft imaginable.

Rudy built a dock complete with ladder and waterslide, and packed the boathouse with twelve tiny boats for water polo. He had eight kayaks, two sailboats, and ten paddleboats for guests to use. His own favorite was the thirty-one-foot Chris-Craft cruiser called "Banjo Eyes," which Eddie Cantor gave him in appreciation for pinch-hitting as host on his radio show.

Eddie and Rudy were a mutual admiration society; they idolized each other's talents. One of Rudy's most treasured mementos is a letter from Eddie, dated December 15, 1931, to the Portland Elks Lodge, apologizing for not being able to attend a dinner: "In honoring Rudy Vallée, the Portland Lodge of Elks is paying tribute to more than an outstanding personality in the theater; Rudy Vallée, to my mind, is one of the finest human beings it has been my good fortune to know. His unselfishness, his ready willingness to help those less fortunate than himself, endears him in the hearts of all the people in our profession. He has many imitators, but there will always be only one Rudy Vallée."

Another guest was Paul Keyes, who later became the producer of *The Tonight Show*. Paul, who came from Maine, was a great fan of Rudy's. He asked him to stop by his high school one time as Rudy was on his way to The Lodge. Paul and his wife, Miriam, became friends of ours, when they moved out to Los Angeles, staying with us until they could find a house to buy.

A fitness buff, Rudy had plenty of gym equipment around The Lodge. Violinist Richard Himber, always a welcome guest, supplied most of it—an Exercycle, a punching bag, and medicine balls.

My husband said he named The Lodge's bedrooms, the den, dining room, living room, even his closet after songs that were identified with him and nailed plaques to their doors. Alice Faye's boudoir, at the top of the stairs under the eaves, was called "Nasty Man," her debut song with Rudy's band. His own master bedroom, of course, was "Vagabond Lover" and was furnished in eggshell blue and deep bronze colors. If he invited a couple up who had recently married or had a special anniversary, he'd lend them his sumptuous bedroom.

Always full of creative ideas, Rudy commissioned carved wood-and-scrolled-silver musical cigarette boxes to place in every room that play a melody to match the room's name. "The tune 'Saxophobia' was really difficult to put into music-box form," Rudy related, "but the little mechanism played it out quite clearly."

The bright red music box in Rudy's exotic cherry-and-black bathroom was named for actress-singer Lenore Ulric and tinkled out the title song of her show, "Lulu-Belle." The little blue one in the Vallée dressing room played "Flying Trapeze"; the room called Americana had a cigarette box that played "America"; and the Blue Room's played the song "Blue Room" from the Rodgers and Hart musical *The Girl Friend*. One or two of those music boxes are in my house today. I treasure these wonderfully historic souvenirs of a bygone era.

One of his favorite gifts was an Indian curio carving from David Randolph Milsten, who played the trumpet with Rudy in the Yale Collegians band.

In spite of Rudy claiming he built The Lodge to relax, my workaholic husband always brought up songs to study, arrangements to rewrite, recordings of auditions to listen to, mail to answer, and ditties to memorize for his radio broadcasts. "At least I got away from the noise and city air of New York," he said. Yet he discouraged his guests, especially the musicians in his band, from discussing business or working while at The Lodge.

Because of Rudy's close association with a number of sponsors for his shows, a variety of products and food began arriving at The Lodge. Heinz sent sacks of beans; a Portland company baked brown bread for Rudy and his guests; Frank Gravatt, who ran the Steel Pier in Atlantic City, sent salt-water taffy and macaroons; and from the Poland Spring Company came spring water, ginger ale, and club soda to accompany liquor from Seagrams, Don Q, and Ronrico. There was never any shortage of Chase and Sandborn coffee, Tenderleaf Tea, Royal Gelatin Desserts, and Planters Peanuts, whose president sent a thousand cans of nuts. Sealtest, of course, contributed milk, ice cream, and cheese.

Although Rudy didn't smoke but enjoyed an occasional cigar, Philip Morris and Old Gold sent a constant supply of cigarettes, and Eli Witt of Tampa, Florida, made sure Rudy had plenty of humidors around The Lodge filled with his favorite Hav-a-tampa Jewels, tipped with a small wooden stem. And there was certainly no need for Rudy to buy cigarette lighters. Each of the boys in Rudy's band generously gave him a lighter with his name engraved on the front. He begged guests not to lift them as a souvenir, according to his book of rules.

Generous with The Lodge's amenities—fishing on Lake Kezar, hiking in his private maple, elm, and birch forests, playing pool on the walnut table Dorothy Lamour gave him as a gift—Rudy was an acknowledged eccentric to his guests. "He was a nut for neatness," said a frequent guest who believed Rudy inherited the mania from his mother. "Especially if we left our belongings at the lake or on the courts."

As each guest arrived at The Lodge, Rudy handed out a copy of an illustrated birch-bark bound brochure called "Lodge Logic and Your Eccentric Host." He'd written it himself and the eight pages set out strict rules and codes of conduct:

* When thru using a face or bath towel please use them to clean the mirror or chromium bath fixtures to delight the next user.
* Don't clog the toilet bowls. Plumbers must come twenty-five miles to undo the damage.
* Don't operate the phonograph; it requires bringing a man forty miles to repair it.
* Don't overeat, overdrink, over-exercise.
* Servants are not here to put caps and stoppers back on your tube of shaving cream.

He also admonished everyone to "stretch like a cat at least twice a day," take a siesta every afternoon, stay limp when awake whenever possible, and above all, "don't talk shop." This final command was, of course, ignored because the Lodge usually hosted musicians, actors, producers, and others in the entertainment industry.

When it was time to leave, Rudy's meticulous planning was still in evidence. He placed a record on the phonograph to play his favorite vocalist, Bing Crosby, singing "The End of a Perfect Day" as he and his guests streamed out the door.

One of the biggest regrets of Rudy's life was selling The Lodge in Maine, long before we met.

"How I wish I could have kept it for you, Buttercup," he'd say. "But I'd moved to the West Coast and, when I enlisted in the Coast Guard, there was no further use for it." At one point he considered writing to his father with the idea The Lodge could be turned into a convalescent base for the returning wounded, but it seems the government was not interested.

I wish Rudy had kept The Lodge. It sounded fabulous, and I'd loved to have owned it. But his later financial woes forced the sale. I once asked Rudy how much he paid for the almost four-hundred-acre estate. "$8,000. I sold it for $38,000."

In 1972, according to a newspaper report, a developer bought an adjoining one hundred thirty acres for $400,000. When he heard the news, Rudy spent a few fiery hours exhausting his vocabulary of colorful expletives.

I still have some old, frayed copies of the Book of Rules he handed out to his guests. The birch-bark covers turned brown years ago, but the handwritten code of behavior is as clear as ever.

FIVE

From Radio to Vallée-Video

The Dizzy Decade, as Westinghouse Broadcasting called it when they hired Rudy to host their radio series, was his most successful and busiest. Stretching from 1929 to 1939, the years encompassed the Depression and the threat of war. Rudy was the most recognized entertainer in broadcasting, and anybody who was anybody appeared on his radio show: Bob Hope, Ozzie Nelson, Carmen Miranda, Larry Adler, Helen Hayes, Katharine Hepburn, Fanny Brice, Bert Lahr, Bea Lillie, Joan Davis, Ken Murray, Joe Penner, Billie Burke, and Kate Smith.

"In his heyday," wrote disc jockey and columnist Joe Franklin in his book *Up Late with Joe Franklin*, "Rudy Vallée was bigger than Michael Jackson and Bruce Springsteen and the Spin Doctors combined. I was very close with Rudy Vallée. He was gigantic. One time he picked up the phone and on the extension heard his wife, Fay Webb, saying, 'Hi lover, I'm gonna poison him tonight.' It made front-page headlines. It was bigger than World Wars I and II put together."

Rudy and Joe were close friends, and in his later years Rudy appeared on Joe's radio shows no fewer than eighty-five times as a guest, often with me, talking nostalgia and playing Rudy's most well-known recordings.

Caricatures and cartoons of Rudy appeared everywhere, in the *New York Graphic, Life*, the *New York Herald-Tribune*, and hundreds of other national publications. His hit tunes included "Sweet Lorraine," "Deep Night," "Kitty from Kansas City," "Betty Co-ed," "If I Had a Girl Like You," " Old New England Moon," "I'm Dancing with Tears in My Eyes," and "Forgive Me."

The week of May 3, 1930, "The Stein Song" topped the New York list of bestselling sheet music and another Vallée hit, "Springtime in the Rockies," was second. "I was so busy running from one engagement to another, Ellie, I once had to dress in a box office in plain view of the customers buying tickets."

On September 10 of that year, the circulation of New York's *Daily Mirror* took a huge jump when its front page headline claimed Rudy was tortured by two bandits outside the Paramount Theater until he gave up $10,000. The story, said Rudy, was untrue.

That fall he visited the University of Maine to present his younger brother, Bill, with an SAE fraternity pin in a formal ceremony; he was invited to meet and chat with Mrs. Herbert Hoover; and broadcast the first performance in America of a new European dance craze called The Moochi.

By now Rudy Vallée had earned unprecedented respect from his peers. Bing Crosby put into words his admiration for Rudy Vallée as "the man who has labored earnestly and effectively for the elevation of the popular American song, who is outstanding and pre-eminent in the radio world."

Impresario George White added: "Rudy Vallée. . .is the outstanding singer of the present day and the greatest radio artist in the world. He can be counted one of America's leading citizens."

On July 28, 1933, Rudy's thirty-second birthday, he made world history as the telephone company's choice to receive the first "singing telegram" sent to him at his New York club.

In 1935 composer Ferdy Grofe honored Rudy by writing a piece of music called "The Rudy Vallée Suite"; in 1936 Suffolk Law School presented him with an honorary masters degree, and in 1937 Rudy was elected president of the American Federation of

Actors, a job he took with great seriousness to advance the interests of fellow performers.

Rudy's hometown of Westbrook honored him by changing the name of the square his father's drugstore was located on to "Rudy Vallée Square." When Rudy showed me a press clipping about the event, I read that Paramount and other studios filmed the proceedings, which were presided over by Ernest Porell. This kind gentleman was startled later to receive letters from as far away as Mexico from people who knew Westbrook and saw Porell's "first and only screen test."

It was during this period that Rudy undertook one of his most generous gestures. Despite his fame and the demands on him, Rudy found time to befriend a young blind girl, Margaret Young, who lived in Chicago in somewhat dire straits.

I was not aware of his compassion for her and her devotion to him until I began researching this book. Martin Getzler, the curator for Rudy's archives at the Thousand Oaks Library in California, showed me the lengthy correspondence the two carried on from 1930 until she died. I am so proud of Rudy for this act of kindness. His whole career was about being able to touch someone and make their life a little happier.

Rudy sent Margaret money for food and other necessities, and she sent him back accounts of where the money went: "6 eggs, 11 cents; milk, 7 cents; medicine," And so on. She had an amazing capacity for accepting her life and never complained. In spite of her youth, Margaret's letters, written on a Braille typewriter, were mature and poetic. In one she wrote, "With this heavy curtain of darkness drawn as tightly as not to allow even the brightest ray of sunshine to penetrate my eyes, the greatest pleasure I have in life is listening to music and, to be sure, the most beautiful music which has ever found its way into my life has come from your beautiful golden voice. It is so soft and sweet and possessing all the while a slight tone of sadness—it seems to cast a momentary spell over me. I feel I have been taken suddenly to another world, and that the voice which was so filling my heart with joy was that of an angel."

Rudy responded and talked about his life. Margaret writes back: "You said in your letter that there are a great many headaches and heartaches connected with your profession. I am so, so sorry. In this lonely, dark life of mine I have always wondered just what I would like to be. I should like to be some sort of an instrument, not a person at all, but the kind of instrument that does not exist anywhere, the purpose of which would be to take away all your heartaches and leave you as happy as you are wonderful."

His friendship with Margaret prompted Rudy to have Helen Keller on his radio show in 1936. She wrote to him afterwards: "Once you said your art was somewhat like that of a physician, and now I realize how true that is, such a multitude calls upon you for the cheer of your songs and the healing balm of your sympathy."

Almost immediately Rudy acquired a Braille fan club and was gifted with a copy of his autobiography, *Vagabond Dreams Come True*, in Braille, a copy of which is in his archives. Rudy was worshipped by these sightless fans. One wrote, "I touch the radio for vibration when you broadcast because I am also tone deaf."

In 1938 the Rudy Vallée name was immortalized in *Who's Who in New York*, and later in the 1946 and 1947 editions of *Who's Who in America*.

During 1939 Rudy appeared in a New York play, *The Man in Possession*, but his radio show for Fleischmann's Yeast ended. Fortunately, another radio program was developed and in 1940 Rudy began broadcasting the "Sealtest Hour." In that year he also became a Hollywood nightclub owner along with Bing Crosby, Fred MacMurray, Jimmy Fiddler, Vic Erwin, and Ken Murray. Run by his old friend Don Dickerman, the club was called The Pirates Den. Among his favorite guests were Martha Raye and Dorothy Lamour, who used to get up and sing spontaneously.

Back in New York, Rudy found a friend from Los Angeles had hit town—Morey Amsterdam. "I met Rudy when I was living in Woodley Heights writing and performing comedy around 1937," he said. "I was always impressed with his choice of words. He spoke so intelligently. He could introduce a guest on his show like no one else ever did, or has since. Rudy told me that if I ever came to New York, he'd show me around. Well, did he ever! He took us to the Broadway shows, the best restaurants and clubs. He was very generous. Anybody who ever told me Rudy was tough with a buck was wrong. He gave me a camera he'd bought in England and sent me all kinds of equipment. When he opened at the Waldorf Astoria, we went out and bought silk top hats to wear. We had a great time."

Morey once told me that Rudy's legacy would always be that of a historical figure in the pop music culture of America because he introduced so many songs. In 1943, buoyed by the success of Paramount's *Happy Go Lucky* with Betty Hutton, Mary Martin, Dick Powell, and Eddie Bracken, Rudy was now considered a true Hollywood celebrity. He was all over town squiring starlets, doing the nightclub scene, and appearing in fan magazines.

Rudy decided it was time to renovate his new home, Silver Tip: heating the swimming pool, excavating cellars to house wines and memorabilia, and motorizing the hand-cranked car turnstile. The door was never closed. Hosting tennis parties on the rooftop court, film screenings in the little theater, formal dinners in the banquet room, and casual soirees in the games room, Rudy lived a charmed life.

Errol Flynn rode over on horseback from his home across the canyon, and stars from all the studios found their way up the hill to the Vallée castle. "Errol came over primarily to play tennis and to see if I had any cute girls around," Rudy told me.

My own meeting with Errol Flynn was many years later when he and his son, Sean, were visiting New Orleans on their way to Errol's home in Jamaica.

Rudy and I were part of "The Hadacol All-Star Caravan Tour," a traveling vaudeville show to promote a vitamin tonic for elderly people invented by Senator LaBlanc. Actually, it seemed to me it was full of alcohol. Hadacol's first promoter was Colonel Tom Parker, who later went on to become Elvis Presley's mentor and manager. Billy Daniels, Carmen Miranda, Hank Williams, Minnie Pearl, Jimmy Durante, Jack Dempsey, Milton Berle, Dick Haymes, and Rudy were signed on for portions of the forty-seven-city show through the South and Midwest.

In New Orleans, Cesar Romero was one of the stars. After the performance Rudy said, "Ellie, I want to fix Cesar up with some beautiful women. He's all alone here." So Rudy went off and came back with half a dozen showgirls, all gorgeous and raring to go out on the town. Rudy phoned Cesar in his hotel room.

"Come down to the club. We've got a surprise for you." When Cesar arrived and saw all the girls, he excused himself and left. So we took the girls out. We never tried to fix him up again.

The next night we were sitting at the long bar in Pat O'Brien's restaurant. "Ellie, there's Errol Flynn," Rudy said. My husband waved and Errol and his son joined us.

"Who's this?" said Errol. "She's terrific. I want a date. Introduce me, Rudy."

"With the greatest pleasure. Ellie, this is Errol Flynn. Errol, my bride." Errol gaped. Then shrugged in a charming way.

"Well, next year, she could be mine." We laughed and spent the evening together.

After playing in thirty-five locations, the Hadacol tour was abandoned and everyone went home.

Not all of the guests at Silver Tip were high-powered tycoons, celebrities, and VIPs, although musicians like Billy Daniels and Lita Baron were among our favorites. One of the biggest and most pleasant surprises came when Nadine Keller, the young daughter of our friends Bill and Mary, came to Los Angeles on a business trip. She had planned on staying in a hotel but Rudy and I invited her to stay with us instead. At the end of her first week with us, she presented Rudy with a check, saying, "If I stayed in a hotel, I'd have to pay." Rudy accepted the check only after she threatened to leave if he didn't, and after that he always enjoyed telling the story of Silver Tip's only "paying guest."

Rudy loved meeting people in all walks of life, as I learned soon enough after meeting him. I never knew who I was going to be entertaining. Rudy invited people on impulse, especially if he found them fascinating, and more often than not, he'd steal off to a quiet room and they'd talk for hours.

When we went to parties, he disliked having to waste time with small talk until he found someone he found interesting. I often went on ahead so I could meet the most fascinating people in the room before he arrived. Then I'd introduce them.

"I always had to hire an extra bartender when I gave parties and you were on our guest list," Diane Abramson, one of our dear friends, reminded me. "Rudy loved to discuss wines—one of his favorites was Moscato Amabile—liquors, and various kinds of exotic drinks. He'd disappear with the bartender for hours!" She was right, and I had the same experience at our own house many, many times. Rudy often sneaked off, an interesting new guest in tow.

I knew this trait was due to another of Rudy's qualities I so admired, his curiosity. Not only was he a walking encyclopedia as far as I was concerned, he never stopped learning. Rudy wanted to know exactly how everything worked, how it was built, how it should be used. Once he grasped this new information, he'd want to make sure everyone else knew it too. Sometimes he made my head spin with all the facts and figures he collected.

It was 1942 and, while most Americans' thoughts were on the war, Rudy's were on his career, which now centered in Hollywood. He considered himself a bona fide resident of Los Angeles, severing most of his business ties with New York and hiring West Coast attorneys and financial advisors.

"Dammit, Rudy, you're a terrific bandleader, but why can't you ever keep in step?" Arnold Wechter's voice sliced through the early morning mists as he and his fellow members of the Coast Guard, 11th Naval District, marched to Vallée's band in San Pedro, California.

"When they give me a commission, maybe I'll get in step," Vallée quipped. Volunteering, Rudy took over as bandmaster, entertaining the troops in every branch of the services and loving every minute of it.

On August 18 of that year, Bette Davis sent a handwritten note saying she was anxious to know if he was going to help with an auction at Pickfair, the home of movie greats Douglas Fairbanks and Mary Pickford, as a fund-raiser for the war effort. Rudy, of course, offered his services.

Busy as ever, he continued his radio broadcasts for Sealtest, encouraging listeners to join the services and buy war bonds. He turned over his Sealtest salary to the Coast Guard Welfare Fund. One radio show prompted a note from Groucho Marx "You whined so plaintively and effectively the other night."

Walt Disney wrote to Rudy from his Burbank studios: "As a lover of military band music myself it is with sincere pleasure that I am sending you these copies of a special studio arrangement of 'The Song of the Eagle' which I think you will find both patriotic and inspirational . . . it is the main theme of the musical score to our picture 'Victory Through Airpower' . . . with kindest personal regards . . . Sincerely, Walt Disney."

After grooming comedians Jack Haley and Joan Davis as hosts to replace him, Rudy's final Sealtest show was broadcast on July 1, 1943. "By the time the war ended a couple of years later, Ellie, and I returned to civilian life, many changes had taken place," Rudy told me somewhat sadly. Radio was beginning to give way to television; interest in ballroom dancing was ebbing; hot jazz was all the rage; and many nightclubs closed.

Yet small film parts continued to come Rudy's way. Whenever he left the club to fulfill movie contracts, he recommended Will Osborne and his band as a replacement, teaching Will to use a megaphone.

On the pop music scene Crosby was tremendously popular and Sinatra's fame was increasing with every record album he produced. Other new singers were emerging as well: Johnny Mercer, Tony Martin, Dick Haymes, Perry Como, Vaughan Monroe, and Mel Torme. The field was now crowded and Rudy quickly discovered he was no longer in great demand.

Although he continued to be tapped for movie roles, Rudy said they were often cameo parts. Still, by the time I met Rudy many years later, he had been in seventeen films already and continued in movies after we were married. One in particular he enjoyed making in 1947 was *The Bachelor and the Bobbysoxer* with Shirley Temple. A letter he sent to Shari Lewis in 1977 reveals that Shirley Temple was the deciding factor in Rudy getting the role of district attorney in the film. "She felt I'd give the part something refreshingly different," he wrote.

Rudy and his orchestra played some nightclub dates in Hollywood at the Cocoanut Grove, where, he wrote to his friend Bill Keller, "I just hope it won't be a repetition of the Roxy. We had a big opening and then there was as nose-dive thereafter." Fortunately, the Cocoanut Grove was a great success.

Ever innovative, eager to try something new when necessary, Rudy tried his hand at comedy. "I admired Jack Benny, Eddie Cantor, and Fred Allen," Rudy said, explaining how he came up with his format. "I studied their style and what made them successful."

"Who's the best, in your opinion?" I asked.

"There is one true comic I glorify, and that is Jonathan Winters. He approaches real genius. Dick Shawn has it at times, too." Soon, Rudy was performing routines based on his own tongue-in-cheek brand of humor. He sang saucy songs and ditties, told jokes, and played the sax.

He was also invited to be a judge to select a beauty queen to compete in the 1945 Miss America contest. There he met W.M. Jeffers, president of Union Pacific Railroad. Rudy subsequently invited Eileen and William Jeffers to his home, where he treated the couple to a live performance of "All Points West," a story of a train announcer who had no where to go—one of Rudy's most famous monologues.

Looking for fresh material, he wrote a letter to Hal Block, whose article in *Variety* appealed to him: "Your style of writing is exactly the type of thing I want for monologues for myself. As you probably know, my approach is that of a restrained Yankee, a straight-faced type of diatribe on various situations, customs, etc. I bemoan what has happened to my beloved radio."

At this point in his career Rudy came up with an idea for a series of sixteen millimeter videotapes for television, although there were only sixty or so stations at that time. He formed a company, Vallée-Video, to produce short films and musical features to bridge the gap between shows not sponsored by advertisers. Vallée-Video has been called a precursor to television as we know it today, and Rudy was in the forefront. He planned to sell these new music video-tapes at music stores. Rudy believed he stood to make millions. Another venture he got into was Vis-o-Graph—"soundies" or brief films of orchestras and singers shown on small machines you looked into through an opening while cranking a handle.

Fired up with enthusiasm for Vallée-Video, Rudy rented a small studio at 5746 Sunset Boulevard and amassed camera equipment. He hired Joe Parker as his vice president. Rudy was Joe's best man at his wedding, then godfather to Joe's first son.

Rudy set to work writing, directing, and often starring in the made-for-TV shorts. He called them "songfilms." Among the first Vallée-Videos produced were "These Foolish Things Remind Me of You," "College Days," and "Under a Campus Moon." Comedian Ed Wynn starred in "It Pays to Exercise."

The company brochure announced that Vallée-Video was the first to cut in canned laughter in its comedy films, the first to announce credit titles, and the first to bring the lyrics of phonograph records to life with sketches, cartoons, live performers. The fledgling TV production company tailored its films for "the budgets of the smallest television stations," with the talents of Pinky Lee, Buddy Lester, Cyril Smith, Mike Riley and his Mad Men, Steve Gibson and His Red Caps, and Don Zelaya.

"My idea," Rudy said, "was to produce 'bumpers' to segue between television programs so viewers didn't have to sit and watch dead air. Remember, this was way before commercials. So I decided to dramatize songs, music that was acted out, just like the videos on MTV today. Unfortunately, Ellie, everything took three times as long to complete, and the delays drove me up the wall," he told me.

At one point Vallée-Video was on the verge of signing a huge contract with Philip Morris, and Rudy rented a larger studio with a sound stage at 6611 Santa Monica Boulevard. But the format for the films became a bone of contention, and what would have been a lucrative deal fell through. Other potential sponsors Rudy approached were Philco, Zenith, and Ralston Purina, and a contract was almost signed with NBC to do a Dick Tracy series. Ralph Byrd, who played Tracy on the screen, was a long-time friend of Rudy's, and he was scheduled to play the same role in the Vallée-Video films. That deal, too, failed to materialize.

Rudy wrote to Francis, Day & Hunter, a British music publishing company, asking for sixteen millimeter television film rights to "Sam and His Musket" and "Albert and the Lion of Blackpool," although records show that Vallée-Video had already produced the films.

My husband was always innovative, a visionary, but often his practical side prevented his ideas from turning into actual projects. Rudy asked Victor Kayfetz, a New York agent who was approaching movie mogul Otto Preminger to film *The Vallée Story*, to help promote Vallée-Video films. Kayfetz suggested selling or renting the videos to the home market, long before anyone heard of home videos. Rudy nixed the idea.

Rudy then asked Bill Keller to represent Vallée-Video in New York. Bill was the brother of orchestra leader Jack Keller, who was also a captain with American Airlines and who Rudy had helped years earlier to be hired at the Milton Point Casino in Westchester, New York. "I met Rudy by chance after World War II, in the Entre Cafeteria at Vine and Hollywood Boulevard, where we both liked the food," Bill told me on a later visit to our home. The remark brought back memories of Rudy's enjoyment of eating at cafeterias: the selections were wholesome and safe, the places were usually clean, and the service was fast.

Rudy's favorite food was roast lamb and turnips. That's why he loved the Horn & Hardart cafeteria on the corner of 42nd Street and Fifth Avenue, New York. Everyone knew America's favorite singer could be found sitting at the counter during breaks from playing at the Roxy Theater.

"So here we were at the Entre," Bill continued, "and Jack looked over and saw Rudy. Jack got up and re-introduced himself, thanking him again for his help before the war. Well, Rudy ended up inviting us both to his house and showing us those incredible archives of his and his memorabilia. It was astounding. And that's when he offered me the opportunity to help him with Vallée-Video."

Nothing came of the association, however. "Vallée-Video could have been the forerunner to the Desilu empire, Rudy had such an inventive mind," recalled Bill. "But he was on the road a lot, and I think mismanagement might have been a factor."

That was one of Rudy's fatal flaws. He was competent in so many areas that sometimes he insisted on handling problems himself. He should have delegated the work to others. We lost many opportunities because of this attitude, and it cost Rudy his big chance to be a television star.

To keep his new venture afloat, Rudy traveled constantly, appearing in supper clubs, dinner theaters and hotels around the country. This forced him to leave the Vallée-Video business in the hands of Joe Parker. Lacking Rudy's dynamic energy and expertise, I think Joe was overwhelmed and had a hard time dealing with the details. Eventually, Rudy decided he was spread too thin and disbanded the company. He was upset about letting Vallée-Video go because he saw that television was rapidly replacing radio.

He continued to guest on a few radio shows but, as the old-guard executives, producers, and directors retired, new decision makers filled the shoes of Rudy's loyal friends. New formats and new talent were demanded. His variety show budget was cut to the bone, and he was often forced to work with talent he knew nothing about and people he didn't know.

"Rudy didn't move forward because he didn't conform to what the kids wanted in music," was publicist Paul Ross's opinion. "He needed to be on television, but he didn't pursue it. Instead, he preferred going on the road."

Then along came the "Sealtest Hour" for NBC, which ran from 1940 to 1943. "I knew I had to come up with something new, something different, a change," he told me. "If you're different, people take notice. Nothing is worse than an entertainment pattern you follow forever."

Although he sang a few songs, Rudy's new format focused on comedy and guest stars: John Barrymore, Phil Silvers, Groucho Marx, Eddie Cantor, and Henry Morgan. He amassed a brilliant team of writers: Paul Henning, Norman Panama, and Mel Frank. The head writer was Ed Gardner, and Abe Burrows was his assistant.

By now, Rudy decided to go out to the "grass roots" and play dates at popular nightclubs, ritzy supper clubs, and hotels around the country as a singer/comedian. "Some of these places were luxurious, and a few were flea-bitten cocktail lounges" he related ruefully. "Yet it turned out to be one of the most fascinating, exciting, and exasperating phases of my life."

My husband himself admitted, "I have an unfortunate knack of embarking on certain phases of my career at exactly the wrong time." Yet Rudy was still a man-about-town in Hollywood. He enjoyed his single status once again and dined often at his favorite restaurants: the Brown Derby, Chasen's, Don the Beachcomber's with his friend Don Beach, Trader Vic's with owner Vic Bergeron, La Rue, and Perrino's.

One of the new friends he made around that time was Paul Caruso, who went on to law school and years later became one of our attorneys. "I was a young seaman billeted at the Hotel Laguna in Laguna Beach, California, barely nineteen years old," Paul said, describing his meeting with Rudy. "At a bar I met a Hollywood type, Vinton Vernon, who offered to take me onto some film sets. That's where I met Rudy Vallée, who was a big hero to me, and we all had dinner together at Don the Beachcomber's."

"One of his favorite restaurants," I told Paul.

"It sure was. Pretty soon, Rudy invited us up to Silver Tip. My eyes popped. I'd never seen anything like it before. I was from a little dairy town called Franklin, New York, and believe me, it was nothing like this! We played pool up at Rudy's house, and he and I made a good team, taking on all his friends and usually winning. We enjoyed each other's company, even though I was overawed by him. Rudy was so kind to me, very generous and giving, as he was to many, many others." Several years later, Paul was the first of Rudy's friends to hear the news that he'd met a girl up north and was going to marry her. As it turned out, Paul's presence at our wedding reception was critical. If he hadn't been there, our lives could have followed a very different path.

SIX

Planning the Perfect Wedding

"History is replete with men and women who were supremely happy although there was a difference in their ages," Rudy wrote when he began courting me seriously. The fact that he was much older didn't bother me a bit. I always enjoyed the company of men a bit older, and even in high school I preferred dates two to five years my senior. I loved being in love. I had not been without a boyfriend since the third grade, mostly because I was such a flirt. Like most of my girlfriends, I wanted to get married and be the perfect wife.

Rudy told me that the moment he saw me at King's Beach, he liked my long legs and long, auburn hair. He said I appealed to him although he could see I was young. He didn't, of course, know just how young I really was. He thought I was around nineteen or twenty years old. "I saw the promise in your eyes, your walk, your attitude," he said. "You had a certain something."

Rudy never seemed that much older to me. His handsome, boy-ish good looks, vibrant energy, and effervescent personality were those of a far younger person. I discovered as our relationship progressed that our ages meant nothing. He walked fast, talked fast, and juggled a dozen projects at once.

At one point he proudly showed me a newspaper column that appeared a couple of months before our engagement that read: "The amazing thing about Vallée is that, like few other artists who have become American institutions, he is indestructible. . . . Even now he still looks like the clean-cut laconic youth who somewhere in the mid-twenties made the United States aware that one of the big things about the University of Maine was *The Stein Song*."

Although Rudy was on the road a lot, appearing on radio and on television shows as guests of Bing Crosby and Ed Sullivan, and I was still in school, we spent as much time as possible together. He'd call me if he was appearing at a hotel or club nearby and I'd sit right in front, gazing up at him like any mesmerized fan. It was a thrill to see Rudy on stage and have him smiling down at me in front of everyone. I'd give him my dazzling smile back and think, that's my man.

Soon, the name Eleanor Norris began appearing in the local newspapers linked with Rudy's as "his new love interest." He didn't try to hide; rather, he seemed very proud to have me with him and often told the press, "She's my girl, but she has a crush on Ronald Reagan."

Rudy's actual proposal was just as much a surprise to me as it was to my parents. Although I had fallen in love with him, I thought we'd have a couple of years of dating before he popped the question. I was staying with Roberta Whitney in Los Angeles. Rudy called to say there was a big party going on. The party was formal, much to my dismay. I only had a short dress with me, so Roberta's sister, Beth, lent me one of her long gowns. Edgar Bergen's wife at that time had a designer boutique where Beth bought many of her clothes, and the dress I borrowed was tight-fitting, sapphire-blue velvet.

"I'm in love with you. I want to marry you," Rudy breathed into my ear as we whirled around the dance floor. Stunned, I could hardly believe I'd heard the right words. Rudy Vallée wanted to marry me! "Will you?" He pressed me to him.

"Yes," I whispered, my knees weak. This was the most romantic moment of my life, and I meant to savor every single second of it. "Ask me again," I said.

We didn't tell anyone about our betrothal because Rudy wanted to ask for my hand in the traditional manner, with my father's permission, so our engagement remained a secret at first. Only later did I remember to tell Beth that Rudy asked me to marry him when I was wearing her dress.

But our joy was tempered with deep sadness. After we returned to the Whitney's house that night, we learned that Charles Vallée had died suddenly of heart failure. The death was unexpected. Four weeks earlier Rudy had visited his father in Westbrook, and he seemed to be in good health. I was just as upset because I could see my new fiancé was extremely agitated and I had no idea how to comfort him.

Then, in his usual take-charge manner, Rudy spent the following day on the telephone making all the funeral arrangements for his father to be buried next to Rudy's mother in St. Hyacinth's cemetery in Westbrook. Rudy, however, did not travel back to Maine himself. "I can't face attending his funeral," Rudy confessed. "I want to remember Dad just as he was, with his jaunty homburg perched on his head and smiling at everything."

One of the few funerals I remember my husband attending occurred towards the end of his life. It was for comedian Doodles Weaver, brother of Pat Weaver, who was head of NBC. Doodles was a comedian with Spike Jones and got his nickname from the little drawings he made between film takes one summer at Universal Studios.

The Weaver family asked Rudy to speak at the memorial service at Forest Lawn in Glendale. Well, for some reason Rudy got off track and rambled on all about himself and his career for what seemed ages. Finally, remembering where he was, Rudy said the only thing he could recall about the dearly departed was this story that Doodles had a big framed photograph of Christ in a prominent position in the lobby of his house. The photo was autographed: "To my dear friend Doodles" and signed "J.C."

Rudy ended his eulogy by saying he understood everyone was invited to view the body. "I want to be first in line because I heard that Doodles shot himself and I'd like to see how the funeral director has patched him up." By this time I was under the pew. Needless to say, we were not invited to the Weavers' home for the wake.

Rudy said nothing more about our engagement, and I began to wonder if he'd changed his mind after the death of his father. Then he invited me to spend a weekend with him at a San Diego hotel, where he was doing a show. I knew my mother and father would never agree to let me stay with him unchaperoned, so I appealed to Mrs. Whitney for advice. I had taken her into my confidence.

"Don't worry, Eleanor," she said. "We'll work something out." And so she did. She called my parents to tell them she would be my chaperone and that Rudy and I could stay at her house. In separate bedrooms, of course.

The weekend promised to be deliciously wicked yet within the bounds of propriety. I was still firm about being a virgin until my wedding night, but I wanted to do something intimate with Rudy, the kind of thing husbands and wives do when they're alone.

I decided that the sexiest thing in the world to start our weekend off right was to bring Rudy breakfast in bed. Seeing your beloved in this private place, where couples share their most secret desires, had to be among the most sensual of all pleasures, I thought. Since I couldn't actually get into bed with Rudy, I loved the image of sitting on his bed as he lay there in his pajamas. Surely this was one of the great moments in daily married life.

Carrying a tray piled high with scrambled eggs, Canadian bacon, toast, and coffee, and trembling with excitement, I gently pushed open Rudy's bedroom door. "Good morning!"

There was no response from the bed. All I could make out was a big lump. "Good morning!" I repeated, this time a little more breezily.

The lump moved, arms flailed, and a head appeared with a thick black cotton eyeshade covering both eyes. Was this my handsome fiancé? "What time is it?" his voice growled.

"About ten o'clock and I've brought you breakfast, darling." Rudy's rumpled form in striped blue pajamas pulled itself up.

"Are you crazy? At ten o'clock? It's too early!" Rudy groaned, flopped back down onto the pillows, and pulled Mrs. Whitney's beautiful red quilted bedspread over his head. Uncertain, I stood there for a full minute holding the tray. This was not going according to my romantic script. Should I tiptoe out? Should I leave the tray on the bedside table? Should I sit there and wait? It didn't occur to me to take offense.

Suddenly, Rudy threw back the covers, ripped off the eyeshade, and burst into laughter. "Sit down, you sweet young thing. Breakfast in bed! What a wonderful wife you will make." He took the tray, gave me a hug, and began to eat the breakfast I'd cooked.

Rudy's eyeshades were a regular part of his bedtime routine, I discovered after we married. He had cases of them, all designed to keep out the light. His normal working day didn't end until 3:00 or 4:00 A.M. so he didn't get up until early afternoon. He relied on the eyeshades to help him sleep. Rudy kept a huge supply at Silver Tip and gave away dozens to friends. After he died, I found sixteen unopened cartons of eyeshades in the attic.

That same weekend in San Diego, Rudy repeated his marriage proposal, and again I said yes. Now I knew he was serious, and I couldn't wait to call my mother.

"Come home immediately!" she said. "Get on the next train! No, take a plane!"

I had no idea of the bombshell I dropped when I called mother that summer morning to tell her Rudy had proposed. My parents knew Rudy and I dated off and on, that we'd spent a lot of time together during the Easter vacation in Palm Springs, and they approved of our relationship. However, neither of my parents were prepared to face the reality of my actually marrying Rudy Vallée. Mother and Dad thought Rudy and I had a nice friendship going but eventually Rudy would move on. I would marry someone like Bill Steer, that nice pharmacy student I sometimes dated, or Ted Gramko, for whom I had deep feelings.

"Rudy's forty-eight years old! You're still a child!" Dad's protestations still echo in my ears.

"He's a man of the world. We love Rudy, we're crazy about

him," my mother said, "but we're afraid of the age difference and you know how fickle you are, Eleanor."

"Besides," said Dad, "you want to be married in the Catholic church, and he's a divorced man. No priest will marry you." I was devastated. My parents went on for days. A lot of their concern was for Rudy, not me. They knew I had no true concept of marriage, and they believed I was still a flighty teenager. But I was convinced in my heart this man was for me. Every intuitive sense in my soul told me marrying Rudy was the right thing to do. My natural stubbornness asserted itself. I'd find a way.

To solve the church dilemma I appealed to priests in as many different Catholic dioceses as I could find in the San Francisco-Berkeley area. Their advice was all negative. Were my parents right? One night, having dinner with Rudy at Trader Vic's, I burst into tears. "We'll never be married," I wailed.

It was all too much. I cried into my Navy Grog. I cried over the Chicken Supreme, I cried over the Flan Caramel, and I cried over my Creme de Menthe after-dinner liqueur, all the time telling Rudy how much I loved him. With tears flowing like a river, my mascara became smeared all over my face. Rudy, for the first time since I'd known him, was speechless. He didn't know what to do. I was crying so hard people began staring at us.

Rudy pulled out a perfectly folded, snowy white linen handkerchief—I'm sure with great reluctance—and tried to stifle my loud sobs. I was not to be comforted. All the pent-up frustration had found an outlet, and I wanted to have a good cry.

"Ellie," Rudy said gently, as I gave him back his handkerchief, "you know I don't go to church, even though I was brought up a strict Catholic. I am a realist, and I don't believe in the dogma of any church. We could get married in a civil ceremony."

"No!" I said, "I am determined to marry you in the Catholic church—somewhere."

The next day I tried one more Catholic priest. He asked, "Has Mr. Vallée ever been married in a Catholic ceremony?" When I said no, he said it was his opinion that there should be no problem then. I raced home.

"I *can* be married! I *can* be married," I shouted, running through the front door at full tilt. That evening Rudy formally asked my father for my hand in marriage.

"Eleanor may change, she may hurt you," replied my father. I could have choked him. "Why not give her more time?"

"Alright," said Rudy. "Let her go out on some more dates. But if she hasn't changed her mind by July fourth weekend when we are all at Lake Tahoe, we can announce our engagement."

July has always been significant in our lives. Rudy's birthday was that month; we met on that weekend, became engaged, and Rudy died during a July fourth weekend. For me now, while I celebrate the nation's Independence Day with sadness over the loss of my husband, I also celebrate it for bringing into my life some of the happiest holiday weekends I have known.

After announcing our engagement with a party at Cal-Neva Lodge, my family returned to Oakland where I spent every waking moment planning my dream wedding and driving everyone nuts.

If Vallée-Video was in a tailspin, Rudy gave me no hint of it. He was too busy negotiating a contract with CBS for personal services and had to drop promotional appearances on behalf of Vallée-Video; he left Joe Parker wondering what to do.

Victor Kayfetz wrote to Parker asking for a publicity shot of "a large group of Vallée-Video employees." Joe responded wryly: "We'd have to inflate Miss Otto and Miss Hall, Dick Alexander, and myself."

Rudy's frantic schedule continued unabated as he played nightclubs and appeared in several movies: *Father Was a Fullback*, *The Beautiful Blonde from Bashful Bend*, and *I Remember Mama*.

He found time to write to George Raft and apologize for criticizing the famous movie star to a newspaper columnist. Rudy told Raft that his success was due to his resemblance to Rudolph Valentino and that he envied Raft for making ten times more money than he did. Rudy ended the letter: "It is a shame we both don't have radio shows. We could have built this up into a terrific to-do."

Booked on three Ed Sullivan TV shows, Rudy was dismayed to hear that, despite Sullivan paying Rudy the highest figure of any guest, agent Ben Pearson claimed he had to heavily persuade Ed to have Rudy on. Sullivan wrote a personal letter back, saying, among other things: "There was no 'selling' involved. I wanted *you*. I knew damned well you'd be an enormous hit . . . and you were. You added considerable prestige to the show and an amazing amount of newspaper space."

Among the business ventures Rudy was considering was an investment in a needle-threader machine company; he gave the owner a $2,000 loan. Rudy spent weeks investigating, asking attorneys, colleagues, and friends for advice. After hearing from his friend Jim Healey, assistant commissioner of the Department of Conservation for the Commonwealth of Massachusetts, Rudy decided not to invest.

"Rudy wasn't a really good businessman," said Valerie Nixon Forman, one of Rudy's accountants for a period of time. "He was a soft touch for anyone who needed money, and he could easily get talked into buying stock in a company or a crazy venture. He bought stock on margin, which is risky." Valerie once saved Rudy a great deal of money by selling his stock one week before the market fell.

Meanwhile, Rudy's attentions to me were constant, filling my mailbox with love letters and calling whenever he had a moment between shows and rehearsals. I'd receive telegrams telling me how much he missed me and loved me. Rudy's nickname for me was "Buttercup." Then, throughout our entire married life, he often referred to me as his "bride." In public or in media interviews he also called me "Mrs. V," which I found rather quaint and gentlemanly.

Sometimes Rudy mailed me pages of sheet music. One was from "Some Enchanted Evening," on which he'd changed the lyric "across a crowded room" to read "across a crowded beach." This was the most romantic time of my life and I was in seventh heaven. My love for Rudy was rapturous and in full bloom. I doubt my heart could have beat faster every time the phone rang and I dashed madly to answer it. I found my cheeks blushing whenever I received one of Rudy's passionate love letters, imagining our dear old friendly mailman could see through the envelope and read the scorching phrases Rudy wrote.

While I couldn't think of anything else except our wedding, Rudy spent his time on the road fulfilling dates, setting up future appearances, and answering business correspondence. He made another movie, *Mother Is a Freshman* and tried to rescue Vallée-Video. In between, he wrote letters to newspapers about something he either vehemently agreed with or opposed.

Along with all of this, Rudy, with his compulsion for organization, found time to become involved in every detail of our nuptials and bombarded me with instructions from New Mexico, Nevada, Montana, Illinois, Ohio, and Massachusetts. The notes were written on hotel stationery and always typed in block capitals on his constant companion, the trusty typewriter.

Soon Rudy played the Cocoanut Grove in Los Angeles again and invited us to Silver Tip for the weekend. After the show, Rudy said he was having a big party at the house. Before we left Berkeley, mother took me shopping for a beautiful navy blue satin, off-the-shoulder, side-draped Ceil Chapman cocktail dress.

During the afternoon of our arrival at Silver Tip, we proudly showed Rudy my elegant designer gown. As soon as mother went into the guest bedroom to hang the dress up, Rudy handed me a bundle of hundred dollar bills. "What's this?" I asked?

"That dress is perfect, and I want you to buy some more," he said.

"What? I could never take money from a man before our marriage!" As it turned out Rudy was to buy me dozens of satin gowns—after we were married.

A day later we went to a dinner party, and Rudy introduced me to Ronald Reagan. "This is my sweetheart," Rudy said. "She's a big fan of yours and has your photo on her bedroom wall. It's the only one she's framed. She doesn't even have my photo up!"

I had a crush on Ronald Reagan since I was a kid and thought he was the most handsome film star in the world. Rudy couldn't resist telling Reagan this when we were introduced. I felt very embarrassed.

Years later, as guests of the Reagans, Rudy never failed to remind them of my youthful crush.

Now that we'd solved the problem of getting married in the Catholic church, we turned to the matter of an engagement ring. Rudy wanted me to have a big, flashy gem that befitted his star status. He asked Ben Barzum and Joe Rudin, some jeweler friends in New York, to send several different diamonds to me.

"I'm going to buy you the most multi-faceted, showy diamond I can find," Rudy declared.

"I prefer a small jewel in a simple setting," I protested.

"Darling, people will think I'm poor!"

As we discussed each other's preferences, and we both made heroic, time-consuming efforts to find exactly what we wanted, the Engagement Ring became a *cause célèbre* on both coasts. "Don't you agree they're much too ostentatious?" I asked my mother, showing her Rudy's diamonds.

"They're very large and beautiful, Eleanor," she answered, "but it's your choice."

Rudy wanted me to take the diamonds to my father's jeweler in San Francisco for evaluation. Although each precious stone was beautiful and very valuable, the diamonds had either a tiny flaw or were "yellow." I wanted a pure blue-white diamond.

"I am going to have a perfect marriage, so my ring must be a perfect diamond," I said.

I asked Carl Priest, part owner of Parker Pen Company, for advice. When Rudy heard Carl was assisting in the search, he wrote to his insurance agent: "I am deeply indebted to Carl for all his energy and excitement engendered in the selection of the ring, entailing, as it probably will, a certain amount of grief until we find the ring we want." But Carl acted fast.

"I know a local jeweler. Let's see what he has." We found a perfectly cut, pear-shaped diamond that sparkled like a thousand stars. It weighed four and a half carats, not the ten carats Rudy wanted.

Telegrams flew back and forth between Rudy and me. He insisted on a larger diamond, I preferred the smaller gem. After finally agreeing to the diamond I wanted, Rudy then changed his mind. More letters back and forth. Finally I repeated, "My engagement ring must be perfect because I am going to have a perfect marriage." He had no answer to that, and I got my little $7,500 stone, mounted with baguettes. Predictably, a few years later Rudy bought me a much larger stone.

SEVEN

Adjusting to Life on the Road

wo hitches loomed in our nuptial plans. Rudy couldn't find the Jane Greer marriage and divorce papers to present to the priest, and we had to juggle the dates around so Rudy's engagements weren't jeopardized. We finally found the papers, set the wedding date for Saturday, September 3, and were married at Corpus Christi Church in Piedmont, California, by Father Edwin J. Keller.

I wore the satin that Rudy loved, in a classic, alabaster-white wedding gown over a hoop skirt. The sweetheart neckline was edged in seed pearls to match my tiara headdress, and I had a long veil. My bouquet was of butterfly and white orchids, lilies of the valley, and calla lilies. Escorted by eight ushers, the eight bridesmaids were in kelly green satin, carrying shower bouquets of chrysanthemums tied with satin ribbons and wearing streamers in their hair. My sister Betty was my matron of honor, and little Gil Jr. was the ring bearer.

Rudy wanted a home-state connection for his best man and chose Ralph French, one of Rudy's road managers and a long-time friend from Maine. My husband later set him up with a camera store on Ventura Boulevard in Studio City.

During the wedding vows, Rudy's responses were spoken in a

precise, well-projected voice, while mine, my mother told me, were almost inaudible. I'm not surprised. This was the most momentous day of my life, and I was overcome by it all.

After the nuptial mass, we were escorted by a police motorcycle parade to our reception at the Orinda Country Club. I was amazed at the crowd of fans and media who mobbed us at Corpus Christi church, where a police cordon had to control thousands of people who then followed us to the reception. "Get used to it," Rudy whispered, noticing my surprise. Our wedding made the papers all over the world.

Once inside Orinda Country Club, the champagne flowed freely. We dined, danced, laughed, and cut the cake. It was a storybook wedding, and I felt like a fairy princess. Towards the end of the wedding reception I suddenly became faint. The dresser from I. Magnin, where I'd bought my wedding gown, had given me a Phenobarbital pill to help me relax when she was helping with my veil. Not used to taking medication, I could now feel the effects, sipping on a glass of champagne as I stood in the reception line greeting our guests. Dizzy, I leaned against one of the candle-lit tables for support. Suddenly my tulle wedding veil, hanging down my back, was engulfed in flames.

I heard a shout. "Oh my God!"

In a flash Paul Caruso, standing next to me, doused the fire but not before my hair and his hands had been slightly burned. A part of my veil had succumbed to the flames, leaving a gaping black-edged five-foot hole. If I'd been standing alone, I know my face could have been disfigured for life. All I could think of was how would Rudy have coped, with his mania for perfection? I've never forgotten Paul's fast response, and we laugh about it today.

The evening of our wedding we left on a twelve-week honeymoon/nightclub tour. I was so happy, my fingers shook as I changed into a deep periwinkle blue going-away suit and perched a tiny little matching hat on my red hair. Luckily, I have a "hat face"—I modeled for Mr. John, one of America's top hat designers. I still have dozens of hats in my closet.

Not only did my new husband have a new wife, he was also embarking on a new career as a nightclub comedian. Over the next twelve years Rudy polished his one-man act into a combination of comedy sketches, singing, and a series of what he called "the best collection of minister, priest, and rabbi stories ever told."

I, too, was embarking on a whole new life. From the time we got engaged, I'd laid down one law to Rudy: I'm coming along. Whisked away from California's casual beach lifestyle with close friends and family into a maelstrom of rushing from one engagement to the next with strangers, I could barely contain my excitement.

As a model and drama student, I'd long had dreams of performing onstage, and Rudy made sure I became part of his show. One of the first songs he'd open with was "The Most Beautiful Girl in the World," which he dedicated to me. Then he'd proudly call me out and introduce me onstage. But I decided at the outset that there would be only one star in this family, and it was Rudy.

Putting aside my own ambitions, I determined to devote all my time to my new husband. A signature tune on one of his radio programs had been "My Time Is Your Time," and taking my cue from that, I knew that my time was completely his time. I thought he was marvelous, I was thrilled to be his wife.

Unlike most married couples after the honeymoon, we did not settle into a daily routine. There was no such thing in our life together. Rudy had his agenda for the day, and that was mine, too. We were always on the road, packing, unpacking, repacking. When we piled into Rudy's azure Chrysler after changing out of our wedding clothes, I knew I was leaving any sense of a normal life behind.

Swept up into his hectic, colorful, complicated existence, which he had only hinted at when we were engaged, I couldn't wait for our first performance. I had always wanted to be a glamour girl; even since I was two years old I'd played dress-up with my mother's clothes and jewelry. Now I was a glamorous wife, married to her dream man.

Rudy had dates to fulfill at The Biltmore Hotel in Los Angeles almost immediately, so my commitment to show business began the week we were wed.

Our brief, two-day honeymoon was spent at the Del Monte Lodge in Pebble Beach, a very elegant resort near Carmel, California. One of our first social stops was in the San Fernando Valley, where Vic Bergeron, owner of Trader Vic's, and Don Beach, owner of Don the Beachcomber's, held receptions for us.

Looking back, I'm surprised we managed to fit in a honeymoon at all. Yet short as it was, it fulfilled every expectation I had: Rudy was a marvelously romantic lover. Far from being jealous over the women he'd courted before me, I was impassioned with his expert lovemaking and he was just as appreciative of my eager response.

"I'm so glad we waited. I knew you'd be terrific in bed. I knew you'd be hot. You're better than any other woman I've been with," he said the morning after our fantastic wedding night. "And it's going to get better now that I've awakened your sensuality." I could only nod numbly, still vibrating from the most wonderful night I'd ever experienced.

We never had problems in the bedroom. I believe that sex, which colors every communication in relationships, is one of the most important and blissful components of a happy marriage. Sex deepens your love and bonds you together. If both partners are loving and giving and have respect for each other, they can work out disagreements. But you must be willing to consider the other's opinions and be fair.

After four weeks of marriage we went to Vancouver, where Rudy received a call from his agent offering him some dates in Cleveland. "But you have to leave pretty quick if you want the engagement," said the agent. Rudy decided to fly to Kansas City and have me follow by train. This was my first train ride in a sleeping compartment. I was excited as Rudy got me settled in, but sad he wouldn't be with me.

Around ten o'clock the train pulled in to one of the stations along the way. Almost before the train came to a full stop, the door to my compartment abruptly swung open. Rudy jumped in, a delighted smile all over his face. I was speechless. "Sweetheart," I said, when I found my voice. "This is the best surprise a bride could have!"

"Well, I was having dinner with the owner of the Sporting Club nearby and I saw the railroad tracks outside the restaurant. I had the strangest feeling that your train might pass through. I called to check it out and here I am!"

After a passionate twenty-minute second honeymoon, my new husband leaped off the train. "See you in Cleveland, darling!" he said, waving goodbye. That was one of the sweetest memories I have of Rudy. Rudy was very impulsive. I loved it.

I realized from the beginning that my husband was a workaholic, but young and naive, I had no idea of the scope of his activities and travel. His work ethic was inherited from his father, and Rudy despised idleness. He never let up. Four days after our wedding, I fell right in with Rudy's routine:

> Awake at 1:00 P.M.
> Walk the poodles
> Confirm bookings
> Answer business correspondence
> Rehearse the show
> Take a short nap
> Have hotel deliver dry cleaning
> Have Eleanor check out clothes for creases
> Perform

We'd have dinner very late after the show, then go nightclubbing or watch a movie. We'd finally fall into bed around 4:00 A.M.

Criss-crossing the country, we did dozens of one-nighters, three-nighters, and week-long stints. We were at the Nicollet Hotel in Minneapolis and the Copley Plaza in Boston for two weeks, the Mark Hopkins in San Francisco for three weeks, then on to Florida, New York, Chicago, Texas, Colorado, Louisiana, Pennsylvania, and Massachusetts.

In Sarasota, Rudy received a telegram from Jimmy Durante, who was to serve as ringmaster for the Ringling Brothers' circus, asking Rudy to donate his performance for the Heart Fund. John Ringling North followed up with a letter, but our schedule was too hectic to fit it in.

On several opening nights, Rudy received telegrams from Eddie Cantor and other old friends. Singer Hildegarde wrote: "Use a few German words or sing a German song. Good luck." Rudy loved driving, so while he took the wheel, I'd read his favorite newsmagazine to him, *US News and World Report*, and we'd discuss the issues of the day. Sometimes I helped him memorize scripts or we'd listen to the radio, but neither of us much liked the current music.

"There are some awful records around," he'd say. "Just listen to those rock and roll songs! They're frenzied, frightening, a cacophony. I don't know how they dare record them!"

We both enjoyed discovering America on our travels and often took the back roads. Yet however quiet it was, Rudy's brain was always working overtime. We'd pass a dairy farm and he'd tell me to make a note; if we were running late he'd come up with a song; he'd overhear a couple talking, and he'd write a new monologue. Every second presented Rudy with a joke, a melody, an opinion, or an idea for a performance. He often did two things at once, wearing special glasses while he was having his hair cut so he could read at the same time.

Not all our travels were by car. On our first long train ride from Los Angeles to Vancouver for a show with Fifi D'Orsay and the Will Masters Trio with Sammy Davis, I was so excited and Rudy was so busy with the luggage, we got on the wrong train and ended up in Sacramento. Fortunately my mother, in nearby Berkeley, drove us back to San Francisco, where we had to start out all over again. We felt like two kids playing truant.

One of our train rides together was tragic, however. Two years later, on our way to Kansas City, I became nauseous. "You're pregnant!" Rudy shouted in delight when I said I felt ill.

"Don't be ridiculous."

"We'll see a doctor in Kansas City and find out, Buttercup." Rudy was so thrilled at the thought of having a child, he jumped off the train at the next station and phoned Hollywood gossip columnist Louella Parsons to give her an exclusive. For the next four weeks, he treated me like a piece of delicate china.

"Put your feet up, Ellie." "Eat more food, Buttercup." "Are you sure you're warm enough?"

After our engagement at the Plaza Hotel in Kansas City, where a doctor confirmed my pregnancy, we took the train back to Los Angeles. The first day I was fine. As the train pulled into Albuquerque on the afternoon of the second day, I started hemorrhaging and believed I was suffering a miscarriage. Rudy was devastated. I was hysterical. "My baby! My baby!" I couldn't stop screaming.

Rudy asked the station master to delay the train until a local doctor could come to the station. After the doctor examined me, he thought I was having a miscarriage but wasn't sure. Rudy grabbed the towels from our bathroom and gently gathered up the bloody tissue into plastic bags so we could take it back to Dr. Skalater, my own doctor, for diagnosis. When we arrived in Los Angeles, Rudy arranged for an ambulance to take us to Cedars-Sinai Medical Center.

When I saw the handsome young gynecologist walk in, I refused to let him examine me. I was too embarrassed and I was bawling like a baby. I wanted an older person. I called Mother to ask what to do. "Let that doctor do his work, Eleanor," she said. "He's a specialist."

A little more than a year later, on our way to an engagement at El Rancho Hotel in Las Vegas, misfortune struck once more. I had a second miscarriage.

When we arrived at the hotel we were shown to one of the lovely guest cottages in back. Although it had its own small, private pool, it was dark and gloomy. I was already depressed after losing the second baby, and I didn't want to stay there. That evening we were invited to the grand opening of The Desert Inn. I was so impressed with its beauty, I asked Rudy if we could stay there instead of El Rancho. Anxious to please me, he agreed immediately, even though professionally it wasn't the right thing to do. No one ever heard of performing at one hotel, and preferring to stay at another. Our situation became the scandal of the strip, and we expected to be fired any day. It was bad publicity for El Rancho, but the management was very understanding.

So we moved over to the Desert Inn and went to El Rancho each evening to perform. Frank Sinatra was staying at the Desert Inn with Ava Gardner, before their marriage, and we'd visit with them at the pool.

Although we were not blessed with children ourselves, Silver Tip was home to several babies. Each housekeeping couple we hired became parents.

Over the years we had five babies living with us at various times. Rudy and I doted on them all and included them on our personalized Christmas cards. We turned one of the bedrooms next to ours into a nursery and helped bring up the little children who called Silver Tip their home.

The first baby was born to Fumi and Johnny Ito, a Japanese couple who worked for us from 1955 to 1960. Fumi was a legal secretary, and her husband was now back in school after serving with the U.S. Army. So we hired them to look after Silver Tip while we were away—which was almost always—and to help us with business correspondence.

A doctor told Fumi she was unable to conceive. "Don't give up hope," I said. "I'm going to say a Novena to St. Francis Xavier for you every day, and God will take care of you." Fumi joined me as we knelt in prayer each morning.

The following week Rudy and I left for New Orleans and another lengthy tour. I continued the Novenas. The day before we returned to Silver Tip, Fumi phoned.

"I'm pregnant! The doctor says I'm pregnant!"

When Rudy and I arrived home, she fainted in Rudy's arms; we all got so excited. They called their new son Taro Vallée Ito. Three years later, Fumi gave birth to a little girl, Sono Vallée Ito.

We always preferred to hire couples who were young and wanted children. Our next housekeeper Amalia, was Mexican. Her husband, Enrique Rosenblum, was half Jewish. They lived with us for seven years. When Amalia's unwed sister got pregnant in Mexico, Rudy and I flew her in. She named her baby Eleanor after me, as her godmother, and they lived with us, too. The Rosenblums had two handsome sons, William Rudy and Mark Paul. Tragically, Enrique was killed in a plane crash a few years later.

I was surprised to find myself thriving on our hectic schedule even though it was a totally new world to me. Besides, the only thing that mattered was that I was at my husband's side morning, noon, and night. He included me in everything he did, whether it was meeting with booking agents, hotel owners, sponsors, musicians, or friends.

My respect for Rudy's many talents grew. He was incredibly thorough in his preparations for his shows; he knew as much about lighting as the experts, often insisting on using his own equipment if it was superior; he knew as much about direction as most directors, and as much about what was appropriate for his act as the writers.

My youthful exuberance and outgoing personality was put to good use as soon as we hit the first stop on the tour. Rudy sent me down to the local radio station to promote the show. I barely knew what promotion meant and had little idea of what to do but I willingly handled it alone.

"Hi! I'm Eleanor Vallée and I'm here to talk about my wonderful husband Rudy who is appearing here this week," this brash new bride said to the interviewer. Faced with my obvious newness to publicity, he was more amused than annoyed as I extravagantly praised Rudy's various talents. "Rudy Vallée sings fantastically, he keeps you laughing like crazy with his jokes, and plays the saxophone better than anyone else in the world," I proclaimed. "Everyone has to come and see the show. They must!"

"Sounds like you're a fan," he said, smiling at my seriousness.

"A fan? I love him the most of anyone," I replied passionately. "He is my hero, my idol, the most romantic person I've ever known." I could barely stop talking, my words tumbling over each other as I lavished one compliment after another on my husband.

When I returned to our hotel room, Rudy was still laughing uproariously over the interview, which he'd listened to on the little red radio we carried with us. From then on, he sent me out to handle all advance publicity interviews.

With twenty-four pieces of luggage, living on trains and in cars, I quickly learned how to pack sun lamps, the Waring blender, a steam iron, a hotplate, portable refrigerator, musical instruments, tennis racquets, sheet music, an exercise machine, half a dozen hats used in the act, letters, scrapbooks, clippings, four tape recorders, slide projectors, lights, the typewriter, and Rudy's megaphone. We had a dozen suitcases for our show costumes and street clothes. We literally carried our home on the roof of the car.

Rudy designed a much-admired luggage rack and container so we could fit everything in. Like an architect, Rudy worked out a specific way to load and unload each item, arranged a particular way so our five-foot-tall rooftop carrier was as compact as possible.

We had boxes, equipment, and suitcases piled up, and three very special containers for Rudy's three dummies, Ezry, Sally Ann, and Linoleum, used in his ventriloquism act.

These hand-carved, wooden dummies were made back in the 1930s by George and Glenn McElroy in their Harrison, Ohio, workshop, for Rudy's ventriloquist vaudeville acts. Later on, Rudy resurrected the dummies and included them in our act. He was surprisingly good at ventriloquism and earned much applause. I'd dress in a slinky, satin gown and high heels, and carry the dummies out on stage.

In addition to our props, we also carried around little beds, dishes, and supplies for our three poodles. We were both dog lovers, and Rudy was a certified judge for dog shows. An ardent supporter of animal rights, Rudy addressed many humane society meetings, and in 1970 took to task Walter J. Hickel, the Secretary of the Interior, regarding the clubbing of seals in the Pribiloff Islands.

In Miami he once pulled out a pile of personal snapshots to show a journalist: "Look at these poodles. What charm! What naiveté! Who could resist them?"

When we stopped touring decades later and took up permanent residence at Silver Tip, Rudy once asked a waiter at Lawry's to give us some dog bones. We were presented with a huge sack, which we took home for all the neighborhood dogs. From then on, whenever we came home, regardless of the hour, there'd be a large group of canines waiting to greet us. Some of them never did go home.

When Rudy learned about vivisections being performed at one of Hollywood's top hospitals, he launched a scathing campaign in the press, asking his movie star friends at the studios for help. He recorded a tape for broadcast: "I have read a report concerning the mutilation of vocal cords and other hurts and wounds inflicted on these dumb animals too horrible to describe. I am personally appealing to others in the movie colony, more powerful than me, to aid the members of Animals Allies in their fight to alleviate the suffering and torture inflicted on our pets by sadists who call themselves scientists."

My husband owned three dogs, a dachshund, a German shepherd, and a poodle.

At my parents' home, we bred Pekingese and I was so delighted that Rudy loved small dogs, too. After we were married, Rudy left two of his dogs at Silver Tip, and we took Mr. Pom Pom everywhere we traveled. I'd fallen in love with the tiny poodle and spoiled him like crazy.

When fourteen-year-old Mr. Pom Pom had heart trouble and lay gasping on the floor, Rudy instantly knelt down and administered mouth-to-mouth resuscitation! The dog survived and lived four more years. At Mr. Pom Pom's funeral service at Silver Tip, our friends Joanne Kosrog and Mary Dunphy, the former wife of newsman Jerry Dunphy, were delighted to read the mourners' cards signed by other pets.

While we were driving from San Francisco to Los Angeles one time, we had one of our later poodles, Mimi, with us. She was pregnant and made signs she was about to give birth. "Stop the car! She's going to have her puppies!" I shrieked. We were in the middle of rural California, outside Fresno, surrounded by miles and miles of cultivated fields in the San Joaquin Valley.

Rudy pulled over and gently wrapped Mimi in a car blanket. "Okay, now she can have her babies," he said.

"Rudy, she can't give birth wrapped in a blanket on the back seat of a car. She needs to be in a box or something. We have to find a vet."

"All right, sweetheart. We'll drive on in."

Back behind the wheel, Rudy turned our police siren on full blast, and we drove at one hundred miles an hour towards Fresno. Suddenly, behind us we heard another siren. The cops were on our tail. Rudy called out, "My dog's having puppies!"

"Follow us, Mr. Vallée!" yelled the police in the squad car, recognizing my husband. They escorted us into town to a veterinary, lights flashing all the way. While we left Mimi to have her pups, we called our friend George "Naz" Mardikian, who owned Armenian restaurants in San Francisco and Fresno. He had baked our three-tiered wedding cake.

Then we went in search of eye droppers and baby formula. "We have to make sure they have enough to eat," Rudy told me. He delighted in feeding the palm-sized puppies with the eye dropper, and once again I hoped we'd be parents ourselves.

Our life up to now had been great fun and, with our hearty sense of humor, Rudy and I laughed at everything. I guess Rudy's deep love for me made him indulgent to my carefree attitude towards life. My upbringing had been one where I always felt safe, secure, and loved. I had doting parents, a wonderful sister (who had all the common sense in the family), and an easy life. I assumed marriage would be no different.

Since my parents enjoyed a very loving relationship, and I never once heard either of their voices raised in anger at the other, I expected the same from my marriage. But I was in for a shock with Rudy.

There were times early on when adjusting to living with a man as creative as Rudy had me in despair, and I shed many tears. "Ellie, I've always had passionate feelings and a lot of temper," Rudy would say by way of apology. "It's my Irish-French genes."

Sometimes, it was like living with a hurricane that rushed in, committed chaos, and rushed out, leaving me to pick up the pieces.

On two occasions I even went as far as sending him pathetic little notes of apology, although the fault was not mine.

Impatient with incompetence in others, Rudy was hardest on himself when he'd done something foolish—made a poor decision, lost an investment, or put his foot in his mouth. Then he'd become red-faced and so angry he'd beat his head against the wall, chastising himself for being stupid. The first time it happened we were newly married and Rudy was performing at the Mark Hopkins Hotel, San Francisco. I was scared to death. I thought he was going to have a concussion.

I wear my heart on my sleeve and get very emotional when there are problems. But I wanted to help my distraught husband. Eventually I managed to calm him down and he apologized for flying off the handle. These head-banging sessions didn't occur often and stopped, thank goodness, after a year.

Ever since I was a little girl, I had sought solace in the Catholic church if I was upset. With my strong convictions, I knew there were always answers, so I'd talk to God, asking what to do. The first four years of my marriage God and I had many, many conversations. Conversely, I know for a fact that there were many times Rudy needed the patience of Job to live with me. Believe me, I'm no angel either.

It can be difficult on both partners to spend twenty-four hours a day together, every day, but my faith helped me to handle my Vagabond Lover with sympathy and compassion. Many times I had to be the strong, protective one. Our relationship evolved into making life together comfortable, and I did everything I could to ensure others didn't upset Rudy. I did all this willingly because I loved him so.

I washed his shirts and my underwear, not so easy in a hotel room, while Rudy took care of combing and feeding the poodles. We shared the chores, we shared the pleasures, we shared our most intimate thoughts. We reminisced about our childhoods and our young dreams. The loving bond between us was unbreakable.

"My goodness, Eleanor," Alice Faye said a few years after Rudy and I married, "you've made a new man out of him! He's so happy!"

The interesting aspect of our marriage was that I never was a homemaker in the traditional sense because we traveled constantly. I went straight from living with my parents into a marriage where, for the first twelve years, we lived on the road. Room service, I discovered, was very, very nice. Some people who have been at the receiving end of Rudy's acerbic remarks have wondered aloud to me, "How do you stand it?"

Stand what? Two and a half decades of the most exciting and turbulent years of my life? I wouldn't change a single minute. We had great fun, and life with Rudy was always exciting. We both loved people and enjoyed entertaining. Everything he did was different, unexpected. He could be the greatest flatterer in the world, and one of the most critical people as well. I loved him when he was the former, and I loved him when he was the latter. He was my Rudy, for better or worse, and nothing could shake my love for him. Many times I had to go back into meetings with booking agents, nightclub owners, and businessmen to smooth the ruffled feathers Rudy stirred up before storming out. He'd say the wrong thing at the wrong time. The worst incident was when he was being interviewed in our suite at the Park-Sheraton Hotel in New York by executives putting together a new television show called *The 64,000 Question*.

He was a shoo-in, Rudy was told. Articulate, intellectual, handsome, charming, Yale-educated, and self-possessed, Rudy was the first choice as host of the show. "For appearances' sake," the TV director said, "let's do a brief audition."

Rudy handled the mock questions well. Then, as lead-in casual conversation between host and contestant was called for, he balked. "I hate this chitchat. These contestants are probably going to be plain, ordinary people, and I can't stand making small talk with people like that. I'm not in the least bit interested in them!" As his agent, Walter Craig, listened in horror, Rudy went on, "I'm just not interested in strangers." As soon as I heard those fateful words, my heart plummeted. I knew he'd just done himself in.

"If you're looking for a Bert Parks-Milton Berle type—big smiles, peppy, jumping all over the place," Rudy said, "count me out."

They did. After those remarks, his transition to television was doomed—by his own hand. Rudy knew it and tried to explain that while he loved audiences, he disliked chitchat. But it was too late.

Most of the time, though, every day was a new experience for me, and Rudy got a kick out of my enjoyment and seeing things fresh through my eyes. When he took me to New York for the first time, I was amazed at the canyons formed by skyscrapers.

He was very protective, too. The first time I was backstage with him for a show, I went in to chat with the young showgirls in their dressing room. "Ellie, where are you?" I heard him calling.

"Up here, dear, talking to the girls." Rudy ran up the stairs, grabbed my hand, and took me back to his room.

"Buttercup, you mustn't hang out with those girls. Their language is terrible. You'll learn some very bad things." But I had lots of fun with the dancers and singers, and I always spent time with them, trying on their makeup and wigs, gossiping about the performers, and enjoying "girl talk."

I'm often asked what magic we possessed to make our marriage so perfect. Well, it wasn't perfect, of course, and I challenge anyone to say there is such a thing as a perfect marriage. We had our fights. We made up. I'm told by friends who knew him long before we met that I was a calming influence on him. The fact that I was not a demanding wife made a great difference in his attitude towards me. All I know is, he was the center of my life.

Rudy once told a newspaper reporter: "The nightclub and hotel field is the most difficult of all. But I have been fortunate in having a very understanding, patient, sympathetic, and loyal companion, who has made this grueling grind more bearable."

I discovered early on that one of Rudy's major flaws was inflexibility, which he didn't try to hide. It was almost impossible to change his mind once he'd made it up, unless he changed it himself. Rudy believed that nostalgia was ridiculous, that people should move on and live in the present, yet much of his conversation, and his solo shows in his later years, resurrected his past successes and early fame.

As he aged, my husband became even more outspoken—if that were possible!—about himself. In a lengthy profile with *Esquire* magazine in 1962, he announced, "I cannot tolerate inefficiency and lack of knowledge of a job. But what really brings me to a boiling point are people forgetting messages or phone numbers; cruelty to animals and children; people who block the sidewalk; talking; insolence; drivers and passengers not wearing seatbelts; and people who talk during an entertainer's performance in a nightclub. I live by the Golden Rule, and so should everyone else!"

Visiting my aunt and uncle while Rudy finished up a date in Kansas City, I was interviewed by their hometown newspaper in Marshalltown, Iowa. I told them I majored in psychology but that "I've learned more about psychology in one year as an entertainer's wife than anything I learned from my professors!"

And to a reporter in Phoenix, where Rudy was appearing at the Playboy Club, I confessed, "I'm happy in Rudy's shadow."

Generally, our life was idyllic at this stage. I loved to swim, spending most afternoons at the hotel pool. When Rudy joined me an hour or so later after finishing correspondence and other business chores, he always brought along wine or champagne. We drank champagne like lemonade during the day, inviting everyone to join us before Rudy's evening performance. He'd buy cases and cases from the wineries and have most of them delivered back home to Silver Tip for our return.

Although Rudy enjoyed rum drinks—a favorite was the Rudy Vallée Special: two kinds of rum, milk powder, and pineapple juice—he also loved wines. He'd manage to arrange nightclub tours in the Napa and Sonoma Valleys where his favorite wineries were located and introduced me to his friends, the owners. We were feted by Fred Abruzzino at Beringer, Mondavi, Louis Martini, and others. Then he taught me to enjoy Chianti, the raw, red Italian wines that are so wonderful with pasta, Rudy's favorite cuisine.

I also discovered on our honeymoon and tour that Rudy could be sensitive about his height. We were dancing cheek to cheek after one of his shows at the Shoreham Hotel in Washington. My lips brushed the top of his ear. "Rudy, am I still growing or are you bending your knees? You seem shorter tonight."

"No, sweetheart, I'm just wearing my regular shoes. When we were dating I wore Adler's, those shoes with lifts in them. Now that we're married I don't need to wear them so often."

I did share Rudy's dislike of phonies. When we returned to Silver Tip, Rudy hosted a huge party to introduce me to all the people who didn't make it to our wedding. As the actresses, singers, and musicians came up to shake hands, one elegantly gowned film star asked, "And what do you do, dear? Do you sing, or dance, or act?" in the most patronizing tone.

"I can do all three," I replied coolly. "But now I take care of Rudy, that's what I do. I can't imagine a better job than that."

EIGHT

Making Movies

Aﬀter three more months on the road I was anxious to get home to Silver Tip where, on our return, we found a mountain of mail. One package contained a book by David Dunn called *Try Giving Yourself Away*.

Delighted with the gift, Rudy wrote a letter of thanks, noting: "Frankly, I have been sort of an amateur in the art of giving myself away, but upon reading the book, I realize only too well that the author has really brought this particular subject to a fine art. Many of these little things that I did unconsciously will now be multiplied and carried out with the enthusiasm, the timelessness, and with the sincerity that unquestionably go into giving yourself away from the heart."

Our wedding presents were still at my parents' home in Berkeley so, while Rudy attended to some Vallée-Video business in Los Angeles, I took the station wagon and drove up to Northern California. I had another joyous reunion with my parents and friends, then loaded up the car with our gifts and headed back down to my new home.

Just outside Fresno, almost halfway to Hollywood, the station wagon broke down, fortunately near a ramshackle Mexican saloon. I had no idea how to handle this crisis, the first I'd ever had on the road by myself. A friendly Mexican offered to drive me into town in his pick-up to get a tow. At the garage, I called my husband to find out what to do.

"Find the best hotel in town," he instructed, "and ask for the bandleader. Tell him who you are, and see if he's planning to drive to Los Angeles in the near future, so he can drive the station wagon down here for us. Give him a blank check to pay for the car repairs. I want you to get on a plane today and come home."

Sounded simple enough. I sought out the bandleader, who was kindness itself and delighted to help out Rudy Vallée's wife, he said. Then I remembered all the sterling silver, crystal, and valuable wedding gifts in the car. Worrying how to protect it, I had the bandleader sign a note I wrote: "I am now in charge of and responsible for Mr. and Mrs. Vallée's wedding gifts."

The check, as it turned out, bounced. My busy new husband had neglected to have the Bank of America add my name to his account, and I was not authorized to sign the checks. We finally sorted everything out, paid the bandleader, and thankfully unloaded our gifts. From that day on, my name was on all Rudy's bank accounts.

The best wedding present Rudy gave me was a house in Palm Springs. It had four bedrooms and a magnificent swimming pool. We'd invite familiy and friends to use it as a vacation home. David and Mertice Rubinoff, Earl Muntz and his wife, Paul and Monique Fisher of the Fisher Pen Company, and many others spent time there. In fact, guests stayed in our house more frequently than we did, because we were always on the road.

One of Rudy's oldest fans around that time was an elderly widow, Mrs. Cochran. She wrote saying she had nowhere to live and was practically homeless, so we took her on as a housekeeper for the Palm Springs house. She refused to live in the house itself, preferring to occupy the apartment over the garage. After twenty years there, she became too ill to take care of herself, so Rudy and I moved her into Silver Tip, where she died a few years later.

One of the longest periods we stayed in Palm Springs was when Rudy starred in a revival of Jean Kerr's comedy, *Jenny Kissed Me*, at the Palm Springs Playhouse. The play had enjoyed a short run on Broadway with Leo G. Carroll in the lead. My husband was tapped to replace him for the summer stock production back East, with sixteen-year-old Lee Remick, for twelve weeks. Now, a couple of years later, Rudy was offered the opportunity to re-create his role as the Irish priest, Father Moynihan.

Jenny Kissed Me was his all-time favorite and one of the highlights of his acting career. When we went on the national tour with the comedy, Rudy also took on the job of co-director. We premiered the revival with Ruth Buzzi at the Pasadena Playhouse to rave reviews and standing ovations. Rudy brought the house down. I had a small part as a young sophisticated street girl, dressed in a cute black miniskirt, black stockings, and of course, high heels.

After we returned from the tour we performed *Jenny Kissed Me* three or four times on television, including NBC's "Matinee Theater." When Jean Kerr saw it on TV, she wrote to Rudy: "You were wonderful. You had a charming, buoyant quality that lifted the whole proceedings." CBS was so impressed with Rudy's acting they began searching for a part for him in their popular *Playhouse 90* show. Unfortunately, they never came up with just the right part.

Rudy invested a considerable amount of his own money to take *Jenny Kissed Me* to the Geary Theater in San Francisco. We opened during Lent, which made it difficult to attract full houses, but it was still a success. Ruth Buzzi and I shared a dressing room. She had me in hysterics with her antics. She'd tell me dozens of jokes, and as Rudy drove us home—we were staying with my parents at the time—I'd relate them to him. Rudy was very impressed with Ruth, and predicted she'd make it big in show business, which she did on *Laugh In* and other shows. Several years later Ruth bought a house down the hill from us on Pyramid Place, and she's still a good friend.

Now in residence at Silver Tip, though only for two weeks, I was anxious to give this bachelor pad a feminine touch. While my husband took care of his business interests, I set to work making plans to remodel a few of Silver Tip's rooms, put in a new kitchen, update the bathrooms, and brighten the house with Oriental rugs, cream silk wallpaper, and red easy chairs and sofas. The master bedroom was to be refurnished in pink and white French provincial, with silk damask drapes designed for the six windows.

I was still exploring the vast mansion, and one day found a closet that could have stocked a drugstore. "That's a habit from my days in Dad's pharmacy," Rudy said when I asked him about it. True to form, Rudy had multiple boxes of aspirin, Alka-Seltzer, Band-Aids, and gauze, which we often needed when someone was too energetic on the tennis court.

In the patio and garden I planted masses of bushes and trees, as well as scarlet and yellow roses, red bougainvillea, pink hibiscus, all hues of orchids, and purple irises. The red-tiled rotunda was filled with lush green plants. "What's all this?" asked Rudy when the pots and plants were delivered.

"They'll make our home look warm and beautiful."

"Ellie, flowers in the house remind me of funerals, and you know how I hate funerals."

"Rudy, you were brought into this world with flowers—every mother giving birth receives them—and you leave this life surrounded by them," I reminded him.

"Buttercup, what a wonderful thought. Okay, fill the house with flowers. Just make sure they have no bugs on them!"

Back on the road, Rudy performed several benefits including a show at the U.S. Naval Training Station in Newport where Rudy had trained as a fifteen-year-old.

I wrote excited letters to my parents each week, describing our adventures and enclosing newspaper clippings as we traveled north, south, east, and west: "Rudy is astonishingly polished and witty." "What a show!" "How I love him."

Some of the newspaper interviews focused on me. I was called Mrs. Vagabond Lover and asked every kind of personal question. "What do you sleep in?"; "What does Rudy wear to bed?"; "What is his diet?" To the last question I answered: steak for breakfast, two eggs for lunch, two prunes for supper. And what do I wear? I sighed, winked, and said, "You guess!"

One of the most exciting engagements of my life was spent in Texas. Glenn McCarthy, owner of Houston's Shamrock Hotel, and his wife invited us to his ranch outside of town. Flying there in his private plane and landing in the middle of a vast prairie that, as far as the eye could see, belonged to Glenn, I felt as if I'd dropped into the middle of *Giant*, the movie starring Rock Hudson and Elizabeth Taylor. I soon learned how close my imagination was to reality—Rock Hudson's character in the film was actually based on Glenn.

Dozens of private jets flew in, filled with tycoons in cowboy hats and gorgeous women in skin-tight designer jeans. I learned some of them were mistresses, and married just two years, I was somewhat shocked at these goings-on. One of these beauties was Ilsa Ray, recently arrived from Sweden. Her mentor was Bob Hope, and here she was in Texas with Glenn McCarthy.

The party was one of the largest, most fabulous, and memorable I've ever experienced. There were magnums of champagne, every kind of barbecue, every kind of food, wine, beer, and liquor. This was Texas, all right.

Back in Houston, after Rudy's show, we were invited to dinner with Glenn and his wife. I realized as soon as I saw this stunning and charming lady, we'd never met before! This was the real wife.

That evening, after Rudy left for his performance, I took the dogs out for a walk. A man approached. "Excuse me, Mrs. Vallée, Mr. McCarthy would like you to have lunch with him tomorrow."

"How kind. Tell him Rudy and I will be delighted."

"Well, you see, Mrs. Vallée, the invitation is for you, not Rudy."

"Tell Mr. McCarthy thank you, but no," I said, and kept on walking. When I related the incident to Rudy, we had a good chuckle. Before we left the Shamrock Hotel we bumped into a friend, W. Howard Lee, who confided over drinks that he was in deeply love with Hedy Lamarr.

"Let me talk to her," said Rudy. "We know her quite well." My husband called Hedy in Los Angeles and urged her to fly to Houston. Wonder of wonders, she did. And ended up marrying Howard. Texas is a wild, wild place.

During an engagement in New York, we hosted a wedding at our Essex House suite. Rudy woke up one morning and said to me,

"Oh, by the way, Ellie, we're having a wedding here today for Cliff Steward and his fiancée, Helen. Judge Hymie's officiating."

"Here? Here? Are you crazy? There're no flowers, no champagne. What are you talking about? We can't have a wedding here!"

I called Marilyn Abrams, the first friend I'd met in New York, and we ran downstairs to the hotel florist, bought flowers, and ordered champagne. Seconds later, it seemed, our attorney, Hymie Bushell, came in from his suite next door and the wedding began. In the middle of the ceremony the telephone rang. "It's for you, judge." Hymie took the call. And talked. And talked. And talked. We all stood patiently waiting. Except for Rudy.

"Come on, Hymie, get off the phone!" yelled Rudy. Hymie knew that tone of voice. He hung up and completed the ceremony.

At Cliff and Helen's reception, our friends included Mayor Paslliateri, a lot of cops, and numerous members of New York's Mafia. We called it "The New York Connection."

For their honeymoon, we offered the newlyweds our homes in Los Angeles and Palm Springs for three months. Rudy knew Cliff from way back, and at one point had asked him to be the New York manager of Vallée-Video, bringing him to Hollywood for training. Over the years we became a foursome, traveling around the world together, with Cliff acting as Rudy's manager.

We also saw a lot of Marilyn and Stanley Abrams during this time. Before we were married in 1948 Stan, president of Emerson Radio and Television, asked Rudy to replace Ed Sullivan after Ed debuted his show. Rudy was the first guest. But Rudy declined, saying that Ed was a friend of his and he could never take his job away from him. "It just wouldn't be right," he told Abrams. Had Rudy accepted, the course of his career would have changed dramatically.

But that guest spot inspired a letter: "I saw you on the Sullivan show and enjoyed your monologue. Actually, it wasn't a monologue, it was a collection of wheezes from the Stone Age to the Orbit Age. It was very funny and delivered magnificently. Paste this carefully in your book of memories along with my best regards. As ever, Groucho Marx."

Within two years of my marriage to Rudy, I received sad news. My mother had a car accident, suffering chest and head injuries. I rushed home from New York and spent her last two weeks with her. I visited every day dressed in a different outfit because she always loved to see me in pretty clothes. Mother's unexpected death was a terrible tragedy for me; we were so close, and she had always been my confidante and anchor.

As the top real estate agent in Oakland, she was prominent in both business and social circles, and I always admired her style. She never went out without a hat to match her outfit and was always impeccably groomed.

Mother's membership in the Opera League of Oakland introduced me to the fascinating world of classical music when I was a child. She had a tremendous impact and influence on my life. She was also very active in volunteer work, especially one-on-one. We visited less fortunate families loaded down with turkeys she cooked, and spent time trying to help where possible.

The charity work she did for children was my inspiration to become involved in children's charities in Hollywood as president of Operation Children, formerly known as WAIF, founded by Jane Russell. I was also a member of the Muscular Dystrophy Association as well as other charities. After marrying Rudy, I was president of the Women's Auxiliary of the American National Theater and Academy.

Soon, Rudy was offered a part in the movie *The Admiral Was a Lady*. Although I'd visited film sets as a child to watch Alice Faye and others, this was my first time as a star's wife, and I was determined to enjoy every moment of it. A few hours into filming, the director called a break. Immediately, a flashy young blonde went up to Rudy, curled herself around him and began flirting. I marched over and glared at this forward young woman, who soon slunk away under my withering gaze. What did she think she was doing? Rudy laughingly explained over lunch that it was the custom when a new movie began for the leading men and second-strings to select themselves each a member of the cast as a girlfriend for the duration of the movie.

"I don't think she knew we were married last year," Rudy said, trying to calm me down.

"She does now!"

The tables were turned a couple of years later when we went to France for five months, where Rudy filmed *Gentlemen Marry Brunettes* with Jane Russell, Jeanne Crain, and Scott Brady. As Rudy was studying his lines on the set early the first morning, Scott arrived, scanned the room, and made a beeline for me. "This one's mine!" he announced to the cast, wrapping his arm around my waist.

Rudy's head jerked up. In his haste to rush over to correct Scott's claim, Rudy tripped on the chair leg, but that didn't stop him. "Excuse me, Scott, she's taken."

"Oh, Rudy, go and find someone else. She's the best looker here," Scott said.

"You don't understand. She's my wife!" Scott's mouth fell open.

"You old devil! How do you do it?" Scott Brady went off in search of a different gal, and soon he and actress and dancer Gwen Verdon were inseparable. The four of us had great fun together. When the film was finished, Scott and Gwen came back to New York with us on the *America*.

Our time in Paris, especially off the set, was enthralling. It was my first visit abroad, and Rudy was a terrific guide. Besides sightseeing, we often wandered through narrow, cobblestone streets searching for hidden little music stores where Rudy would spend hours talking about saxophones. He'd end up buying reeds after discussing the merits of each one at length with the shop owner.

Interested, as always, in fashion, I was delighted when Jane Russell and Jeanne Crain took time off from filming so we could visit the designer salons of Dior, Givenchy, and Yves Saint Laurent, although their prices were beyond our budgets.

Often Rudy and I dined at small, out-of-the-way bistros where only blue-collar French people ate, talking in fractured French and laughing with the waiters. Rudy loved meeting these down-to-earth locals, whatever country we were in. "They're the real people, Ellie. You know where you are with them."

After shooting was over for the day, most of the cast went out to Paris nightclubs where Rudy often sat in with the musicians and sang. He did a marvelous imitation of Maurice Chevalier complete with straw hat, which brought down the house.

One night at a restaurant some of the male stars in *Gentlemen Marry Brunettes* began complimenting the Parisian hookers on their beauty, class, and elegance. I'd never seen a hooker, much less a sophisticated, cosmopolitan one. "Where do these hookers hang out?" I asked Rudy.

"Right over there, at the bar."

"But they look just like I do! They're gorgeous!"

Rudy's eyes twinkled. "Yes, Buttercup, they are."

"How much do they cost?" I asked him. "Go over and ask!" My curiosity was really piqued. But my husband declined.

To celebrate our first Christmas in Europe, Rudy decided we should spend a few days in Germany, where he'd lined up a weekend date to entertain the troops stationed in Weisbaden. Although the *Gentleman Marry Brunettes* cast was requested not to leave Paris, we played truant and hopped on a plane.

As soon as we entered the Schwartzbach Hotel lobby, the manager greeted us with the news that Ava Gardner was also a guest. Rudy knew Ava from his early parties at Silver Tip. Later she became a client of Rudy's close friend and lawyer, Paul Caruso, who represented her for the last fifteen years of her life.

That evening, after Rudy's performance for the troops, we invited the military brass up to our suite for a party. "You know," confided General Tunner, "We heard Ava Gardner's in town. Boy, wouldn't it be fantastic to meet her!"

Taking up the challenge, Rudy winked at me and left the suite. When he returned I expected Ava to be on his arm. However, he was alone. Rudy told me later he ran into her in the lobby, but poor Ava was so inebriated she had to be held up by her Air Force escorts. He made a hasty retreat.

While the exteriors for *Gentlemen Marry Brunettes* were shot in Paris and Monte Carlo, the interiors were filmed in England, so the entire cast packed up and headed for London. Our stay at the Mayfair Hotel was to stretch into six months.

Rudy had fallen in love with English marmalade from the time he played at the Savoy Hotel in the 1930s, and our floor waiter, tired of bringing up yet another jar from the kitchen, finally gave us a key to the hotel's private pantry near our suite. "Please, help yourselves," he said, smiling, "but don't tell anyone!"

To make sure we'd have a marmalade supply in Los Angeles, we bought several cases from Fortnum and Mason, London's ritziest specialty store.

Rudy took me to his favorite hangouts from his early years, the Savoy, Simpson's Restaurant, and the Cafe de Paris, his favorite nightclub. I met the owners and managers and they made a big fuss over Rudy. When I visited them in 1992, after Rudy's death, I was amazed to be remembered by some of the same waiters.

Off the *Gentlemen Marry Brunettes* set, Rudy rekindled his friendships with Noel Coward, Bea Lillie, and others British celebrities. During a fall weekend, we took the opportunity to enjoy one of our favorite means of travel: we went by train to Scotland, where Rudy was honored as a performer at the Regal Cinema in Glasgow.

The greatest honor Rudy and Jane had in England was being presented to Queen Elizabeth II, along with every major American star who was in London at the time. Jane's husband, Bob Waterfield, and I dressed formally for the event and watched from our elegant chairs. Afterwards, we went out and celebrated with champagne. Rudy was so excited he said he completely forgot his actual conversation with Her Majesty. And this from the man with the phenomenal memory!

A few years later, back in Hollywood, Jane remarried and invited us to the wedding. When Rudy heard Jane's brother sing during the services, he was so impressed he wanted to help him get started in show business, so he called a couple of agents and managers he knew in New York and helped him to get some bookings.

Then Rudy invited the newlyweds to Silver Tip for one of our weekend tennis parties. On the court, I decided to give Jane a little advice. "Now don't forget," I said quietly in her ear, "Rudy likes to win, so take it easy, okay?"

Either Jane's competitive spirit got the best of her, or she completely forgot my advice, because pretty soon Rudy was red-faced. When the score against him continued to mount, I could see he was ready to blow up. Not for the first time, I ran onto the court and held up my arms.

"Now look here," I shouted to the players, "this is Rudy's tennis court. These are Rudy's racquets, and you're at Rudy's house. When Rudy plays tennis here, he wins, dammit!"

NINE

The Roller Coaster of Fame

Back from Paris, Rudy was booked at the Belmont Manor Hotel in Bermuda. This was the kind of vacation with pay Rudy enjoyed. By day we explored the island, sailed in Hamilton Harbor, and hit the cabarets late at night. Rudy was introduced to the Belmont's famous Swizzler Rum Recipe, which he pasted in a scrapbook. It's still there.

Our trip to Bermuda had a dramatic effect on Rudy's wardrobe. He fell in love with Bermuda shorts. My husband ordered them by the dozen. From then on Rudy wore his shorts, complete with white shirt, formal tie and jacket, to as many places as he could get away with.

Once at the Beverly Hills Hotel, he was refused permission to enter because of the knee-length shorts. I happened to be wearing hotpants that showed far more of my legs than Rudy's outfit did of his, yet I was allowed in. The management was adamant about the Bermudas and insisted on sneaking Rudy in through a back door and seating him in a dark corner of the Polo Lounge, where he was told to keep his naked knees out of sight. In Bermuda Rudy also discovered the multicolored, plaid cotton fabric called "madras" and had several jackets tailored to his measurements. Because the fabrics were hand-woven and hand-dyed, they needed to be dry cleaned and kept away from moisture. I didn't realize this when Rudy asked me to have the jackets pressed. I figured I'd be a good wife and save him some money by hanging them up in the hotel bathroom, and letting the shower steam the wrinkles out. When I opened the door half an hour later, the jackets had all fallen into the bathtub, and the colors had run into each other. Panicked, I called the desk. "My husband's jackets for the show tonight are ruined! He's going to kill me!"

The housekeeper ran out to the dry cleaner with them, who, fortunately, was able to repair most of the damage.

Catching up with Rudy in New York, I plunged back into the social whirl. Rudy's name was always one of the most recognized in Manhattan, where his early successes made him a star, and he was in great demand at charity events and dinners. I was excited to read Rudy's telegram from Gloria Swanson inviting him to be an honored guest at the Henry Rosenfeld Tribute for the American National Theater and Academy. We attended the premieres of friends' shows, going backstage each time to offer congratulations. Entering Dolores Gray's crowded dressing room after her opening night in *Two on the Aisle*, she hugged Rudy hard, shouting, "Here's my first discoverer!" and poured us champagne in Dixie cups.

A booking at Miami's Driftwood Room took us down to Florida, giving Rudy an opportunity to try out one of his crazy ideas. He brought a microphone onto the plane and, standing in the aisle, entertained the passengers with his favorite songs as we flew south. He may have been the first airborne entertainer, as far as I know.

We looked up friends Charlie Donnelly and Bill Jenkins, who took us sailing and fishing. One evening Bill hosted a dinner for us at the Lauderdale Yacht Club, and the next night we dined with Mamie and Bob Grewsham at the Nautilus Club, where Bob was performing.

We'd met Bill Jenkins in Paris during a rather amusing incident. Dining at the restaurant atop the Eiffel Tower, Rudy whispered to me, "I think that's my favorite film director, John Huston, over there at that table. I'm going to introduce myself."

Rudy went across the room and approached the white-haired gentleman. "Excuse me, Mr. Huston, may I have a word with you?"

The man turned around. "I'm not Mr. Huston, I'm Bill Jenkins. But I know who you are. You're Rudy Vallée," he said, a big smile on his face. "Sit down and have a drink."

"I'm delighted to accept your offer. Let me bring my wife over." We sat with Bill and his party for hours, drinking Grand Marnier. It was my first experience with this potent orange liqueur. The more we talked, the more we drank. We had tickets to the Moulin Rouge that night but I became ill from the liqueur and, wisely, we decided to cancel and go to bed.

During the next several years we were frequent guests at Bill's parties on his luxury yacht, and he gave us free use of his estate's guest house whenever we were in Florida. Bill owned a chain of theaters in Georgia, and his winter home in Fort Lauderdale was next to an alligator farm. He loved boating, which was one of Rudy's hobbies when he had time for it. I managed to catch a shark off Nassau the first time I had a rod in my hand. Rudy couldn't believe it. My husband wasn't a keen fisherman himself because he didn't want to kill the fish—but he had no problem eating them.

Shortly after returning from Europe, Rudy was booked into the Chi-Chi Club in Palm Springs. The third evening he made his appearance on stage, he discovered his voice had gone. He couldn't sing. Baffled, we went to the doctor. "You have a tiny nodule on your vocal cords, Mr. Vallée. There's no need to remove it if you rest your voice."

While we were dining with Frankie Laine, Rudy sought his advice. "If you keep quiet for a few weeks, you won't need the operation," Frankie said.

"A few weeks? That's much too long!"

The next day Rudy said, "Ellie, how can I walk around with a less-than-perfect throat? I can't get up in the mornings and know I have something wrong with my vocal cords. I'm a singer. My voice is my life. Besides, I'm due to perform in Santa Barbara next month. I have to be ready for that."

After the operation to remove the nodule, Rudy woke up and complained of a terrible headache. "Buttercup, I'm having a brain tumor!"

When I called the doctor, he explained that because of the position they'd held Rudy's head in during the operation, he'd developed a crick in his neck. "It'll soon go away," I was assured. It did. Interestingly, Rudy's voice dropped a full pitch after the operation, giving him a deeper, better tone. Impatient as always to hasten his cure, Rudy decided one morning to open his mouth wide and aim his sunlamp at the back of his throat. The result: a mouthful of blisters!

After appearing at the Roosevelt Hotel in New Orleans, Rudy was offered an engagement in Panama. The prospect excited Rudy. He could practice the Spanish he'd majored in at Yale. Leaving our car in Louisiana, we flew to Panama City and completed the engagement at the Panama City Hotel. Planning our return, Rudy discovered we could travel back to New Orleans by ship through the Suez Canal and the Caribbean. We sailed out of Panama on the *TES Chiripi*, one of six sister ships of the Great White Fleet owned by the United Fruit Company, the largest conglomerate in South America at the time.

At every stop—Honduras, Dominican Republic, Guatemala, Costa Rica, and Jamaica—Rudy was the first to disembark and break into song standing on the dock, entertaining the bewildered but delighted port workers and enthralling the departing passengers and the families who'd come to meet them.

Rudy loved these opportunities to perform, even if the local people had no idea who he was. But they soon joined in, clapping and dancing. Then we'd go into town and buy out the tourist shops. Returning to the ship laden down with half a dozen woven baskets along each arm, three straw hats on his head, and colorful beach mats rolled up under his elbows, my compulsive shopper and I usually got to the ship minutes before weighing anchor.

Rudy experienced his greatest insecurities whenever we were apart. I missed my sister and father very much and made several short trips back home alone, with Rudy reluctantly but generously agreeing. By now Rudy had become accustomed to having me constantly at his side. His previous wives had never traveled with him but with me he found it to be a happy new experience.

During my trips back to the West Coast, I made sure to write or call Rudy every evening. He seemed to have an insatiable need for constant contact between us. He wrote back daily on his trusty typewriter, mixing humor, romance, household instructions, and minute details of his activities. "Baby Dzzzzzaaaaahling, another day without you . . . Lee asked if he could include my name for a Nixon ad . . . next time you write include a check to pay for the wines . . . don't forget Pinky Herman is using the guest room for week . . . hurry back, don't stay away so long next time . . . Patrick's girl is short! . . . Betty fixed hearts of lettuce so I have no need of the bran my baby prescribed . . . had a little sherry last night . . . I read David's synopsis, don't think too much of it . . . I need you in my arms . . . I want to greet my lovely one soooo badly. I'm no good without you, my lovely lady of the evening with the shining gold legs."

I think he sat in his hotel room dreaming up tasks for me to do back home because he was bored. One of his favorite occupations was choosing various black-and-white color combinations for our car. One day his letter would instruct me to have the front doors white and the rear doors black. The next day, he'd change his mind, and a third letter would tell me of a different color combination altogether. Then he'd call and say, "Stop! Stop! I've changed my mind!" My solution was to wait about four days, then make the decision myself, which was not to repaint the car at all.

Even ten and twenty years into our marriage Rudy sent me telegrams urging my return from a trip home. "Dear Darling Buttercup, it has been hard being away from you. Reunion should be tremendous," read one of his telegrams after we'd been married fifteen years.

During one of our interludes at Silver Tip, Rudy's brother Bill and his young son, Bill Jr., came to stay from the East coast. A brilliant artist, Bill was making a career as a magazine writer and illustrator. We were remodeling our kitchen and several other rooms, and the bedrooms were stacked to the ceiling with furniture. We had no way to use the stove or refrigerator, and we were eating out of cans on a table in the garage and drinking instant coffee.

Because of the upheaval, when it came time to show Bill to his room, Rudy and I led him out of the main house and down the mountain to the lower building where celebrities, senators, and our friends played tennis and partied. But poor Bill thought we were relegating him to Siberia. "I'm one of the family. Why can't I stay in the house?"

"We're camping out up there. We thought you'd be more comfortable down here because it has a full kitchen for you and little Bill," Rudy shot back, miffed. For the next two days the two brothers refused to talk to each other and I had to smooth over two sets of Vallée feathers. Their French-Irish tempers were at full blast, and I could see where they were miscommunicating. Seeking a solution, I wrote little notes to both of them and finally they made up. The rest of the visit was wonderful.

In 1979, three years after Bill Sr. died, his son came to visit us at Silver Tip. Bill Jr. was now in his late twenties and arrived sporting a full beard that covered most of his face. A few days later he declared he was ready to shave it off. To commemorate the event, Rudy gave Bill Jr. an electric shaver and took "before" and "after" photos. Bill was trying to find his own way, and we took him everywhere with us. "Do you like this lifestyle?" Rudy asked him. "Then you need to go back to college. I suggest you study law." Today Bill Jr. practices law in Connecticut, where he lives with his wife and two children. We are still extremely close.

After we left New Orleans, where Rudy was playing at the Roosevelt Hotel, we flew to Puerto Rico to perform in Ed Gardner's show, "Duffy's Tavern." By now Rudy had realized his finances were not too rosy. We had many financial problems. Vallée-Video had drained the coffers; some club owners were unable to pay him for previous appearances; and a couple of agents neglected to pass along the fees they had received for Rudy's shows. Rudy wrote to his attorney Sam Zagon, "I'm in the midst of a crisis," inquiring about his IT&T

stocks and Third Avenue Railway bonds as well as the possibility for tax breaks on his losses with the needle-threading venture. "I'm going to have to cut and retrench everywhere, as failure of securing a picture or a steady television or radio show leaves me at the mercy of nightclub work, which is sporadic at best. I've got to come up with $25,000 to $45,000 for past taxes, too."

Rudy was also chagrined to read in columnist John Crosby's column that "Rudy Vallée as a bigtime radio entertainer disappeared long ago." A few other critics took pot shots, claiming his show was "unhappy . . . confused." This was perhaps one of the worst times in Rudy's career, when it seemed all his agent could book was one-night stands. On one occasion, the hotel was really a seedy motel, our room was a dump, and the "nightclub" was a small bar. Depressed, we were both practically in tears. "Oh, Buttercup, what am I doing here?" said Rudy, his head bowed.

"Dearest, nothing can touch us if we still have each other," I said, giving him a hug. "It's us against the world."

"Hey, is that the title of a song?" he quipped, his mood instantly changing. And we burst into laughter.

Yet there were a few bright spots to cheer us up. Rudy was presented with 330 shares of Coffee-Time, an iced coffee product, by the New England company's president as an incentive for Rudy to promote it, and Phil Harris asked his permission for a Rudy Vallée impersonator to recreate his discovery of Alice Faye, Phil's wife. Then Rudy was offered Edgar Bergen's spot as host on the "CBS Kraft Music Hall" radio show in New York for ten weeks. Rudy broadcast the show live from our Park Sheraton hotel suite, and each week I invited thirty or so guests as an audience.

The lengthy stint gave us a chance to live a more normal life. We bought black bowler hats and wore them in the Easter parade and dined and danced almost every night at the Stork Club, El Morocco, the Copacabana, or the Peppermint Lounge where we danced the Twist. Rudy performed at a champagne benefit for the ASPCA where dogs, dressed up by Gimbel's pet department, paraded around the Plaza Hotel.

Another encouraging engagement was when Rudy was hired by Texas millionaire and fraternity brother Al Hill, who was married to one of the Hunt daughters, to perform opening night of Colorado Springs' exclusive new Garden of the Gods Club. In a telephone booth in the club's lobby, newly wall-papered in a pocket-watch design, Rudy posed in a white dinner jacket for a publicity shot singing, "My Time Is Your Time." The photo became one of his most famous.

As competition between performers grew hotter, some of Rudy's routines grew bluer. He began reciting a few risqué jokes to spice up his act, raising some critics' eyebrows. Rudy also incurred the wrath of little old ladies in the Midwest, who sent him letters, and he received an occasional warning from his booking agents. Yet his manner of delivery, acting out the off-color humor, was devastatingly funny. He was still considered one of the finest storytellers in show business.

One show business principle Rudy always held to was never to demean people—except himself. Some of the funniest segments of his act included poking fun at himself as the young crooning idol. Yet in spite of his delicious, self-deprecating sense of humor, we were often amazed when audiences took his tongue-in-cheek remarks seriously.

By 1958, in spite of a part in another movie, *The Helen Morgan Story*, my Vagabond Lover's star was starting to dim. But Rudy was considerably cheered by an article in *Modern Man* magazine: "Despite anything you have read to the contrary, Frank Sinatra was, for sheer popularity, never in the same league as the curly haired Vagabond Lover."

After so many years on the road, Rudy lamented to a Wilmington, Pennsylvania, newspaper reporter, "Night life is dying in the U.S. Nobody goes out any more. It's all about television, and all entertainers suffer."

While Rudy was ready for change, to me life was still tremendously exciting. I was never bored. I told the same reporter, "I enjoy the nomadic life with my Vagabond Lover, whether we're in luxury surroundings or a quiet motel. As long as I am with Rudy, nothing else matters."

We were appearing at the Petti Arms and staying at the Lord De La Warr in Delaware with our friend Fred Cirello. Formerly a pianist, Fred was now an accountant. Rudy related to Fred his experiences with Lucille Ball and Ann Southern, both of whom he'd just appeared with in one of the Desilu Playhouse TV series, "Lucy Takes a Cruise to Havana." Rudy played a natty skipper. This show was a pleasant experience for him, but a later one was not, although he did three or four Lucy shows. I didn't get the whole story, but I feel certain that Rudy was insisting on perfection.

One film legend I enjoyed meeting was Gloria Swanson. During a formal New York charity event, I went into the ladies room with my friend Alice Bernstein, whose husband owned a large advertising agency in Providence, Rhode Island. I noticed Gloria at the counter, fixing her hair. Eyeing me up and down, she said, "Listen, dear, close your eyes or turn sideways when you go out the door because that tall, handsome guy outside is my boyfriend, Frank Farrell!" Farrell was one of New York's top columnists.

"You don't have to worry," I responded, smiling. "I'm married to Rudy Vallée." Gloria joined in our laughter.

On a quick trip home Rudy became embroiled in a battle to permit RCA to erect two fifty-four-foot radio towers on our property in exchange for a monthly fee. Frank Jacobberger put the deal together, but our neighbors protested that the towers would be unsightly, and the deal fell through. Rudy was unhappy, but he understood.

Other ventures close to his heart also failed to materialize. An LP recording of the humorous part of his shows to be called *Is This Our Rudy?* was never made; Warner Brothers proposed an album of his radio shows with John Barrymore, Orson Welles, and Lionel Barrymore, but this project, too, was abandoned. Small gestures from other stars, however, cheered him considerably.

"My many good wishes for a very happy birthday," telegraphed Frankie Avalon on Rudy's sixtieth birthday.

With no time for regrets, we left for Cleveland and a date at the Tudor Arms. Coincidentally, Rudy's third wife, Jane Greer, was filming a test there for Dick Powell's "Zane Grey Theater."

"I'm so happy to hear they like Rudy in Cleveland," she told the *Plain Dealer* newspaper a few days after a story on Rudy was printed.

I met Jane Greer at the Indy 500 races. She was escorted by a close friend of Rudy's, Earl Muntz, and we were all invited to a pre-race party. "Buttercup, sit at the pool all day and get yourself a great suntan. I want you to be really lovely on my arm tonight."

I did as my husband asked, and stayed under the hot sun for hours. When I came into our hotel room to change, my fair-complected face had swollen and blistered so badly I had to wear heavy makeup to conceal the redness! Rudy still told me I looked beautiful, bless him.

With a break between bookings, we headed for Silver Tip. Here, an upheaval was taking place. After five years with us, Fumi and her husband were leaving, with little Taro and two-year-old Sono. We had helped Fumi's husband Johnny with his education and he had recently graduated from college. Rudy offered to build the Itos their own house on our estate, but it was time for them to move on and make a life in their own home.

Fumi and I had become as close as sisters. When I was away, we exchanged letters several times a week discussing everything under the sun including our husbands.

When she left she wrote to me: "Living with you and knowing you has taught me so much. I hope that what I learned from you will not be lost, and that I will be able to pass on some of your goodness to others." We kept in touch. When Taro went to high school he joined the school band as a saxophone player, like "Uncle Rudy." When my husband heard about it, he sent Taro one of his saxophones, which Taro says he treasures to this day.

Although our travels continued and our dates every June at the Inverurie Hotel in Bermuda were ongoing, bookings became scarce. At times Rudy berated himself for sinking to accepting appearances at smaller clubs. "Nightclubs are the dreary court of last appeals, a nickel-and-dime existence," he remarked sadly. Was it time for my talented husband, now in his sixties, to accept the inevitable and hang up his party hats?

"I want you for our new musical comedy on Broadway." That magical announcement from Abe Burrows was a bombshell. We knew Abe, a scriptwriter for Rudy's early radio shows, was now a dynamic name in show business. He and songwriter Frank Loesser had teamed up on blockbuster shows: *Guys and Dolls*, *The Boyfriend*, and *Where's Charley?* If they were mounting this new production, called *How to Succeed in Business without Really Trying*, it was almost guaranteed to be a smash. And when Abe said he wanted my husband for a starring role, I thought I'd died and gone to heaven. But Rudy took some persuading. When he was first approached with the story, he thought his character was too one-dimensional. He turned the part down. A month later, he was asked again. He still said no.

Producers Cy Feuer and Abe Newborn, desperate enough to charter a tiny private plane piloted by a sixteen-year-old, now tried a third time. They tracked us down to the Iroquois Hotel, an obscure Canadian hotel in London, Ontario. This time they wanted him to read Act I. Rudy liked it immediately. "Ellie, it's a hit show. I can smell it!"

I was stunned by this turn in our fortunes and excited at the opportunity for my darling Rudy to regain public recognition for his incredible talent. What a showcase this would be for him. Rudy boarded the plane for New York to meet the young unknown lead, Bobby Morse, and female lead, Michele Lee, along with Virginia Martin, Charles Nelson Riley, and the rest of the cast.

A lifelong friend I met through *How to Succeed* was Marilyn Clark, one of the lead dancers. She had a little white poodle she brought backstage. Pets weren't allowed in the dressing rooms, but she and Rudy sneaked the dogs in, and they took turns hiding their pets whenever the other was onstage.

Burrows wanted Rudy to play the part of fuddy-duddy millionaire J.B. Biggley. Within a few days the contract was signed. Before rehearsals began, we had time to fulfill our annual date in

Bermuda, where Rudy studied the show songs he was to sing by listening to his own recordings on acetate discs. This was a focusing technique he had perfected decades earlier, when it was common practice for musicians.

We also spent a couple of days in El Paso visiting friends, where I thought we'd be incognito. No such luck. Before I knew it, Rudy met up with County Judge Woodrow Bean and found himself an honorary Texas Ranger!

Just before he returned to New York for rehearsals, we headed to Yale for Rudy's thirty-fifth reunion, and then I went back to Silver Tip to organize packing for what we both hoped would be an extended East Coast stay.

Fumi and I went over lists and lists of "Things To Be Done" and dealt with a daily bombardment of instructions and sketches from Rudy. Fumi was careful to follow his orders. When we first hired Fumi, Rudy's first written note to her said: "I am taking a nap!! Do not disturb me for anyone, *Not even God!!*" I think exclamation points were invented with Rudy in mind. It was the most used key on his typewriter.

I looked into hiring additional staff and instructed Evelyn Young, our secretary and confidante, how to handle our bank accounts and business papers while we were away. We asked her to make sure the accountant had all the figures necessary to handle the ledgers, pay the bills, and keep everything running smoothly. Rudy had four differently colored checkbooks: red, yellow, green, and white. When he sent instructions for invoices and statements to be paid, he would specify which color check to use. At one point Rudy wondered if we should just hand everything over to an accounting firm, but Evelyn and Fumi were handling things so well, I told him—and they were so trustworthy—I insisted on keeping them on. We did.

Bob Fosse joined the Broadway production to stage some of the dance numbers, and the cast plunged into the grueling routine of daily ten- and twelve-hour rehearsals at the Variety Art Studios in the Edison Hotel building. Rudy joked on the phone to me that the studio had the atmosphere of a funeral parlor. This proved a prophetic statement. Three days later during an evening rehearsal break Abe pulled Rudy aside. "Let's go down to the Green Room and grab a coffee."

"Sure," Rudy said.

Once seated, Abe got down to business. "You're fired. Frank wants you out of the show."

"What's wrong?" Rudy told me later his heart was pounding like a sledgehammer.

"It's your voice. You're not projecting."

When you tell a veteran entertainer who made millions with his vocal talent that his voice is at fault, it's not surprising to hear an instant reaction. In Rudy's case, his face turned purple but he couldn't utter a word! "Ellie, I finally spluttered I wanted to prove something to them, but only if we went next door to the Lunt-Fontanne Theater." Rudy knew that if he read and sang his part in a theater instead of the cramped rehearsal rooms, Frank would change his mind.

"I used to fill the Paramount Theater with five thousand people packed in and, even without the megaphone or a microphone, everyone could hear me. When you listen to me tomorrow, sit at the back, gentlemen. You'll learn something," Rudy instructed. They agreed to meet in the morning. As usual, I called Rudy at 1:00 A.M. from California. Totally unprepared for his devastating news, I choked up with tears. How could this happen? I was heartbroken at the pain I could hear behind my husband's words as he related the events. At the end of the phone call we were both crying and wishing we were together for this crisis. Then Rudy assured me there was no way he going to leave the show and that he'd call me after the Lunt-Fontanne theater tryout the following morning.

It worked. Rudy kept his part.

In a 1977 letter to Rudy, Abe Burrows wrote: "Anything unpleasant that happened . . . on *How to Succeed* was part of the general hysteria that happens on all Broadway shows. Crazy things happen . . . a sort of fright. The main thing is that *you* were sensational.

The critics thought so, the audience thought so, and I thought so. No one who played Biggley after you could even approach your performance." Burrows also confessed in the same letter that he had always had a sense of awe working with Rudy.

I arrived in New York loaded down with luggage and Mr. Pom Pom, Pitou, and Michelle, the poodles. We quickly rented a furnished apartment on East 56th Street, close to the theater so that Rudy could walk there each evening. Later we moved to 55th Street, across from the Blue Angel Club, where Barbra Streisand was appearing before she became the megastar she is today.

Then another crisis developed before opening night on Broadway.

How to Succeed in Business without Really Trying would open at the 46th Street Theater. Prior to leaving for the comedy's first tryouts in Philadelphia, we'd checked out the dressing room assigned to Rudy. It was a filthy dump. "This is a broom closet!" Rudy said. I was outraged they would treat my husband this way. But it was the only other single dressing room apart from Bobby Morse's; otherwise, Rudy would have to share a large room with the rest of the cast.

"Rudy, this is a disgrace. There's nothing to sit on and the paint's peeling off the walls. At least let's have them fix it up." We wrote a polite and reasonable note to the show management asking for a fresh coat of paint and an armchair so that Rudy could rest. We also asked for the removal of the sagging shelves and dressing table in front of the mirrors. Rudy had no use for them since he never wore makeup; instead, he used his sunlamp every day to maintain an even tan. We were assured the dressing room would be taken care of.

In Philadelphia we received a flurry of good luck phone calls and telegrams from our families—Dad and Irene and Bill and Dorothy, Rudy's brother and sister-in-law—and from Mertice Rubinoff, Betty Comdem, Adolph Green, Jule Styne, Hermione Gingold, Kathryn and Arthur Murray, and Paul Caruso, our old friend who'd put out my wedding veil fire. The telegram Rudy treasured most read: "All my best wishes to you for a great success. Noel Coward."

~THESE ARE THE GIRLS AND WOMEN I HAVE MET OVER THE PAST SXITY YEARS, AND IN TH
WRITING WHICH MAY BE TITLED EITHER " TALES OF A VAGABOND LOVER " OR
                    " THE DOLLS OF THE VALLEE "

SOME OF THEM (LINDA DARNELL) WHO DROVE ME CRAZY ON THE DANCE FLOOR WHEN I ME
HER AT CIRO'S FOR ONE DANCE WOULD NEVER GIVE ME A DATE AND THOSE WHO WERE   ...
UNATAINABLE SHALL BE DESIGNATED AS " THE GIRLS WHO GOT AWAY " !!! MARKED *
THOSE INCLUDED IN MY 3RD BOOK, " LET THE CHIPS FALL " DESIGNATED BY A CHECK
                SO HERE THEY ARE, WITH MORE TO COME.

1. LUPE VELEZ
2. ANN (MRS. JACK WARNER)
3. DOLORES DEL RIO *
4. CORA CANNING (THE DENTEYNE GIRL)
5. GLORIA YOUNGBLOOD (1/8 CHEROKEE)
6. HEDY LA MARR
7. DOROTHY LAMOUR
8. LINDA DARNELL *
9. GENE TIERNEY *
10. CAROL LANDIS
11. BEA LILLIE
12. YVONNE De CARLO
13. GLORIA DIXON
14. GAIL PATRICK (THE HALITOSIS GAL)
15. LIBBY HOLMAN
15. ADELA ROGERS ST. JOHN
17. MARIE WINDSOR
18. PAT DANE (MY LOVELY KITTEN)
19. GINGER ROGERS
20. AGNES O' LAUGHLIN *
21. BETTE JANE GRIER (WHOM I MARRIED)*
22. ALICE FAYE *
23. FAY WEBB * (WHOM I MARRIED)
24. MARY McBRIDE * WHO CHANGED MY TASTE IN WOMEN SO COMPLETELY !!
25. JUDY STEWART * THE GIRL WHO COULD HAVE BEEN MRS. V.
26. LEONIE CAUCHOIS * THE FIRST MRS. VALLEE (BUT WE HAD IT ANNULLED!)
27. LENORE ULRICH (MY IDEAL BEAUTY, MY COLLEGIATE CRUSH, A SUPERB ACTRESS.
28. AINAS ERICKSON THE GIRL WHO BROUGHT ME TO NEW YORK IN 1927.
29. MARY ANN NYBERG * WHO PUSHED ME INTO ELEANOR'S ARMS, BECAME MRS. ARTHUR KNIGHT.
30. JUNE KNIGHT A CHARMING GIRL ONE OF THE STARS OF COLE PORTER'S " JUBILEE "
31. NITA NALDI MY PERFECT BRUNETTE IDEAL WHO STARRED WITH VALENTINO
32. LILLIAN DUVAL AS HEAVENLY DESIRABLE AS A WOMAN COULD BE THE WIERE BROTHERS
    HUNG THEIR DERBIES ON HER BEAUTIFUL BREASTS IN AN EARL CARROLL SHOW
33. HARRIET HLLIARD WE MET MAKING A FILM, OZZIE LOVED HER SO MUCH HE DIED DENYING
    THAT SHE HAD EVER MARRIED BEFORE SHE MARRIED HIM.
34. JOAN CRAWFORD HOW I ENVIED DOUG FAIRBANKS JR. AND YET WHEN THE OPPORTUNITY
    WAS MINE, I DIDN'T GRAB IT!
35. LYDA ROBERTI WE ROMANCED IN THE WINGS JUST BEFORE I WAS TO PRESENT HER ON STA

36. SHIELA RYAN A LOVELY IRISH BEAUTY WHOM I WOULD HAVE MARRIED, BUT SHE REJECT!
                                          ME FOR DEAR PAT BUTTRAM!

37. ANN JEFFRIES *

38. JANE WYMAN, (REAGAN'S FIRST WIFE) WE WERE BOTH WORKING ON FILMS AT WARNERS
                 IT WAS A QUIET RELAXED DINNER. I DON'T REMEMBER IF WE KISSED!

39. SUSAN HAYWARD, WHO DROVE ME UP THE WALL AS I SAW HER IN A FILM BUT WHO WAS
    SO DIFFERENT ON OUR ONE DATE!

40. GRACE POGGI, JOE SCHENK'S GAL, WHO DROVE ME WILD AS I WATCHED HER DANCE WITH
    GEORGE MEXTAXA ON THE EL MOROCCO DANCE FLOOR ONE SUNDAY NIGHT !

41. JEAN HARLOW, RKO SUGGESTED IN 1929 BEFORE I WENT TO MAKE MY FIRST FILM THAT
    I BRING HER TO THE VILLA VALLEE. I PUT HER ON A CAB AND SENT HER HOME.

42. WENDY BARRIE, A WONDERFUL, CRAZY DARLING GIRL WHO DESIRED ME VERY MUCH, BUT
    WE ONLY BECAME THE BEST OF FRIENDS BEFORE SHE DIED SO TRAGICALLY IN NEW YOR'

43. JOAN CAULFIELD, WE ENJOYED SEVERAL PARTIES AT THE RADIO KING'S BEL AIR MAN-
    SION AND WAS A DELIGHTFUL ARMFUL!

44. MARY BRIAN, WHO FELL FOR ME AT A YALE DANCE AFTER HER FIRST PICTURE, BUT WHO
    SADLY NAMED THE GIRL SHE SAW I ADMIRED AND WHOM I KNEW I WOULD MARRY AND
    REGRET IT SO TERRIBLY!

45. MADAME OUSPENSKAYA, I ARRANGED FOR A GIRL TO STUDY WITH HER ONLY TO FIND TH/
THAT THE OLD GAL REALLY HAD A CRUSH ON ME AND HAD SHE BEEN YOUNGER WOULD HAVE
    SEDUCED ME!!!

46. CLARA RUSSELL, (ROSALIND'S SISTER WHOM THEY CALLED " THE DUTCHESS " AND WHO
    WAS ONE OF THE MOST HEAVENLY DATES OF MY ENTIRE LIFE (WHILE AT YALE)

47. CLEATUS CALDWELL, A BREATHLESS BEAUTIFUL FACE, SHE BECAME " MISS BLUE PACIFIC
    AND MARRIED KEN MURRAY, WHICH WAS A MISTAKE!

48. ADRIENNE AMES, WHO WOULD HAVE MADE A FINE WIFE AND A BEAUTIFUL ONE, BUT I
    LET HER GO TO STEPHEN AMES AND BRUCE CABOT WE WORKED TOGEHER IN A FOX FILM.

49. RITA RIO, WHO WAS THE THIRD GIRL TO CALL ME AND ASK TO "COME OVER " BUT I
    WAS AFRAID TO DO SO. YEARS LATER WE WORKED IN " SO THIS IS NEW YORK WHEN
    SHE HAD CEASED TO LEAD HER ALL GIRL ORCHESTRA AND HAD BECOME " DONNA DRAKE ".

50. MARY HEALY, A CHARMING, GIRL WHOM I MAY HAVE KISSED ONCE BEFORE GETTING HER
    INTO A FILM " SECOND FIDDLE " AND LEFT HER TO BECOME MRS. PETER LYND HAYES.

51. MERCEDES MARLOWE, WHO ASKED A WEALTHY NEW YORKER TO BRING HER TO MEET ME
    AT THE COCONUT GROVE. WE BOTH LOVED TENNIS BUT HARRY COHEN HAD US WATCHED
    AS WE PLAYED, IF EVER I MAY CLAIM A REAL FRIEND AND LOVER, IT IS SHE!

52. ANN SOTHERN, WHOM I SPOTTED AS A STAR AS I WATCHED HER WORK IN CHICAGO,
BUT SHE WAS MAYBE A LITTLE AFRAID. LATER I ATTENDED A PREMIERE OF A FILM IN
    WHICH SHE HAD CHANGED HER STAGE NAME FROM HARRIET LAKE TO ANN SOTHERN!

53. GAYLE ROBBINS, WHO AT FIRST WAS DEFINITELY NOT INTERESTED, BUT ONE NIGHT
    SHE BECAME AN ENTIRELY DIFFERENT PERSON, ALMOST FRIGHTENLY SO!

54. JUDY CANOVA, WHO DURING A SUMMER DANCE ENGAGEMENT ON LONG ISLAND TRIED SO
    HARD BUT IT JUST WASN'T TO BE !

55. BETTY GRABLE * JUST ONE DATE AND I CHASTISED HER FOR DIVORCING JACKIE

56. KAY SPRECKLES GABLE (THE LAST MRS. CLARK GABLE   COOGAN.

57. BETTY MURRAY WHO ALMOST MADE IT!!

58. FRANCESCA SIMS   COURTESY OF AL JOLSON

Rudy and Robert Morse singing "Grand Old Ivy" in the Broadway smash How to Succeed in Business without Really Trying.

Pat Nixon, shown here celebrating my birthday with me, and I were introduced through a mutual acquaintance and quickly became fast friends. We enjoyed many afternoons in New York shopping, dining, visiting museums, and seeing Broadway shows.

RICHARD M. NIXON
20 BROAD STREET
NEW YORK, NEW YORK

December 11, 1967

Dear Rudy:

    Several friends have called me with reports of how you came to my defense on the Merv Griffin show--and bested Mr. Susskind while doing it. This is just a note of personal appreciation and thanks for the effort--as well as for your kind note and continued support. I have asked my side, Pat Buchanan, to write you a brief note with any help he can provide for your idea.

    With warm regards,

Sincerely,

Mr. Rudy Vallee
7430 Pyramid Place
Hollywood, California 90046

P.S. I taped a show with Merv Griffin myself which will run on the 18th of December, I believe, and which also features Mr. Susskind.

R.M.N.

When Pat first took us to her apartment to meet her husband, he and Rudy hit it off immediately—Dick wanting to discuss show business and Rudy all politics. From that night on they remained good friends, and Rudy never hesitated to come to his defense, even during the Watergate fiasco.

The Beverly Hills Hotel swimming pool was the perfect spot for a relaxing afternoon with Lyn Uchitel, Jack Benny, and Hy Uchitel—the Uchitels were the owners of Voisin, our favorite restaurant in Manhattan.

A mural at the 1964 World's Fair featured Rudy and his famous megaphone.

I was constantly bombarded with requests to model; here I'm shown modeling hats with Paulette Goddard for Bergdorf Goodman in New York.

I did numerous commercials, including this one with Charles Nelson Reilly for Met Life. Based on its success, they hired me as their national spokesperson.

October 5, 1962

Mr. Rudy Vallee
46th Street Theatre
New York, N.Y.

Dear Rudy:

      As I told you, I saw you on the Sullivan show and enjoyed your monologue. Actually, it wasn't your monologue, it was a collection of wheezes from the Stone Age to the Orbit Age. But that is unimportant. It was very funny and delivered magnificently.

      Paste this carefully in your book of memories along with my best regards.

          As ever,

          Groucho

          Groucho Marx

Astronaut John Glenn came back stage after a performance of How to Succeed in Business without Really Trying *to meet Rudy—their admiration was obviously mutual.*

Rudy and I first met Elvis when he and Rudy were filming movies on adjoining sets (here we're pictured with Stella Atkinson and Millicent Trent); the two later teamed up in 1968 for Live a Little, Love a Little.

Returning to New York to celebrate Rudy's sixty-second birthday after a trip to the Bahamas gave us a chance to catch up with some old friends, including actor Jack Lemmon.

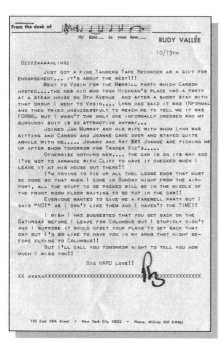

Following the success of How to Succeed, Rudy starred in the touring production of Jenny Kissed Me.

172

I had the honor of meeting Cary Grant at the Theatre Owners of America dinner at the New York Hilton.

Always a source of great joy to Rudy and me were our lovable poodles. Mr. Pom Pom loved singing along as Rudy played his saxophone.

I had a cameo appearance in the movie version of How to Succeed, *which starred many members of the Broadway cast, including Rudy, Michele Lee, and Bobby Morse.*

Rudy and I enjoyed entertaining our friends at Silver Tip; shown here are some guests at a dinner party: Edgar Bergen, Ken Murray, Frances Bergen, Jimmy Durante, Billy Gilbert, Rudy, Lolly Gilbert, and me.

The death of my father, Harlie Norris, in 1965 was one of the most tragic events in my life, but my stepmother, Irene (pictured here with my father, Rudy, and me), and I helped each other through it; she remains an important part of my life.

This picture of Rudy and me was his personal favorite, and he always carried a copy in his wallet.

Pounding away on his typewriter was the one place I was sure to find Rudy; whether keeping up with his correspondence, writing his diary, or responding to the latest editorial, he always had something to say.

We first met Johnny Carson when he was doing the television show Carson's Corner in California. He remained a good friend of ours for many years until Rudy admonished him for firing a staff member in the late '60s; even though Rudy wrote a letter of apology, our friendship never recovered from the incident.

The always lovable Morey Amsterdam knew Rudy as well as anyone—they first met in Los Angeles in 1937.

Rudy and me enjoying cocktails with the poodles on our balcony at Silver Tip.

Each year Rudy and I considered it a challenge to come up with a unique idea for our Christmas cards; here are just a few of them.

Richard and Pat Nixon remained valued friends of ours throughout the ups and downs of Dick's political career.

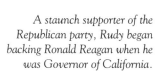

To Ellie Vallee
With appreciation and best wishes,

August 27, 1972

A staunch supporter of the Republican party, Rudy began backing Ronald Reagan when he was Governor of California.

Rudy relished sifting through the amazing archives he amassed over the seven decades of his career, and he would gladly show them to anyone who stopped by the house.

Always ready to have a good time, Rudy and I are shown here twisting the night away in the 1970s.

Phyllis Diller and me enjoying a party with friend Byron Clark in the background.

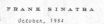

FRANK SINATRA

October, 1984

Dear Rudy,

I have only just now returned from what seems like a century on the road.

I read through what you sent me, and it's all very very interesting, I assure you.

As for your question regarding my irons I might have in any of the recording companies, the easiest way to answer that is to say not as I used to.

I am not heavily into recording these years and on those rare occasions when a recording project interests me enough, it's usually put together as a separate package on an ad hoc basis.

The recording industry is so different today than it was when you made records and when I made records that I sympathize with you on your project regarding the 34 songs culled from your 56 years of recording. I have no question that you do have a "gold mine" as you say, but from what I have gathered over the recent years today's recording guys aren't panning for gold. I wish I were in a position to help you, but I am not. But be assured I will drop kind words should the occasion arise and keep you in my prayers.

Warmest regards,

Frank

Mr. Rudy Vallee
7430 Pyramid Place
Hollywood, Calif. 90046

THE WHITE HOUSE

WASHINGTON

May 15, 1981

Dear Eleanor and Rudy:

I can't tell you how happy Nancy and I were to receive your message. Making that speech to the Congress was a great pleasure for me, almost as much as having the House of Representatives approve our budget resolution last week.

Nancy and I certainly feel our share of homesickness from time to time, but days like these and the outpouring of good wishes from dear friends like you provide a perfect cure. You're a part of that "memory we'll treasure forever," especially now when everything means just a little bit more.

With our heartfelt thanks and best wishes,

Sincerely,

Ron

Mr. and Mrs. Rudy Vallee
7430 Pyramid Place
Hollywood, California 90046

Rudy and me at home with Ginger in April 1984, just over two years before his death.

Coward, whose writings included the monologue "Mad Dogs and Englishmen," which Rudy often performed, was revered by Rudy.

Returning to New York after opening night rave reviews in Philadelphia, we went directly to the theater to inspect the dressing room. Not a thing had been done. That night at rehearsal, I knew I had to speak my mind. With my friend Helen Steward, I walked up the aisle to Abe Burrows, Bob Fosse, Frank Loesser, Cy Feuer, and Ernie Martin as they stood talking in the foyer of the theater. I was ready to do battle. No mother tiger could have matched my fury. But my words were spoken quietly and to the point.

"How could you do this to my husband! You boys don't know him at all. To know Rudy is to love him. You didn't listen to him, you didn't spend time with him. You treat him like dirt! All he asked for was a coat of paint and a chair. What did you do? Nothing! If you'll just give him one percent he'll give you back ninety-nine. He's liable to walk out on that stage and screw everything up, the way he feels. You're cruel, cruel! And one more thing, if you ever tell Rudy I talked to you about this, I'll call you all liars!"

Then I ran back down the aisle, trembling, tears of rage streaming down my face. By the following afternoon the dressing room had been completely transformed. Rudy knew nothing of my outburst. As we met to go to Sardi's for dinner that night, Rudy said, "Sweetheart, look, they've fixed up my dressing room."

"Oh, that's wonderful, darling," was all I responded. Three years later, Cy Feuer said to Rudy, "Everyone should have a wife like yours," and the whole story came out.

TEN

The Darling of
New York
Once More

I gave Rudy a pair of gold cufflinks to wear on opening night. They were inscribed "My Time Is Your Time," with a bar of music. Another pair of cufflinks he wore that week depicted the masks of tragedy and comedy. "I'm going to wear these every night we perform, Buttercup, whether it's seven times or seven times seven," he said. As it turned out, Rudy wore his cufflinks for a total of 1,144 performances.

To celebrate the excitement of opening night we invited sixty of our friends to one of New York's most famous Italian restaurants, Mama Leone's. "Ellie, sweetheart, this is Robert Morse's night. How about we go to Mama Leone's, run over to Sardi's for the reviews, then come back here and party?"

Gene Leone was a friend of Rudy's, and he set up a huge table for us. Once settled, we excused ourselves and walked over to Sardi's, the traditional show business hangout where cast members awaited the critics' reviews. As we walked in, everyone stood up and applauded. "Rudy! Wait till you see what the critics say about you!"

183

The sensational success of *How to Succeed* is now show business history. It was a smash hit, as Rudy predicted. From the first night, October 14, 1961, until its end three years later, there were standing ovations after almost every performance. The public began calling it "the Rudy Vallée show" because the title was so long and Rudy's performance so remarkable.

If we received dozens of telegrams in Philadelphia, we received thousands for the Broadway opening. Dore Schary, Kaye Ballard, George Gobel, Phil Silvers—the list was endless. By now the press was in hot pursuit. Rudy was hailed as "the star of the biggest hit on Broadway," in the *New York Mirror*, which ran a four-part series on "a sax-playing, wise-cracking legend."

The praise embarrassed Rudy. "Bobby Morse is the lead, not me," he reminded columnists Earl Wilson, Joe Franklin, Cindy Adams, Jim Bishop, Louis Sobol, and many others. In fact when columnist Herb Caen panned Morse's performance and Loesser's musical score, Rudy wrote Caen a letter of protest. Caen wrote back: "Rudy . . . you were splendid."

My Vagabond Lover was now on a roll and his quotes and anecdotes were all over the newspapers, magazines, television, and radio, which hailed his "comeback." "Comeback? This isn't a comeback! I never left!" shouted Rudy Vallée with glee at a young reporter from *The New York Herald Tribune*.

Rudy's return to Broadway was his first since 1935 and the press made the most of it. They pulled out all the old stories they could find about Rudy—the incident when a heckler threw a grapefruit at him and missed, the Al Capone episode, his sell-out crowds at Brighton Beach—and they reminisced about his great early fame.

Journalists welcomed this new Rudy Vallée, and they loved writing about him again. He was so popular with the media, he was invited to perform at the press's own awards banquets for writers and photographers. Rudy was still one of entertainment's most colorful characters. He always had a quick riposte and never failed to provide the media with snappy "sound bites." On top of that, of course, is the fact that Rudy was still his own best press agent.

We were interviewed grooming the poodles; barbecuing in aprons and chef hats on our apartment balcony; shopping at Bergdorf's; exercising on our stationary bicycle; and dining at our favorite restaurants. During an interview at Le Pecheur restaurant Rudy became so impassioned about the value of seatbelts, the reporter said Rudy fell off his chair. Rudy was serious about drivers and passengers wearing seatbelts because we had a serious accident ourselves. One night, on our way to Omaha in a heavy snowstorm, we skidded on a winding curve, crashed over an embankment and headed down a slope. "Sweetheart," Rudy said in a tone I'd never heard before, "this is it!"

I grabbed the poodles. I, too, was sure this was it, yet I had no fear. As the car thrashed through the bushes a tree loomed up ahead of us. We hit it head-on, but it stopped us from further disaster. Our guardian angels must have been watching. While Rudy stayed with the car, I walked into the town we could see from the car. After getting help, shock set in. I became violently ill. Rudy ordered seatbelts for our station wagon. After Rudy finished his engagement at the Hill Club in Omaha, he flew to New York for a television appearance. As soon as the seatbelts were installed, I was to drive the wagon to Las Vegas. Frank and Jane Jacobberger, our friends in Omaha, followed me all the way in their car. Rudy and I never rode in a car since then without our seatbelts firmly fastened.

During the first few months of *How to Succeed*, Rudy made time to re-create some of his free Sunday concerts at Brighton Beach in Brooklyn, and the press traveled to New Jersey to record Rudy's return to the rebuilt Atlantic City Steel Pier, where Rudy headlined a vaudeville show twice a day, three times on the weekends. Pier owner George Hamid Sr. treated us like royalty. Our manager, Cliff Steward, and his wife Helen came along. The LaFayette Hotel hung a thirty-foot "Welcome Rudy Vallée" banner from the roof and reserved a suite for us. On the door was a shiny plaque, "The Rudy Vallée Suite." It was a sumptuous apartment with marble decor and its own swimming pool outside.

The bar was already stocked with wines from Renault, a local vineyard, whose owner remembered Rudy from his early days. This wonderful Italian family entertained Rudy during his many visits to perform at the Steel Pier and sent along cases of sparkling champagne so we could entertain our guests. None of us lacked gourmet food, either, because the Hackneys, who own the Hackney Fish House in Atlantic City, sent lobsters, oysters, clams, and shrimp to our suite each day.

Dean Martin was performing at the 500 Club nearby, and I was a big fan of his. I kidded Rudy that I had a crush on Dean, so Rudy took the Stewards and me to see the show. We had a front table, and I sat there cooing and batting my eyelashes at Dean to tease Rudy. Unknown to me, Rudy called Dean after the show and asked him to call our suite to say he was crazy about me. When the call came, it was around 1:00 or 2:00 A.M. I picked up the phone. "You talk like an angel talks, you walk like an angel walks," Dean crooned into my ear.

"Oh, I can't believe it!" I squealed, like any young teenager.

"I just want you to know," said Dean, "that I saw you tonight out front, and if you ever think of leaving Rudy, I'll be here waiting for you."

The next day Rudy, Cliff, Helen, and I took a case of sparkling burgundy to Dean's hotel, where he and Frank Sinatra were staying. They invited us in for drinks and autographed pictures for us. That episode was one of the big moments of my life and proved once more that my husband had a terrific sense of humor.

Our social life was overflowing. Walter Winchell held a Damon Runyon Fund Easter Brunch and wrote to thank Rudy for adding to the fun; Freedomland USA hosted a "Rudy Vallée Tribute" at its amusement park and circus, where my husband was inducted as its mayor and a parade was held in his honor.

I was inundated with invitations to model and judge fashion events. One of my favorite press photos, in *The New York Herald Tribune*, showed Paulette Goddard and myself modeling big-brimmed straw hats from Bergdorf Goodman, designed by Baroness Radvansky. One young designer I discovered at that time was Mr. Blackwell, who was just starting out as a couturier. His designs were classic, very sexy, and elegant. I bought dozens of them.

Rudy, too, bought in quantity. He was a compulsive shopper and could never buy just one of anything, whether it was suits, books, sunglasses, or toilet paper. We never ran out of anything. I tried to avoid sending him out to buy something we needed.

If he found a dress he liked me to wear, he'd order it in black, blue, green, and white. Then he'd buy the high heel shoes to match each dress color.

Reporters wanted to know Rudy's health and youth secrets and how we managed to keep our marriage alive. These were the only occasions when the media seemed surprised, when Rudy and I talked of our great love for each other. After several years of marriage, it was apparent to everyone who interviewed us that we still had a close, passionate relationship. If they showed skepticism, I produced some of the love letters we'd written to each other over the years to prove it. One was a note I sent Rudy a week before *How to Succeed* opened: "I still feel like a bride—your bride—and always will remember our wedding day."

"She still manages to make my poor old heart beat furiously with desire," Rudy told reporters. "Look at her! She's beautiful, statuesque, long-legged, gentle, always smiling, and the perfect companion."

Rudy knew I was devoted to him, even now in the twilight of his tumultuous, star-studded life. "She's my Buttercup," he quipped to a journalist, "and she has the sweetest temperament I've ever encountered. She's crazy about me. I waited years to meet my ideal woman and here we are decades later still acting like honeymooners."

Rudy was amused at the media attention. Asked by *The Star* if he was amazed by it all, he said, "I'm not amazed at all. After all, I'm a living legend!"

One of our greatest pleasures was dining out after the show at New York's fabulous restaurants—Sardi's, the Stork Club, the Four Seasons, Voisin, El Morocco—and dancing to the music of the best bands in town at the Copacabana, the Rainbow Room, and the St. Regis and the Plaza Hotels.

That's how I met one of my dear friends, Lyn Uchitel. She and her husband, Hy, owned the Voisin restaurant on Park Avenue at 63rd Street, one of the most exclusive French dining spots in Manhattan. We went there the first time as guests of Rudy's tailor, Al Heimann, who made all of Rudy's hand-tailored suits. Our dinner companion was one of the Uchitel brothers who made the inner linings for the suits. When we met Hy and Lyn, they adopted us, so to speak. Rudy and I enjoyed Voisin's elegant atmosphere, Wedgwood blue-and-white decor, and cosmopolitan clientele, and it became a home away from home for us. Rudy ate a pretheater snack there most evenings, and Lyn gave him her limo to take him to the theater or pick him up to meet us later. When the Uchitels told us they were planning a huge Christmas party in Rudy's honor to celebrate the first year of *How to Succeed*, we insisted on taking the Voisin owners to our favorite Italian restaurant, Mama Leone's, as thanks.

Rudy enjoyed walking all over New York, being an exercise enthusiast, so he suggested that instead of riding in the Uchitel's limo the few blocks to Mama Leone's after the show, we should walk there, even though the sidewalks were wet and slushy with snow. Lyn slipped on an iron grating and we all ended up at Dr. Maxwell Maltz's office, where my poor friend needed stitches for a cut above her right eye. Rudy dubbed her "Alice Faye," as a reminder of Rudy's auto accident with Alice many years before.

A magnet for every international star, Voisin was where we first met Richard Burton, when he was playing Hamlet in New York. He and his wife, Elizabeth Taylor, were sitting in a booth as we entered the restaurant. Waving at Rudy, Richard gestured us over, jumped up, and kissed my hand. "Stand up, Elizabeth! Stand up! This is Rudy Vallée!" urged Richard. Elizabeth graciously rose to meet my husband and me. She was very sweet.

I met Pat Nixon through my good friend Ann Duggan, the wife of journalist and one-time Nixon speechwriter Tom Duggan. Rudy had guested on Tom's television show in Los Angeles, and we were delighted when Ann Duggan decided to move to New York. About a week after we met, Pat Nixon, Ann, and I dined at Trader Vic's. Rudy joined us there after *How to Succeed* and we walked Pat back to her apartment on Fifth Avenue where she invited us in.

"Dick is back from playing golf and attending a formal dinner, so come on up," she said.

"Oh, no. It's so late. We don't want to disturb him."

"But Dick would love to meet you both."

As soon as we entered the apartment, Pat went back toward the bedroom, calling out that Rudy Vallée was here. "Rudy Vallée? Wait right there!" Dick came out wearing a beautiful blue silk robe over pajamas, and we were introduced. Then he took us into the kitchen and mixed up a batch of gimlets.

"Now, Rudy," said Dick, "I want to know all about show business. Tell me what's going on these days."

"Forget show business. I want to know all about politics, Dick. What's the latest?" After that meeting, we spent a lot of time with the Nixons, and with their friends Bebe Rebozo and Rosemary Woods, Dick's secretary, both in New York and later at the White House and the western White House, his home in San Clemente. The Nixons were living quietly in New York at the time. Their daughters, Julie and Tricia, attended private school. We all knew Dick was being urged to make a run for the presidency, and Pat wasn't keen on the idea.

We went shopping at Bloomingdale's, visited museums, and saw Broadway plays. Pat was a warm, charming woman, not at all the cool person that many people thought her. We'd go laughing and dancing arm in arm down Fifth Avenue after seeing a new musical.

One play we saw together was *A Program for Two Players* starring Helen Hayes, who invited me to bring Pat backstage afterwards. Unfortunately, I had to leave early to meet Rudy. The following day I received a note from Helen saying she was terribly disappointed that Pat and I didn't stay because she was anxious to know Pat's feelings about the play.

Now the new darling of Broadway for three consecutive years,

Rudy could have rested on his laurels. Instead, with boundless energy he embarked upon a heavy schedule of guest shots on radio and television, charity performances, judging dog shows, and driving or flying to neighboring states to fulfill scores of engagements. He did a TV show called "On Broadway Tonight," and I'd take the Nixon daughters to the studio to watch. All this in addition to starring in *How to Succeed in Business without Really Trying*.

Rudy was constantly in demand at opening nights, galas, luncheons, testimonial dinners, tributes, cocktail parties, even fashion shows. We managed to get away with Hugh Downs to a New Year's Eve party in Morristown, Pennsylvania, where we enjoyed a wonderful evening with our friend Regis Philbin. We took a quick trip to Washington, where Rudy was awarded the first annual "Big M" award by the Maine Station Society.

After coming to see *How to Succeed* with her guest, Elizabeth Arden, celebrity hostess Perle Mesta invited us to a luncheon honoring the Olympic coaches and the ambassadors of their respective countries. We read in the paper that small radio stations around the country, like WSAF in Sarasota, Florida, were saluting Rudy with hour-long tributes, broadcasting his records or rerunning interviews.

He was asked by NBC to host a birthday tribute for Bob Hope "since it was on one of your early programs that Bob Hope first appeared on NBC Radio in 1933." Ed Sullivan asked him to keep four dates open for his show, and Nelson A. Rockefeller invited Rudy to join Helen Hayes and Richard Rodgers at a meeting of the New York State Council of the Arts. The Ziegfield Alumni selected Rudy as "The Outstanding Man Performer of the Year."

In the second year of *How to Succeed*, Rudy appeared on Ed Sullivan's "Toast of the Town" television show, telling jokes, performing dramatic sketches, and singing "Alouette," an audience-participation song. "Just think, Buttercup, Ed paid me $800 in 1949. Now I'm getting $7,500!"

Rudy was such a success with Sullivan's studio audience that the critics and Ed predicted that he would be the next TV megastar. If my Vagabond Lover was unavailable, some television hosts found other outlets for Rudymania. Paul Keyes, the producer of *The Tonight Show* with Jack Paar, flew Rudy's sister, Kathleen Lenneville, into New York to be the "mystery relative" on the show. Every talk show host wanted him—Johnny Carson, Steve Allen, Jack Paar, even quiz shows and variety shows.

In his 1995 memoir, television talk-show host Joe Franklin called Rudy his best friend in the world after Eddie Cantor died. Joe, who often stayed at Silver Tip, had Rudy on his show eighty-five times. I met him and his wife Lois in New York, when Joe's show at WOR-TV was a big hit.

Lois and I went to exercise and acting classes together, and we'd lunch with "the girls" at the 21 Club. It had been a favorite restaurant of ours for some time. My friend Ann Duggan and I used to frequent the popular restaurant, and although ladies weren't allowed to dine alone without escorts, the manager was nice enough to allow us to eat there because they knew Rudy and Tom would be joining us later. When Lois and I lunched there, sometimes I had Mr. Pom Pom with me. I'd check the little poodle with the hatcheck girls, and they'd admire his jewel-encrusted dog collar and the cute little fur coat I'd had custom tailored.

Looking back, it sounds so corny, but at the time it was so much fun for me to "play Hollywood." Rudy loved New York, and he gave it to me on a silver platter. There wasn't a better way to live in New York than to be a celebrity and enjoy Rudy's rejuvenated fame. We appreciated every second of it. Fan mail poured into our apartment and to the theater. Many of the letters and notes reminded Rudy of former shows and performances around the country, and others came from original fans who were delighted to see this "reincarnation" of their early idol.

One note was from Al Siegel, owner of Club Miami in Keansburg, New Jersey. We did a one-night stand at this little seashore nightclub about a year before Abe Burrows beckoned Rudy to Broadway. It was around the time when Rudy was becoming disheartened and he almost passed up Siegel's date. But, trouper that he was, he didn't want to let the club down. After Rudy opened in *How to Succeed*, Siegel wrote that Frank Sinatra's parents had been at Club Miami the night he performed, and that he, Siegel, was now buying dozens of tickets to see Rudy in the Broadway show.

We celebrated Rudy's sixty-second birthday with a quick trip to Bermuda, where Rudy couldn't resist accepting welcome-back engagements at the Inverurie Hotel. On our return to New York, the entire cast joined in birthday congratulations, and Dick Nixon sent a telegram. Ivan and Mary Obolensky, who published Rudy's and Gil McKean's book *My Time Is Your Time*, gave us a party; Johnny Carson's celebration was at Rudy's favorite Chinese restaurant that Rudy called Won Hong Loe.

Our friend Bill Black, chairman of Choc Full o' Nuts, asked Rudy to act in some coffee commercials; Joseph Papp wanted to use his name for the New York Shakespeare Festival; and Jack Benny invited us to his pre-Broadway opening party. One of the most elaborate events we attended was hosted by Secretary of State Robert McNamara in honor of His Royal Highness, Prince Peter of Greece.

We appeared at benefits at the Sutton Place Synagogue; at a ball in honor of the State of Israel's fifteenth anniversary; at Elsa Maxwell's April in Paris Ball; and at the United Nations' Broadcast Pioneers dinner along with Peter Ustinov, Jack Pearl, and Smith and Dale. We were guests of honor at Ella Fitzgerald's opening at the Americana Hotel. Julian "Cannonball" Adderley, noted alto sax player of the 1960s, asked Rudy to appear on behalf of CORE, the Committee for Racial Equality. My husband accepted immediately and gave a lengthy performance.

Out-of-towners remembered us, too. At the 1963 World's Fair William Wallace Barron, the governor of West Virginia, designated Rudy an honorary mountaineer in recognition of meritorious service based on Rudy's contributions to the nation. We spent several days at the World's Fair when General Motors hired Rudy to stand outside their tent, singing through his megaphone.

An interesting episode occurred on the West Coast during our success in the East. The press reported in several newspapers and magazines that pianist Liberace had just bought our home, Silver Tip. This was ridiculous, of course. We had no intention of selling, and our home was never on the market while Rudy was alive. But the media went crazy and almost every publication in the country ran the story. The truth was, Liberace purchased a home similar in architecture to Silver Tip, and it was wrongfully identified as the home of Mr. and Mrs. Rudy Vallée. In fact, the pianist's new home was far larger than Silver Tip, but the exterior resemblance was striking. We often kidded Liberace about this years later when we saw him in Las Vegas or Hollywood.

Rudy's previous home on Sunset Boulevard was sold to Jayne Mansfield when she married Mickey Hargity. The two turned the swimming pool into a heart-shaped lagoon, and photos of it appeared all over the world.

Alice Faye, in town to rehearse for a Perry Como TV show, came backstage, and we caught up with friends Rudy hadn't seen in decades: Jimmy Durante, George Jessel, Abbe Lane, Joe Levine, Eartha Kitt, Sammy Davis Jr., Anita Louise, Mary Martin, Ethel Merman, Carol Channing, Jack Lemmon—the list was endless.

Norman Corwin, a revered veteran of radio, sent an amusing fan letter (though we'd known him for years), and *Vogue* magazine included Rudy in its 416-page anthology, *The World in Vogue*.

President John F. Kennedy showed up to see *How to Succeed* one evening, slipping into an aisle seat just before curtain time. We visited with him later that night at Voisin, and we expected to meet Angie Dickinson, as she was rumored to be in the wings at the show. But only the Secret Service men were at Voisin with the President.

The next time I met President Kennedy was after I received a call from Lyn and Hy Uchitel to bring Rudy over for Sunday brunch. When we arrived, Lyn seated us right next to the President's table. We exchanged general conversation, and I told him that he and Rudy looked alike. Jackie Kennedy laughed, then mentioned that she was born on the same date as Rudy, July 28.

I hosted many luncheons at Voisin, but one luncheon stands out: Lyn's birthday on Saturday, November 23, 1963. I wanted it to be a very festive event, with a fashion show by Marusia. One of the noted fashion designers of the day, Marusia was in fact Princess Toumanoff, a friend of Lyn's and mine. We spent weeks discussing her beautifully beaded designs, accessories, and the menu for the big bash. Lyn and I decided to invite the forty-five most wonderful women we knew, from all over the country. They included Pat Nixon, Jolie Gabor, Ann Duggan, Bob Rockefeller, Pamela Mason, Creta Deek, Ramona Treffinger, and Perle Mesta. The day of Lyn's birthday luncheon, Pat repeated to me she hoped Dick would say no to a try for the White House. I often wondered afterwards if the tragedy that week gave her even more reason to hope her husband wouldn't run.

On Friday, November 22, the day before the celebration at Voisin, President John F. Kennedy was assassinated. We were not sure how to handle this delicate situation. Most of our friends had already flown in. Should we cancel? Shouldn't Voisin be closed as a mark of respect for our president? As we read the press reports about Kennedy, we noticed that several newspapers mentioned Voisin as one of his favorite Sunday spots for brunch after attending mass at St. Patrick's Cathedral on Fifth Avenue. We decided to go ahead with the celebration and include a tribute to our beloved young leader by inviting George Jessel to give a eulogy.

As we wiped away tears at his eloquence, George felt he needed to lighten the atmosphere, so he launched into some of his famous comic routines and we ended up with tears of laughter mingled with those of sadness. Thereafter, Lyn decided she would celebrate her birthday on New Year's Eve instead of the day after President Kennedy was shot.

Paul Whiteman wrote from a hospital bed in New Hope, Pennsylvania, saying how delighted he was with Rudy's Broadway success, and thanking him for sending galley proofs of a manuscript, *Jazz: A History of the New York Scene*, another project Rudy was working on. To my knowledge, it was never published.

One Sunday, the only day off for the cast from *How to Succeed*,

Rudy performed a benefit at the Fairfield County prison in Connecticut. Bill and Mary Keller introduced us to the High Sheriff of Fairfield County, Bill Berlund. During the run of the play, we left our blue Chrysler station wagon with Berlund, since we couldn't make much use of it in Manhattan. The sheriff fixed it up for his own use as a sheriff's vehicle complete with siren, air horn, side decals, and all the official regalia.

When it came time to collect our car, we left the decals and horns on. "It's perfectly legal, and it'll be safer for us traveling like this," Rudy said. "Besides, Bill made me an honorary sheriff."

From then on, whenever we drove cross-country, we had a lot of fun playing cops and robbers, wearing police officer caps Rudy found in a Hollywood costume store. If we saw a driver speeding or changing lanes dangerously, Rudy would drive up alongside and wag his finger. Other times I'd dress up as a nurse, and pretend we were driving an ambulance.

In Santa Barbara, where my sister lived, we'd switch the siren on just for fun. Rudy was like a big kid playing make-believe. I had just as much fun as he did, joining in the stunts he pulled. Later, Rudy had the horn rigged to blast out "My Time Is Your Time," and he'd play it each time we drove into a new town.

While we were staying with Bill and Mary Keller in Bridgeport, Rudy offered to perform at the local prison, playing excerpts from "Jenny Kissed Me," as he often did at federal prisons. He'd sign autographs and give away miniature flashlights and pens to the inmates. For the female prisoners, he took a satchel filled with vials of perfume. Rudy was a walking gift shop.

Sheriff Berland died not long after, but we kept the black and white car, bringing it back to Los Angeles, sounding the horn, and fooling around. We were pulled over a few times until finally our good friend Sam Yorty, the mayor of Los Angeles, phoned. "Look, Rudy, these little games have been fun, but it's time to paint your car a normal color." We finally took his advice—a few years later.

Later Sam offered an olive branch. "I think we should make you the Traffic Commissioner for the City of Los Angeles." Rudy agreed, and he'd show up at the commission meetings in his black-and-white car, parking in red zones, double-parking, and never getting a ticket.

But Rudy did have advice for other drivers. He had small cards printed up to leave on the windshields of parked cars reading, "Please Be Courteous and Leave Space for Other People."

When I took the car myself to visit my sister Betty in Santa Barbara, the gas station attendant came over quickly. "Well, now, who are you?"

"I'm a sheriff from Fairfield County," I announced. We both laughed.

On most Sundays off from *How to Succeed*, Rudy had complimentary tickets to other Broadway shows. We'd take along newly-divorced Johnny Carson and Joanne, his fiancée. We took turns hosting dinner beforehand at each others' apartments. One night it was the Carsons' turn. Dinner was a little late so we had plenty of time to drink a variety of cocktails. Finally, Joanne served up our chicken dinner. She'd ordered the stuffed birds from Kenny's Steak House. Kenny and Joanne, we learned later, were having an affair, unknown to any of us. However, she didn't realize that the stuffed chickens from her lover were not cooked. "What the hell is this?" exclaimed Rudy as he stuck his fork into his serving of chicken. Needless to say, we all went off to a Chinese restaurant instead.

We met Johnny when he was just starting out in television in California with a show called *Carson's Corner*. Rudy and Tony Martin were among its first guests. Johnny lived on Tampa Street in Reseda, and he and his wife loved barbecuing. Rudy and I fell in love with their two little boys, who were six and eight years old at the time. After Johnny moved to New York to do *Who Do You Trust?*, a year before he took over *The Tonight Show*, we became even closer friends.

When Johnny married Joanne, we gave the couple a set of Baccarat wine glasses. Many years later those same glasses were a bone of contention during their divorce proceedings. Both Johnny and Joanne laid claim to them, and we were summoned to the attorney's office to relate the details of their purchase.

One day Rudy learned that John Glenn and his three fellow

astronauts were coming to see *How to Succeed*. Rudy was tremendously excited. They were his heroes. He immediately called Stan Abrams and his wife Marilyn to the show. After the curtain fell, Rudy came out front and invited the astronauts and our private party onto the stage so we could meet these American heroes.

By 1962, the second year of the show, my father had married a delightful lady named Irene. She was the mother of one of my closest friends, who died in a car accident the day we graduated from high school. Irene brought great happiness to everyone in our family, especially to Dad.

Their Christmas letter that year described their trip to New York, and the great time they had seeing Rudy in the show, then coming backstage to meet the cast. Rudy was able to pull a few strings to take my father and his wife on a private tour of the United Nations. At lunch, they were seated next to Eleanor Roosevelt and Adlai Stevenson. Rudy knew Adlai through our mutual friend, Illinois Secretary of State Edward J. Barrett. After winning the Illinois gubernatorial election, Adlai invited us to his inaugural ball. During the early 1960s, just after the United Nations was established, Adlai frequently invited Rudy and me to lunch.

A highlight for me that year was dancing with Peter O'Toole at the Waldorf Astoria Hotel after the premiere of *Lawrence of Arabia*. I was dancing with someone else, and he cut in. I was so thrilled, I stepped on his toe. "So, tell me who you are," he said.

"I'm Rudy Vallée's wife."

"Rudy Vallée? Rudy Vallée? I love him! Take me to meet him, please!" That was the beginning of our friendship with Peter. When he came to Los Angeles a year or so later, we invited him to dinner. Rudy was almost salivating at the thought of showing one of his idols through the archives. Unfortunately, Peter had to cancel.

Rudy was so happy to be in *How to Succeed*, he wanted to make sure all our friends came to see it. Getting tickets to the hottest show on Broadway was not easy. At one point he got so frustrated he had his own little folding chairs made, so at least our friends with standing-room-only tickets could sit down at the back of the theater.

We managed to squeeze everyone in somehow, including columnist Pat Karch from New Jersey. Pat had been one of Rudy's most
loyal fans since she was a small child, attending his East Coast performances and writing him up in her column in the *Cherry Hill News*. In
1976 she drove out to Los Angeles from her home in Cherry Hill,
Pennsylvania, to stay with us. "Rudy has married the most fantastic
woman in the world," was Pat's greeting to me as I opened the door,
"He's the king, you're the queen, and you're the only one who can get
Rudy out of those irascible moods." Last time I saw Pat, she reminded
me that Rudy once told her: "Ellie would love to love everybody. She
just doesn't know everybody."

In 1962, Virginia Martin was replaced by Joy Claussen in *How
to Succeed*. Joy was famous for the Aim toothpaste commercials.
When she moved to the West Coast, she stayed with us at Silver Tip
while I helped her househunt. In fact, when our friend Frank Bresee
was single, we invited them both to a party in an attempt to set them
up. But he brought along Bobbi, who is now his wife. Not too long
after, Joy married writer Tony Scully.

Two years after *How to Succeed* opened, young Darryl Hickman
replaced Robert Morse, who went off to Hollywood to make movies. I
discovered that Darryl and Rudy were born on the same day, so I
tossed a double birthday party that year, lighting both birthday cakes
with trick candles that couldn't be blown out.

It was during this period that Rudy was asked to write several
magazine articles, including lengthy stories for *Esquire* and *Playboy*.
Abel Green, editor of *Variety* magazine, asked Rudy to write a guest
column for an anniversary issue. But Rudy decided to turn it down.
"It isn't justified by what I do in the musical itself and I cannot
accept that which is not really deserving," he wrote to Green in one
of his fits of honesty. Then, in one of his famous mood switches, he
added that he was annoyed he was only being asked to do the guest
column because he was currently a hot Broadway property rather
than a veteran entertainer.

A highlight of 1964, the last year of *How to Succeed*, was a
telegram from Jane Morgan inviting us to meet Charles Aznavour.

Rudy was thrilled to have dinner with them, two of his favorite singers. The evening was filled with talk of music.

Rudy was also honored by a watch company as one of the "Most Interesting Wrists of the Year" along with Ted Kennedy, Shelley Winters, Douglas Fairbanks Jr., and Hermione Gingold.

In December my father had another bad spell. This time it was an ulcer and his leg had to be amputated. I flew to Berkeley. My sixty-four-year-old husband's love letters arrived daily, expressing sympathy and reminding me to come back to him as soon as possible. His written words continued to sizzle: "Dzzzzzaaaahhhhling, Baby, am I ever hot for you today! Kept dreaming about you and wanting you sooooo much! Damn it! I'll have to wait until after I've opened at the Shoreham (Washington, D.C.) . . . People still want to host farewell parties for me, but I said, 'No! Not without my gracious bride . . .'" The rest of the letter was filled with details about a new Tanberg tape recorder and a K.L.H. record player he'd acquired.

"Dzzzzzzaaaaahhhhhling" was a word I called Rudy while we were making love, and it became our salutation to each other whenever we exchanged letters. One is truly memorable. Six months after our wedding, I received a note while he was on the road. The words and graphics were so hot they should have burned my fingers, and I still blush decades later at the sight of the pencil tracing of Rudy's lower anatomy included on page two of his embossed linen letterhead.

Just before we gave up our apartment and left New York, we spent every night attending social events at all our favorite places. One was Joe and Rosalie Levine's party at the Four Seasons after the premieres of *The Carpetbaggers* and *A House Is Not a Home*. Rosalie Levine had been a singer with Rudy's band when he performed in Boston. Another night, Joe and Rosalie hosted an evening cruise around Manhattan on the yacht they kept docked in New York. I was thrilled to meet Sophia Loren that evening; her beauty and quiet demeanor greatly impressed me.

ELEVEN

Life after Broadway

ow to Succeed set a record with a three-year, seven-week run on Broadway. It won the New York Drama Critics Award, the Pulitzer Drama Prize, and seven Tony awards. After the final curtain on October 13, we had one last dinner with Lyn and Hy at Voisin, where we bumped into Vivien Leigh who was being feted on her return to New York. Among her guests were Joan Fontaine, Olivia de Havilland, and Cyril Ritchard, with whom we shared a good-luck champagne toast. Saying a sad farewell to the cast, we headed back to the West Coast in the gold Lincoln Continental Rudy bought me.

Never one to let the grass grow under his feet, Rudy set up a series of supper club bookings along the way. At our stop in Buffalo, our three poodles went sniffing around the grounds of the hotel and found some rat poison. Two of our darling poodles died in my arms. It was a terrible experience. Only Mr. Pom Pom survived.

This time on the road, our reception was sensational everywhere we went. Fresh from his Broadway success, Rudy was lionized. As soon as we drove into town the press was there, mobbing the hotel. One of Rudy's funniest lines to reporters who asked if he thought he was too much of an old-timer to be remembered was: "My fans still swoon over me. It just takes them a little longer to get up."

We finally made it back to Silver Tip. The following March, when my father passed away, I mourned the loss of the dearest, sweetest man in the world. Still distraught at my father's death, I stayed on for several days with Irene in Berkeley after Rudy left to fulfill engagements. Finally she said, "Eleanor, your place is with your husband. It's time to go back to Rudy."

Then we started the road tour of *Jenny Kissed Me*. For six weeks we took the play to various theaters, where Rudy's reviews were so encouraging he made several attempts to bring Jean's Kerr's comedy to Broadway again. Unfortunately, we were unable to line up any "angels."

During our time in New York with *How to Succeed*, Rudy began hosting a weekly television show, *On Broadway Tonight*, as a summer replacement for *The Danny Kaye Show*. Rudy's celebrity guests included Robert Goulet, Marilyn Grasshoff, and Tony Martin, who joked he and Rudy liked the same kind of women—tall, slim and beautiful. Tony had married Cyd Charisse after divorcing Alice Faye, who then married Phil Harris. Both couples were frequent guests at Silver Tip parties.

In between shows, we took on other engagements. At one point, Charles Nelson Reilly and I were hired for a Metropolitan Life Insurance commercial. Later, because of its success, I became a spokeswoman for the company. Among other companies I did commercials for were American Tourister Luggage, Yuban Coffee, and New York Telephone. I could have pursued this career, and did, in fact, turn down many other offers, but being Rudy's wife was my main job.

One date we played included two nights at the U.S. Air Force's Tactical Air Command headquarters at Langley, Virginia, where my husband was hailed as "The 'New' Rudy Vallée," bringing him great amusement.

In the fall of 1965, Rudy finally decided he would semi-retire the following year. "I haven't been home, really lived at home, for four years," he told a Lynn, Massachusetts, journalist. "So I'm going to quit performing. We're doing the road tour of *How to Succeed* for the next few months. After that, it's goodbye."

I didn't believe him. Nor did anyone else. Rudy Vallée retire?

Many of our friends had retreated to their ranches or second homes in Palm Springs and Florida after a lifetime in show business, but I knew Rudy would never stop performing.

As 1966 came and went, there was no further mention of Rudy retiring. I think at the time, that day, Rudy really did feel like quitting. But I knew that after just a few days at home, he would pace restlessly around Silver Tip, eager to start performing somewhere, anywhere, again. So I just ignored his statement. Pretty soon, he'd forgotten all about it, too.

During rehearsals for the road tour of *How to Succeed*, Rudy had a falling out with the new director, Robert Nichols. After three years on Broadway, my husband felt that a grueling round of daily rehearsals was unnecessary for his character. Nichols disagreed. Charges were filed with Actors Equity. Rudy was fined $1,000 and censured for his "unprofessional attitude."

You can imagine his reaction. Quick as a flash he lodged an appeal. Among those who testified on Rudy's behalf was young Rick Nelson, who played the part of Finch when *How to Succeed* was at the Melodyland Theatre, Anaheim. "He has helped so many people throughout his career. That seems to epitomize all that is truly professional in the industry," said young Nelson, who was making his first stage appearance. A majority of the Appeals Committee agreed the fine be suspended. Rudy was extremely pleased that justice had been done.

Another time, Rudy decided that rehearsal time was too long. Alex Grasshoff had asked producer Sy Chernak to give Rudy a part in the NBC television series, *CHiPs*. Rudy failed to show up for an early rehearsal, claiming that since he didn't have a starring role he didn't need much rehearsing. "Remember, Ellie," said Grasshoff, telling me about the incident, "Rudy was such a professional, always perfectly prepared with his lines, that he knew he didn't need to spend hours rehearsing. But of course, acting on TV is different than stage and film. And if you're booked for a job, you should be there, if you're a professional."

A few years later Robert Morse and Rudy were reunited in a

summer stock production of *How to Succeed*. Again, there were a few problems. Rudy's costumes for the road production were not up to his standards.

I happened to be back home visiting my sister and her family in Santa Barbara. Rudy mailed me a long list of clothing he wanted sent from Silver Tip: an old plaid suit he'd had made in the '40s would be ideal for the show's "Brotherhood Song" scene; some gray shirts we'd had made in Hong Kong for the roof dance scene; two black homburgs for the elevator scenes; and his favorite Bermuda shorts for Rudy's grand old Ivy scene with Robert Morse.

During the road tour, he received a phone message purportedly from Jean Nelson, Gene Nelson's wife, now known as Jean Martin-Nelson. The caller asked Rudy to fly to San Francisco to appear in a charity performance at the Circle Theater in San Carlos to raise funds for "Ship Hope." Filled with volunteer medical personnel, "Ship Hope" aided children with deformities in South America. Rudy immediately booked a flight and arrived at the airport. "There was no one to meet him," recounted Jean, "so he called me and said, 'Here I am! Why aren't you here?'" The truth was, Jean knew Rudy was touring with a hit show and didn't believe he'd have time for the benefit, but another lady had taken it upon herself to invite him. Rudy, as gracious and as generous as he always was, had not hesitated to answer the call, and ended up doing his vaudeville act to great applause.

The film version of *How to Succeed* was made in 1967 by the Mirisch brothers at United Artists. It was not without a few heart-stopping moments for Rudy, even before the cameras rolled. Rumors flew that first Bing Crosby, then Mickey Rooney, were being considered to play the part of J.B. Biggley. After several sleepless nights, Rudy received a phone call from producer/director David Swift: "Rudy, I've told United Artists that if they want me for this film, they'll have to sign you, too." Rudy got the part.

Back in the mainstream of Hollywood, Rod Steiger invited us to his girlfriend's home for an "All-White Costume Garden Party." Rudy wore a dazzling white linen suit, white shoes, and spats, and I dressed in a long cream-colored, antique lace gown. On my head was a large brimmed hat to rival any in *My Fair Lady*. Toward the end of the affair, I saw Rudy and Rod deep in conversation. Aha, I wondered, could another movie be on the horizon?

As it turned out, Rudy was describing his archives to his host. The following evening Rod came to Silver Tip for dinner, bringing his German shepherd. Afterward the two men took off for the lower building and I knew I wouldn't see them for hours. The dog and I became such fast friends, Rod later asked if we'd give him a home, which we did willingly.

Taking time out to visit our favorite restaurants, one dinner at Don the Beachcomber's was written up in a Los Angeles newspaper. *The Los Angeles Herald-Examiner* reported that when Rudy, a glorious sight in his colorful Madras jacket, Bermuda shorts, and knee-length black stockings, pulled out a credit card to pay the dinner check, the card turned out to be the first ever issued for an account at the restaurant. Because of Rudy's loyalty and patronage, Don presented him with a pair of sterling silver chopsticks engraved with Rudy's famous signature.

In the late 1960s, Joseph E. Levine at Embassy Pictures wrote a note to one of Rudy's press agents, Harry Paul in Boston, and sent a copy to us: "I have been giving much thought to Rudy for one of my films. I think he is one of the most talented men in show business." But for some reason, the film offer never firmed up.

Rudy had similar luck when he tried to interest Darryl Zanuck at 20th Century Fox in making a movie of a musical, *Of Thee I Sing*. "While I love the original play," Zanuck replied, "I am very dubious about its success in the market today." Undeterred, Rudy wrote to Abe Burrows, who passed the idea along to Jack Warner. Jack wrote back with similar regrets. Undaunted, Rudy took to the road again, this time for a few days in Dallas, then Oklahoma while I visited my family.

Returning to Hollywood I began taking care of some maintenance to our home. The flagstone by the pool and the driveway needed repair. "Tell Tom Hicks I like flagstone with a *red* color," Rudy instructed from Dallas. In the same letter Rudy asked that Reed Sprinkle, a good friend and contractor from Newport Beach, be hired to do the concrete work. We had a lot of laughs when the driveway was being fixed. Ken and Joanne Kosrog and Rudy and I, put our handprints into the wet concrete, making our own Hollywood Sidewalk of Stars.

Rudy also wrote that he wanted to make sure he voted for the upcoming Oscar awards since he was a voting member of the Academy. "Mail me the list for the Academy awards so I can make my choices, as I think the deadline is not far away." As usual he remembered exactly where he kept this material. "The Academy booklets are about level with the top of my chair, inside the book case, back of my office chair, on a book."

Another time Rudy forgot some sheet music. He wrote to me: "Look in the copper-colored cabinet to the left of the door leading into the office and on the lowest shelf. You'll see two folios of piano music marked First Show B . . ."

One of the saddest telegrams Rudy sent that year was to Tom May, chairman of May Company department stores: "My dear Tom, some time ago you appealed to me for my aid for one of your charities. I am appealing to you with all the fervor at my command that you do not prosecute Hedy Lamarr. Am thoroughly convinced she did not know what she was doing. I join her hundreds of friends in this plea. Cordially."

Hedy had been caught shoplifting. It turned out she was psychologically ill. Everyone in show business organized telegrams and letters on behalf of Hollywood's former glamorous star, and she received the medical help she needed. We were so glad we'd joined the effort to help her.

Soon after, Johnny Carson and Rudy clashed when Johnny decided to fire one of his staff. "Johnny, you can't get rid of him. He's helped you for many, many years," Rudy said. Although my husband had great integrity and valued loyalty, he probably should have minded his own business. Johnny was adamant and after that conversation, Rudy was never invited on Carson's show again. Although Rudy wrote an apologetic letter, Johnny didn't respond.

As far as I was concerned, the incident was regrettable, because Johnny and Rudy respected and liked each other. However, Dick Carson, Johnny's brother, continued the friendship, including his membership in The Dirty Club, an informal group of us that sat around our homes in Hollywood, had dinner, and told risqué jokes. The club included actor John Myers, Pat McCormick, writer Buddy Atkinson, and their wives. Sometimes the guys dressed up and acted silly, and we had loads of fun. The meetings were often black-tie. One time McCormick arrived in formal tails. In place of pants he wore a jock strap.

Another club we had was called The Society of Ate. Fil Perell, entertainment columnist and publisher of a Beverly Hills newspaper, was one of the eight members; we'd dine together at various area restaurants. Other members included Gia and Gilbert Roland and Jack and Elaine LaLanne.

After the road tour of *How to Succeed* wound up, we were both relieved to return to Silver Tip. But Rudy discovered that time hung heavy on his hands. With few bookings, he began drinking more and more vodka at our cocktail hour. He put on weight, wasn't exercising, and became increasingly irritable. I knew it was the liquor. He mailed out stinging rebukes to all and sundry, wearing out typewriter ribbons by the dozen.

Seated in his huge green leather chair, Rudy watched television every day from 5:00 P.M. to 2:00 or 3:00 A.M., the vodka close by. It was time to put my foot down.

"Rudy, the vodka's out."

One of our greatest friends, Dr. Marvin Jensen, backed me up. Marvin came into our lives when he was arranging speakers for his fraternity's founder's day. He discovered that Rudy was a Sigma Alpha Epsilon fraternity brother. Marvin contacted us, and of course we invited him over. "I felt tremendously privileged to meet Rudy," Marvin told me after Rudy died. "He was such a legend. But I really did get worried about his drinking, even the wine. Rudy pointed out to me that he only drank one glass of wine, but the goblet was huge and looked as if it could hold half a gallon!"

When the day of the fraternity dinner arrived, it was pouring down rain. I didn't think Rudy should go, so we called Marvin. "Don't worry," he said, "I'll rent a limo." Rudy and Marvin hit it off immediately, to the extent that Marvin, one of the most generous people in the world, bought himself a limo just to take Rudy and me around town. The two loved classic films and spent a great deal of time watching Rudy's old movies. One time Marvin stayed with us at Silver Tip for a few days. He went to bed early because he had early surgeries at 6:00 A.M. Rudy would go into his room around midnight, turn on the light, wake him up, stick a note under his chin, and tell him to read it in the morning. The notes were invitations to Jimmy's restaurant or the Bistro Gardens, advising Marvin what to wear, and to be ready at 8:00 P.M. If Rudy didn't like Marvin's tie, he'd pull down the attic trapdoor and rifle through the boxes until he found one he preferred.

Surprisingly, my husband gave me no argument at all about the vodka; perhaps he realized it was time to quit the hard liquor. We agreed to return to drinking wine. Exploring the wine cellars in our lower building, we came across cases of Korbel champagne. "This is it!" exclaimed Rudy. "I'd forgotten all about Korbel. And here's some of Bob Mondavi's great wines."

So champagne became our habitual drink. Rudy counted out exactly six ice cubes for each glass when we drank champagne during tennis matches.

We still hosted dozens of parties and attended those given by Mike Douglas, Earl "Mad Man" Muntz, and many other friends.

One of my favorite Silver Tip parties was the "Rudy Vallée Special: A Billy Gilbert Film Festival" for Billy and his wife Lolly. Billy made many classic film comedies and was the voice of Sneezy in Disney's *Snow White and the Seven Dwarfs*. Rudy gathered together Gilbert's film clips and broadcasts, and we invited Billy's friends to share in the reminiscences.

For some reason Rudy now decided he didn't want any more parties celebrating his own birthday, so I arranged a surprise birthday party, inviting close friends who were also celebrating milestones. I ordered five different cakes. Rudy's, of course, was decorated with a miniature saxophone. Two other cakes celebrated Henry Fennenbock's and Hank Taecker's birthdays. And two others celebrated wedding anniversaries for Gloria and Gene Lester and Los Angeles detective Carl Clark and his wife.

Harry and Sybil Brand were guests, as were the Sam Yortys, Phil Ford and Mimi Hines, Lew Parker, Betty Keane, Edgar Bergen, Jimmy Durante, and Paul Keyes. One of my cherished possessions from that day is a birthday gift of a solid gold pocket-knife engraved "To Rudy, Love Sybil Brand."

We also spent time with our neighbors. Jack and Elaine Lalanne had moved to Hollywood Hills from San Francisco and lived a few streets down. Rudy and Jack spent hours talking about health, nutrition, and vitamins. I was really pleased about this new relationship because it stopped Rudy's bad eating and drinking habits and turned him on to vitamins. He and Jack exercised on the patio. Once, Rudy was so pleased with the number of push-ups he could do, he raced indoors to tell me. Unfortunately, he'd forgotten the glass door was closed and smashed into it. Thank God he wasn't seriously hurt.

Marilyn and Alex Grasshoff were also neighbors. Marilyn had been the lead dancer in *How to Succeed*, so we renewed our friendship after they bought a home off Mulholland Drive. Alex is an award-winning movie director, and the Grasshoffs are avid tennis players, so they became fixtures at our weekend tennis parties. As usual, we'd bring out the wine and champagne to accompany the tennis matches, then go downstairs to watch new movie previews sent us by the Academy.

One time Marilyn needed to pick up an air conditioner but her truck was out of commission. Rudy, who had to collect some cases of wine, offered to take her in our station wagon. On the way, Rudy's car broke down on the left side of one of Los Angeles' busiest ten-lane freeways near the Hollywood Bowl. "We got out and peered under the hood," relates Marilyn. "Suddenly, Rudy disappeared. Then I realized how quiet it was. No longer were hundreds of cars whizzing by. There was Rudy, in the middle of the freeway, both arms raised to the heavens in a commanding gesture, holding up all the traffic while he walked across to the other side." After he made a phone call, Rudy repeated the feat and came back to the truck.

"I almost had heart failure," said Marilyn. "'Rudy,' I said, 'don't ever do that again. You're a national treasure!'"

My husband liked doing errands, going to the bank, the post office, the supermarket, and to one of his favorite stores, Pic-n-Save. One summer morning at the cleaners he bumped into Joanne Kosrog. "Rudy handed over the cleaning he'd brought," Joanne related, "looked down at his trousers, and took them off. After giving them to the clerk, he left, driving home in his underwear!"

Out of the blue, we were offered engagements in the Orient, at the Hong Kong Hilton, the Tokyo Hilton, and other places along the way. We arranged to sail on the SS *President Roosevelt* on a forty-day cruise, accompanied by Cliff and Helen Steward. The day we embarked, we received dozens of bon voyage telegrams. Rudy was so pleased. It was just like the old days when he opened in *How to Succeed*.

I remember the cruise vividly because it was the one and only time I thought of divorcing my husband. Rudy and I had an argument two days out. Although I don't remember what started it, the disagreement escalated. "I'm going to call Paul as soon as we reach Honolulu and file for divorce," I told Rudy. I went to the Stewards' cabin and Rudy hid out in one of the lifeboats under the canvas cover. He took *Time* magazine, *The Hollywood Reporter*, and a flashlight with him. Rudy's antics made me laugh. It was a funny sight.

After two days in the Stewards' stateroom, I'd had enough. I wasn't mad anymore, and I realized how much I missed Rudy. It was much ado about nothing, I decided. Just before we reached port, Rudy grabbed me as I was going in to lunch and apologized. That night in Hawaii was one of the most passionate since our honeymoon.

By now a few of the famous Rudy Vallée locks had turned gray, and he was using more Grecian Formula 16 than usual to color it. But his energy was as high as ever and he was still a romantic lover. Rudy wanted me next to him wherever we went, and we were still referred to as newlyweds by our friends.

While performing in Phoenix, we decided to buy a new car. Our friend Julian Pegler owned a dealership, and we ended up with a brand new Dodge Monaco station wagon. To celebrate, Julian and Rudy went fishing in the Salt River. Then they changed into swim trunks and rented inner tubes so they could float downstream. As they approached the rapids, Rudy's tube capsized, throwing him into the water. "That's when Rudy told me he wasn't a great swimmer," Julian related to me later that afternoon. "So I jumped in, grabbed Rudy's trunks and hauled him out."

Julian pulled so hard that Rudy's trunks ended up around his ankles. Onlookers were treated to the sight of a completely nude Rudy Vallée scrambling onto the river bank. Rudy immediately got on the phone and made sure the story made the newswires all over the country.

Rudy was a natural when it came to public relations and had an unerring instinct for publicity gimmicks. Once when flying with Ken Kosrog on a 747 from New York to Los Angeles, Rudy and other first-class passengers noticed streams of water flowing into the cabin from under the cockpit door. "The stewardess informed us the water was squirting out above the controls panel and through both sides of the fuselage," said Ken. "Then they turned all the restroom faucets on full strength to drain water from the tanks."

After being denied a request to make an emergency landing at Chicago's O'Hare, the pilot headed for Oklahoma City. "Upon landing, Rudy went directly to the airport bar and ordered champagne to celebrate his survival," Ken told me many years later. "But Sunday liquor laws were in effect. Rudy was a little upset, to say the least, and the cops were called." One of the police officers confided to Rudy that the governor was receiving kickbacks from bootleggers. That's all Rudy needed to hear. The next day headlines screamed: "Governor Is a Crook!" with Rudy's photo all over the front pages.

Another example of Rudy seizing the moment was the stormy night I drove to Joanne Kosrog's. It was my first outing in the brand new Buick convertible Rudy bought me. Immediately above the Kosrog's house was J. Paul Getty's not-too-rustic mountain cabin. During the evening, the heavy rains loosened several rocks around the Getty house and a large boulder rolled down the hill smack into the side of my new car. Tearfully, I called Rudy. "I'll be right there. Don't move the boulder."

Within half an hour Rudy arrived with an entourage of TV news crews and photographers. The next day the picture of us sitting atop my wrecked car made all the papers and television stations.

It was around this time that I was elected president of the Women's Auxiliary of the American National Theater and Academy, known as ANTANS, and I spent much of my time organizing fund-raising events with our volunteers. In a nice letter of congratulations to me Francis Lederer, president of the parent organization ANTANS, told me that in 1933 Rudy had given him his first radio job in New York after Francis opened in *Autumn Crocus* on Broadway. It seemed that everywhere I turned, Rudy's name brought back memories. I was always appreciative of people reminding me how my dear husband helped them.

In the 1970s, one of our longest Las Vegas bookings was at the Desert Inn, when Rudy starred in *Newcomers of 1928*, a nostalgic look back to the famous variety acts, comedy, and music of the late '20s. He shared top billing with orchestra leader Paul Whiteman, Harry Richman, Buster Keaton, Fifi D'Orsay, and Billy Gilbert, the superstar talents of their era. Paul Ross, a publicist, came up with the idea for the show, which was produced by Jackie Barnett. Paul came to Silver Tip to discuss the idea. Rudy, of course, immediately took Paul on a tour and I lost sight of them for several hours. "Ellie, those archives are like a history of the United States!" Paul told me when they finally emerged, "and I've just been treated to the finest talent show I've seen in years. Not once, but three times!"

With six veteran performers signed on for his show, Paul was persuaded that rehearsals were unnecessary—probably by Rudy.

On arrival in Las Vegas, believe it or not, we had another dressing-room argument. The stars were to share three dressing rooms. Rudy was teamed up with Harry Richman but in the cramped space, their personalities clashed. Rudy was meticulous about the way his show costumes were arranged in the dressing room. He grumbled it was difficult to relax in the small room.

Playing peacemaker again, I met with Paul Ross. "Why not just switch them around and let Rudy share with Billy Gilbert?" The suggestion worked perfectly, and Billy and Rudy became lifelong friends. At the same time our friendship with Harry Richman was saved, and he and I had a special relationship after that. In Harry's later years, his health failed, and we did everything we could for him. Rudy helped financially, of course, and Harry was a frequent house guest.

Opening night at the Desert Inn was jammed. And so were the next four weeks. We were ecstatic. The run was extended for another two weeks, then we went on to the Moulin Rouge in Hollywood and then the Fountainbleu in Miami. We wanted to take *Newcomers of 1928* on to New York but not enough money could be raised.

When we returned to Silver Tip, Rudy decided to "clean house." I welcomed Rudy's intention to clear out some of the clutter. His archives were scrupulously organized but bursting at the seams, with several boxes still to be sorted through. After a few days I went down to the lower building to inspect the progress of my husband's new project. "Ellie! See what I've found! I've been looking for this hat for years! And here's the photo of us in New Orleans!" Needless to say, Rudy was like a child in a toy shop, his mementos spread around him. All we ended up throwing out was a pile of duplicate papers.

After Rudy died, I found several of Rudy's favorite saxophones in a closet. One was a 1925 Eb Buescher that once belonged to Rudy Wiedoeft. Word got out that I had it, and I received a phone call from Arkansas. An attorney from Little Rock showed up to buy the saxophone and I was told later that it was a gift for Governor Bill Clinton.

After a few days in Hawaii where Rudy performed at a testimonial dinner for State Controller Houston Flournoy, Rudy was hired to play the narrator for the movie *The Night They Raided Minsky's*. Because Warner Studios was close by, this meant we could live at home.

On an adjoining set, Rudy and I met up with Elvis Presley. The two clowned around for publicity photos, Elvis playing his guitar and Rudy singing through one of his megaphones. We spent a lot of time with Elvis discussing music, and Elvis was obviously thrilled to meet the legendary Vallée. In 1968, Rudy and Elvis appeared together in the film *Live a Little, Love a Little*.

During this period, Frank Bresee, creator and host of "The Golden Days of Radio," had Rudy on many times as guest. In 1971, Frank aired a two-part tribute to Rudy. Frank had a stroke in 1974, and Rudy and I were at his bedside the very next day. He recovered, thank God. Two years later, Frank broadcast several of Rudy's early radio shows.

Rudy began avoiding the many parties, galas, and premieres we were invited to. I was disappointed because I loved dressing up and going out to these glittering, black-tie affairs. But I needed an escort. Fortunately, there was a solution to this dilemma. My nephew Michael Bruce, just graduated as an architect, obtained a job in Glendale, thanks to our friend Charles Luckman. Until he found an apartment, I insisted he stay with us. Rudy was relieved this tall, handsome young man was available to take his place. The first party Michael and I attended together, an opening night, raised eyebrows; everyone thought I was cheating on Rudy. "She's finally taken a lover her own age," was the gossip around Hollywood.

Rudy, Michael, and I kept people guessing for weeks. At one charity dinner where celebrities were donating their time and talents as bartenders, Rudy accompanied us. As he stood behind the bar mixing rum cocktails for Michael and me, a beautifully gowned woman came up and said, "You are such a great-looking couple! Would you be interested in making television commercials? Are you married?"

"Yes, I am married, " I replied. "But not to him, to him," and I pointed at Rudy. The expression on the woman's face was priceless.

By now Rudy had perfected a one-man variety show he performed in dinner theaters and clubs. He sang or lip-synced a medley of his most famous songs starting off with "I'm Just a Vagabond Lover." He showed color slides on a fifteen-foot screen of his career highlights, played the sax, told a series of political jokes, imitated President Roosevelt, and changed into a train conductor's uniform for the lengthy "All Points West" poem. Rudy's show wardrobe included dozens of different hats—homburgs, berets, caps, bowlers—and he carried his own sound system, screen, projection machine, tape deck, megaphone, and microphone. This may have been the first multimedia show ever presented.

To prepare, he spent hours in his archives looking at thousands of color slides, selecting a series of two hundred to be shown on a screen behind him to illustrate his live performance. Some of the shots showed Hollywood's most famous stars dancing: Rita Hayworth doing the conga, Cesar Romero and Carmen Miranda swaying to the samba, and Rudolph Valentino in a typical tango pose.

As Rudy's new idea took shape, I could see it would be an intimate close-up of the Vallée show business career, a kind of history of Americana entertainment a la Rudy. I must admit I found the concept a little inconsistent with Rudy's philosophy of never indulging in nostalgia, because this new act was structured entirely on his previous performances. He re-created the "All Points West" and "Casey at the Bat" monologues and Buddy Lester's "Two-Headed Woman" ditty; he sang his old hits, "I'm Just a Vagabond Lover" and "The Stein Song"; and retold the jokes proven to be his funniest. I didn't discuss this turnaround with him; he always knew what he was doing when it came to entertainment and knew when it was time to give audiences something different.

"I know the show is based on what I've done before," he said, sensing my doubt, "but it is different in that no one else is doing anything like it." I couldn't argue with that. It certainly was different.

Finally, after confirming an itinerary that booked us into dozens of hotels, we once more loaded up the car-top luggage carrier and the Vallées were back on the road.

I had a lot of fun with this show because we were a team on-stage. I helped Rudy introduce the material, reacted to his jokes, and generally performed the part of the female sidekick in a sexy outfit. I also made sure the slide carousel was plugged in and organized and that Rudy's megaphone and saxophone were close at hand.

Rudy often opened with the song, "The Most Beautiful Girl in the World," or "Some Enchanted Evening," and he'd call me out from the wings to introduce his "bride." He was so romantic.

Occasionally, our poodles would show up on stage, tails wagging like mad. We always left them in our dressing room, but sometimes they got out and tracked us down. We'd simply pick them up, and go on with the act.

Only once did I let Rudy down. We were in Hot Springs, Arkansas, and I overslept. Changing straight into costume to save time, I ran madly down the street in my long dress, arriving breathless on stage as Rudy was halfway through his act. "Here she is! Here's my crazy wife! Isn't she adorable? Now isn't this woman worth waiting for?" The audience just loved it, and I gave Rudy a long, sexy kiss as we got a standing ovation.

We discovered, as we traveled to the various engagements, that Rudy's Broadway success was still fresh in audiences' minds, and they held him in high esteem. From our side of the aisle, Rudy was in great spirits and he spent much more time chatting with patrons and sign-ing autographs than he usually did. He was relaxed, and I think that's because he was in total control of his own show once again. He han-dled the pre-publicity and promotions, advised club managers about advertising, and like the tireless hard-working trouper that he was, continually polished his act.

The first few stops we ran into a few difficulties because the lighting was inadequate. We had our own equipment sent to us. Sometimes the screen would fall down, or the recordings would get a little scratchy. Whenever there was a mishap, Rudy turned it into a skit, and the audiences loved it.

Reviews of Rudy's show were mixed but proved my husband still had an instinct for bringing the public what it wanted. My husband asked Leonard Feather, jazz critic for the *Los Angeles Times*, for a private showing but met with a less than enthusiastic response.

My own concerns about the nostalgia concept were, thank goodness, unfounded. A *Philadelphia Daily News* columnist wrote: "It is undoubtedly the nostalgia that provides the appeal." Another reporter enjoyed "a refreshing glimpse into the past."

During this trip, as always, we worked with local chapters of the Shriners, Elks, Rotarians, and other civic organizations, visiting children's hospitals and senior centers, where Rudy cheered patients up with his antics.

Rudy then recorded one of the most stirring, patriotic tributes to our nation ever written, called, "What Is America?" Recited in Rudy's most dramatic tones, it rises to a crescendo as Rudy pours out his love for his country. It is an extraordinary recording.

Before we left the West Coast, we paid a surprise visit to the Motorcycle Officers of California L.A. Ball at the Palladium, and Rudy was invited to sing a few songs onstage. Everyone on the dance floor stopped dancing, crowded over to the stage, and listened, just like in the old days. The applause was tremendous, and he spent an hour signing autographs.

On the East Coast segment of our tour, Rosemary, Earl Wilson's wife, asked Rudy to be a dais guest for a Louis Armstrong birthday tribute at New York's Waldorf Astoria. The event was also a benefit for Tay-Sachs patients, and we accepted immediately. It was a chance to catch up with old friends.

After the tour wound down, we returned to Silver Tip to regroup. I was so pleased to come back to our cozy home, see our friends again, play tennis, and give lots of parties.

TWELVE

A Career in Its Twilight

"Rudy, Rudy, come quick!" I shouted. It was a late fall morning, and I was pulling back the drapes in our bedroom.

"What is it?"

"There's a wild-looking fellow down in the driveway. He's trying to get in the front door!" The man's mane of curly black hair was down to his shoulders. A large nose dominated the long face, and his shabby-looking clothes hung in great folds around him. Rudy looked out the window. "Oh, it's Tiny Tim! Take him down to the pool, Ellie."

"Take him down to the pool? You don't want him anywhere near this house!" I said. "He's the worst looking thing I've ever seen!"

"I'll do it, then," and my husband raced downstairs, still in his boxer shorts, to greet him.

Rudy had never met Tiny, but he'd heard his quivering falsetto voice on the radio and television, and read the newspaper reports that said Tiny modeled his singing after Rudy Vallée's early megaphone days. Very few strangers found their way up our long winding driveway, so we wondered how Tiny Tim found us. "I met Rudy's publicist, Chris Harris, and he knew Rudy was my idol," said Tiny. "He gave me your address."

On the spur of the moment, Tiny decided to pay us a visit. The two entertainers spent the entire day talking, taking a tour of Rudy's archives, and discussing music. Rudy enjoyed Tiny's company, he told me that night, and found him to be an extremely interesting, if odd, character. I think the feeling may have been mutual.

When I told Chris about the visit, he said he'd met Tiny Tim at the Hotel Roosevelt, where the Academy Awards were being presented.

"I told Tiny I knew Rudy Vallée," said Chris. "'Rudy Vallée?' screeched Tiny, in that high voice of his, and he started singing Rudy's songs and playing his ukulele. For an hour and a half we had a news conference with Tiny, and he said if it wasn't for Rudy, Tiny would never have had a career. Then he wanted to meet him." Rudy gave Chris one of his casual jackets, and Chris, in turn, gave it to Tiny, who wore it till it fell off him, I hear.

Rudy's typewriter was still active during this time at Silver Tip. He dashed off letters to various radio and TV announcers, correcting their grammar and pronunciation. He wrote an article, "Don't Go on the Stage, My Darling Daughter," sending it off to *Playboy* magazine, but editor Jack Kessie turned it down.

After a performance at an El Toro club, Rudy received a letter taking him to task for off-color jokes. Still a master of the pen, he responded: "I pity such narrow-minded, blue-nosed, intolerant, bigoted, frightened persons such as you and your two friends. You probably make love in the dark. I delight in shocking intolerant old poops like you." That was true. Rudy took pleasure in deflating what he regarded as self-righteous critics and never failed to respond to them with his inimitable command of the English language.

In 1977, we decided a trip to Las Vegas would hit the spot. Rudy owned some stock in the Del Webb Hotel Corporation, where he wanted to perform, but he was turned down. "Don't worry, Ellie, I'll write to Frank. He owns some stock in the hotel, too, and he's king there."

So Rudy wrote to his old friend, Frank Sinatra, asking if he could help Rudy secure some dates. Frank's reply was immediate, amusing, and compassionate. The letter read in part: "Dear Hubert, I received your letter and my translators are working on it for me.

"I am sorry you're having trouble in Las Vegas, but having been in trouble in Las Vegas, New York, Chicago, Hollywood, and more recently Australia and Berlin, I must tell you, you are an amateur at getting into trouble.

"As for my helping to secure a booking for you at the Del Webb, don't believe everything you read in the newspapers. . . . If you want me to, I'll have Mickey take my proxy to the next stockholders meeting and I will write on the back of it 'Save the Vagabond Lover.'" An end sentence read: "Note to Dorothy: Send this letter to the only two Huberts we know—Vallée and Humphrey—everything in it applies to both of them since they have both written they like me better than Crosby and Como and they both want to work Vegas."

That same year Hugh Queenin, a real estate agent, contacted us. He had Rudy's family home in Island Pond, Vermont, up for sale, and asked if we wanted to purchase it for $50,000. "It's a landmark in the area," Queenin wrote, but at that point our finances were not great. We lived on Rudy's annuities and the rather small income we generated from performing. The house in Palm Springs had long been sold. Everyone except our closest friends thought we were still millionaires. Nothing could have been further from the truth. Rudy's investments had turned out poorly, and Silver Tip was costing us a lot of money. I was seriously worried.

How much longer could we afford to keep up Rudy's generous lifestyle? We never stinted on the parties we threw or the hospitality we offered friends, and just when I'd think we'd no liquor left for one last party, Rudy would go down into the cellar and drag out another case of wine or champagne he'd squirreled away.

Our finances didn't stop Rudy from sending out hundreds of Christmas gifts each year. One of his favorites was a huge can of three-flavored popcorn. Rudy considered himself a popcorn connoisseur. Once, in a supermarket, he found a particularly tasty bag of caramel popcorn, and he wrote to the president of the supermarket chain, advising him always to keep it in stock, "so when I am in different towns, I can look for your supermarket and find my favorite corn."

I was now ready to spend more time in Hollywood, where I was heavily involved with WAIF and other organizations. Rudy's desire to perform still burned fiercely. He hated being idle. Offers came in, but they were mostly for free shows and guest shots. Thanks to Steve Allen, Merv Griffin, and Dick Cavett, Rudy appeared on television shows, but there was no doubt that Rudy was in the twilight of his years professionally.

If he had an out-of-town date and I was unable to accompany him, he wrote and phoned daily, expressing his love for me. But his letters to business associates and the media took on a strident tone. Two subjects galled him. He was extremely outspoken against U.S. participation in the Vietnam War; and he complained that no television special was being offered him as it was to Bing Crosby, Bob Hope, Dean Martin, Milton Berle, and his nemesis, Victor Borge.

It was as if Rudy were now two people: my wonderful affectionate husband and a performer who harbored a lot of anger for what he perceived as a lack of recognition of his early fame.

I must confess I had to agree with Rudy. He was indeed being ignored. His record as a radio pioneer seemed little appreciated. I did all I could to sympathize, but my concern didn't always chase the clouds away.

We spent another wedding anniversary at Lake Tahoe, reliving our fateful meeting at King's Beach and enjoying Cal-Neva Lodge. In my scrapbook—yes, I kept a few, too—are most of the sentimental cards and love notes Rudy and I exchanged. I still get a kick out of reading the silly phrases we signed off to each other: "To the one I love, you, you, you, Mr. Wonderful." "I am yours forever, lucky me, loving you, your Rudy." The words are trite, I suppose, but they conveyed all the sentimentality and deep love we still felt for each other even in Rudy's seventh decade.

Rudy joked to the media that our little poodles were eating us out of house and home, and that's why he stayed on the road. But in truth he believed he still had a lot to offer audiences. At nearly eighty, his mind was as active as a volcano, developing new ideas for scripts, films, books, and shows. He wrote to many of his illustrious friends, seeking a guest shot, a one-night stand, a TV series, or a movie.

One letter went to Fred Silverman, asking for Johnny Carson's show if Johnny were to quit, warning Fred not to give it to "that pompous narcissistic Tom Snyder."

Frank Bresee, then president of Pacific Pioneer Broadcasters, invited Rudy to be his first honoree and presented him with a gold-plated microphone. "People would not have listened to the radio back in the early days, if it had not been for Rudy Vallée," Frank told me. "He made it all happen. He introduced countless songs to the airwaves."

Rudy also contacted booking agents, some of whom were young and had never heard of him. You can imagine how heartbreaking that was for my husband; he felt an entire segment of American entertainment history had been lost.

As the pendulum of Rudy Vallée's career wound down, the demand for his appearances decreased dramatically. Realizing his popularity was at an all-time low, the former idol worked up vaudeville routines and renewed efforts for bookings. But by the late 1970s, Rudy Vallée's talents for song, comedy, saxophone, and leading an orchestra were in demand only at charity functions and small clubs or for an occasional television appearance.

Once or twice a month Rudy found a theater club out of state for his one-man show, and he couldn't wait to start packing. When he was away, the weekly avalanche of letters told me in detail all about his hotel room: "one chair, no TV"; or about the club pianist: "so god-damned loud and awful" or "terrific!!!" He'd tell me about his driving ability at seventy-seven years old: "no accidents today." Rudy always included amusing showbiz gossip in his letters: "one of the musician's poodles is in heat." He usually ended with "Miss you . . . miss you . . . miss you . . . love you! Can't wait to get home and make love to you."

There were some wonderful surprises. A single booking in Minneapolis paid my husband $7,000 for a one-hour appearance; Dick and Pat Nixon invited us to the western White House to celebrate the tenth anniversary of man's first moonwalk. And when Rudy and I appeared at Les Mouches on Manhattan's 26th Street, Mayor Koch joined us for the opening night.

However, too often Rudy's shows were charity benefits or performances at small clubs. Checks tended to bounce, or managers neglected to pay us at all. This wasn't always the case, of course, but too often it was deliberate. When Rudy threatened to sue the Hickory Hill Country Club in Totawa, New Jersey, for nonpayment, the club manager claimed, "Mr. Vallée embarrassed the club audience. . . . He cursed." It was interesting to me that the *Newark Star-Ledger* newspaper sent along a reviewer to see that same show at the Hickory. She reported: "The show was absolutely hysterical. I don't ever remember laughing so long and hard at anything."

Even better was when Rudy appeared for a week at the Queen Mary Dinner Playhouse in Long Beach, where he was introduced by Mickey Rain each night. The *Los Angeles Times* cheered us up by raving, "Vallée at Peak of His Form" and stating the one-man show was "outrageous, eccentric and memorable . . . and a once-in-a-lifetime opportunity."

The truth is, Rudy performed tongue-in-cheek much of the time. He liked to test audiences by shocking them. He did it everywhere, at friends' homes and in public places. Sometimes he'd try to shock people at our parties. Those who didn't know him took it all very seriously, but most realized it was his own special sense of humor. Rudy felt that if you failed to understand his occasionally bawdy brand of humor or his tongue-in-cheek banter, it wasn't his fault.

"He was one of the funniest and kindest men I knew," remembers my brother-in-law, Gil. "Conversations with Rudy were always lively. He'd take an opposing side during a discussion, even if he didn't believe in it, just to keep it going or test your intellect. And watch out if you thought you'd beaten him in an argument! He once kept me up till 4:00 A.M. trying to prove a point."

Betty and Gil told me they always knew my marriage to Rudy would last, in spite of the age difference. "Your love for each other was so evident," Betty said many years later, "we had no doubt you'd be together for life, like us."

"More champagne, darling?" Rudy, elegant in the lavender silk pajamas I'd bought for his seventy-ninth birthday, held up the magnum, leaning across the ivory satin sheets that covered our enormous bed.

I shook my head and lounged back against the cushioned headboard. "Still plenty of bubbles left," I replied, smiling at the man I had adored for so many years. "Just like our life."

"I've been so lucky," said Rudy. "What a life of stardom!" Then, with a typical Vallée turnaround, he snapped, "But it's been darned difficult sometimes!"

At his tone, our toy poodles, silver-grey Michelle and snow white Pepe, raised their heads. Rudy swung his feet to the floor and walked over to check the camera sitting on a tripod, its lens facing us. He paused and looked out through the mansion's Spanish-style windows to catch a glimpse of the city lights twinkling far below, then came back to the bed, carefully arranged himself on the pillows, and handed me a copy of his autobiography, *Let the Chips Fall*.

"Come on, Ellie! Smile for the camera! Fluff out that gorgeous red hair! Hold up the champagne! Make sure the book title is showing! My name's still worth something, you know," said Rudy.

"Did you set the timer?"

"Yes!" he replied testily. "Smile! Smile!"

Click.

This particular December Rudy decided that the Vallées' Christmas card would be a color photo that said it all, to sum up our life together: glamorous, successful, and enjoying the fruits of Rudy's incredible career. So here we were, sitting on satin sheets, sipping champagne, and smiling for the camera.

We usually created amusing Christmas cards to illustrate our year. Once we used a photo of myself in a Chinese coolie hat struggling to pull Rudy along in a rickshaw in Hong Kong; during the *How to Succeed* era, we showed Rudy and me on the phone saying, "Tickets to *what* show?"

Dreaming up our annual Christmas card was a lot of fun. One of my favorites early in our marriage was a cartoon of a couple in a convertible lost on a back road in the mountains, trying to read a map. This summed up our life on the road accurately—we were often on the wrong road. A later card showed us loading up the luggage carrier for yet another tour. When we came back from our first trip to Bermuda together, we had a photo of Rudy in his trademark shorts playing the sax on a bicycle, while I sat on the dock gazing up at him, the sun glinting on my gold Lurex swimsuit.

In 1971, Harry Neigher, one of the East Coast's legendary newspaper reporters, wrote a column consisting almost entirely of celebrity names who sent him Christmas cards. Ours was the only one that Harry picked to illustrate the piece. It showed us in front of our stone fireplace at Silver Tip. In the early '80s, our Christmas greeting was a photo of Rudy and me riding in a red Cadillac down Hollywood Boulevard in the Hollywood Celebrity Christmas Parade. Rudy was one of the first celebrities to be invited to ride in Hollywood's inaugural Christmas Parade, and we were invited back every year thereafter to share in the tradition. It was great fun. If we had houseguests, they'd ride along in the limo with us, and we had armloads of poodles, too.

Unfortunately, Johnny Grant, a new parade organizer came along, and "dis-invited" many of the stars important to Hollywood, including Rudy. As the longest living Hollywood residents active within the community, Rudy and I were really upset. Many other stars moved away to Bel Air or Beverly Hills but not the Vallées or the LaLannes.

My favorite Christmas card of all was a portrait of us both, our heads turned toward each other, smiling fondly. The original oil painting hangs in my bedroom. I have kept up the Christmas card tradition we established during our marriage. My 1993 Christmas greeting shows me seated alone at my swimming pool in California, and in 1994, in front of my Christmas tree, hugging the only dog I had left, Ginger. But even Ginger is gone now, and I'm comforted by a fluffy little white poodle I call Princess Valentine, who was given to me by actor Byron Clark. Princess is pictured with me in my 1995 Christmas card at our new home in Beverly Hills.

On his eightieth birthday on July 28, 1981, Rudy declared he had three dreams. "I want to take my one-man show to Broadway, Ellie, make an album of my twenty-five top hits, and write another book." He also wanted to star in a TV series he was thinking of developing. "I'll call it *The Scold*, and it'll be a sort of Supreme Court of the air with Richard Nixon, Bella Abzug, Gore Vidal, William Buckley, and myself as chief justice. Believe me, it would be a hit!"

With eight decades behind him, the birthday celebrations I arranged for Rudy were the occasion for international media attention, with requests for interviews from Japan, Australia, India, Canada, Britain, and Singapore.

Mertice Rubinoff, who was now working as a publicist, spent a month with me planning the tribute. We were rewarded by a week-long stream of reporters, photographers, and TV crews making their way up to our hilltop home, including Kelly Lange, a TV newscaster and neighbor, who did an in-depth interview. The television networks taped Rudy playing tennis, while *U.S. News and World Report* newsmagazine caught him in a more serious moment touring his archives.

In addition to the hundreds of birthday cards, we received a flood of congratulatory telegrams. Lloyd Bridges wrote: "Sorry we can't be there. Dorothy and I are proud to know you. Truly a remarkable man." Vic Bergeron's greeting was true to form: "Congratulations, you old fart." Phyllis Diller reminisced in her telegram: "Dearest Rudy, it must have been 1934 or earlier when I first got hooked on your voice. Once a week I glued my ear to the Atwater Kent and thought about breathing in your ear."

Diane Ladd sent along a lyric she'd composed; Paul Keyes wrote: "I hope you live forever and that the last voice you hear will be mine"; Frank Sinatra telegraphed: "As you celebrate your eightieth, I am performing in Bophuthatswana, Southern Africa"; and Barry Goldwater wrote: "Thank you for all the happiness you have brought Americans."

Among Rudy's old friends who sent congratulations were Dick Clark, Earl "Madman" Muntz, Dave Rubinoff, Stan Popeil, and half of Hollywood.

Vanloads of gifts poured into the house: tennis balls, crazy hats, and magic tricks, the kinds of offerings Rudy reveled in. More than six hundred guests wandered throughout the estate and it seemed the celebration went on for days. Rudy posed for pictures on the patio, at the pool, inside the house, outside the house, and even in his bathroom—he showed journalists the Grecian Formula #16 he used for years to touch up his gray hair. But one gift Rudy yearned for never materialized. Los Angeles mayor Sam Yorty suggested changing the name of Pyramid Place, the street we lived on, to Rue de Vallée. (While the name change would be a tribute to Rudy, the main reason was that there were two similar street names, Pyramid Place and Pyramid Drive; Sam frequently got lost on his way to our home.)

There were only a few other houses besides ours on Pyramid Place, and the owners appeared to have no objections. When the matter was brought up to Councilman John Ferraro at Los Angeles City Hall, we expected an easy approval. We had always chosen to remain in Hollywood and we were among the longest bona fide residents. Surely this was one big argument in our favor.

I'd forgotten, though, that everything Rudy was involved in seemed to turn into a mountain of problems. This project was no exception. Initially the City Council appeared to be on our side, but Councilman Robert Stevenson was up for re-election, and according to news reports, he was the subject of an investigation. To create a smokescreen, it seems that Stevenson made the street name change, which he was against, a big issue. Rudy went to the press to state his case, and the controversy made headlines all over the world. In the end, the street name change was voted down. Soon thereafter, Stevenson died.

We were amused, however, to see that the publishers of the *Thomas Street Guide* for Los Angeles jumped the gun. In every subsequent edition, the map shows the street name "Rue de Vallée" with the notation that it is a private road. Now that Stevenson has gone to meet his Maker, perhaps it is time to officially recognize Pyramid Place as Rue de Vallée.

Another interesting episode stands out for me that year. Rudy was approached to invest in a "pure drinking water" venture to manufacture distilling machines. After doing some research, he sent out a flurry of letters to friends, touting the product. But most people, like Art Linkletter, responded by passing on the proposal. Undaunted, Rudy wrote to multimillionaire oil baron Armand Hammer, suggesting he "open a chain of shops in Russia dedicated to helping human beings whip the polluted water problem," but to no avail.

Rudy's attention, however, was quickly diverted to other matters—he was about to be honored in New Orleans—and he forgot all about purifying the planet's drinking water. Larry Smith, a Louisiana attorney and Captain of the Bards of Bohemia, which helped run the Mardi Gras, put Rudy's name up for an award. The "Great American Award" is given each year to a person who contributed to music, to the American way of life, and to charity. Larry knew Rudy's reputation as a patriotic American and musician and had seen Rudy and me perform in the 1960s at the Roosevelt Hotel's Blue Room.

Rudy loved New Orleans and had played at the Sanger Theater in the mid 1930s. The Krewe honor meant we would lead the 1984 parade, and Rudy decided to make the most of it. The day before the parade, Larry arranged a press conference and arrived wearing a mask—the Captain's identity is secret.

Rudy was asked to make a few comments about being a great American. As Rudy began lambasting President Reagan about the budget and the economy, sweat started running down Larry's neck from under his mask. The rest of us looked at each other in horror. When we got back to the hotel, Larry was a bit upset. "What got into you?"

"Wait until you see the newspapers tomorrow morning," Rudy replied, laughing. "You want publicity for the parade? You've got it." The Mardi Gras and Rudy's remarks about the president made national headlines and TV news all across the country. There was no doubt the nation's eyes were now on New Orleans.

We dressed formally for the big day, with Rudy resplendent in tails, sitting on a float fashioned in the shape of an eagle to represent The Great American. At the Bal Masque that evening, a slide presentation of Rudy's career was a highlight. Rudy was tremendously proud and talked about the tribute for months. The next day, people everywhere along Bourbon Street stopped Rudy for an autograph as we strolled among the shops. At one point a telephone truck stopped in the middle of a street and two young repairmen got out and asked for his autograph. After signing his name, he gave them both a "Gratefully yours, Rudy Vallée" pen.

Larry Smith and his wife, Dianne, became frequent guests and they still visit me. "When I had a business in Los Angeles, I always stayed at Silver Tip," Larry told me on a recent visit. "One night, while I was sleeping, Rudy took my battered old briefcase and transferred my files into a brand new leather case. He had a big heart."

Another New Orleans story Rudy enjoyed telling was when Huey Long came backstage at the Sanger Theater to see him before the show. "I've got laryngitis. I don't know if I can perform tonight," Rudy told Long.

"I've got just the thing." The governor disappeared and came back with a glass full of dark brown liquid in his hand.

"Drink this."

"Within thirty seconds, Ellie, my throat was on fire. I thought it was going to knock me on my ass, but it did the trick. I tried to find out what was in that glass but never could."

The following year, as his birthday approached, Rudy pronounced a total ban on any celebration. I managed to persuade him to have a very small party. "Well, all right. But it has to be really, really small." As most of my friends know, when I plan a party, it just seems to grow. Pretty soon, I realized we'd be quite a large crowd. I didn't, of course, tell Rudy.

In the late afternoon, he decided to visit the Grasshoffs. When Rudy returned a few hours later, our driveway was lined from top to bottom with cars. Without a word, Rudy turned around and went to a double-feature movie, then for a late-night snack, and finally arrived home around 2:00 A.M. The guests missed Rudy, but they'd had a great time, and nothing more was said.

Tributes for Rudy filled 1985. He was crowned "Irishman of the Year" at the Los Angeles St. Patrick's Day Parade, and the American Film Institute inducted him into its Hall of Fame at the Kennedy Center in Washington, D.C. We stayed at the Watergate Hotel over-looking the Mall and the Potomac River. Our nephew, Bill Jr., joined us, along with Peter Craig, his college roommate who was editor of *American Film* magazine.

Washington Mayor Marion Barry declared "Rudy Vallée Day" in the nation's capital and presented my husband with a silk, hand-stitched embroidered jacket.

One of the highlights of the trip was the showing of Rudy's 1942 film, *The Palm Beach Story*, at the Kennedy Center where rock star Linda Nardini serenaded him. Rudy and Linda had recently complet-ed "Girls Talk," a new rock video in which Rudy appeared. Rudy rarely listened to rock and roll music, but Linda's tribute meant a lot. "See, Ellie, there *are* a few young people who know who I am and what I meant to show business." He got such a kick out of the video that when we went to a luncheon in Rudy's honor the next day at Duke Zeibert's restaurant, Rudy played a tape of it. However, his old friend from Catholic University, Reverend Gilbert Hartke, thought it a little loud.

Back home at Silver Tip, Rudy went through the stack of mail that always piled up while we were away. "Ellie, look at this! Ed Lozzi is looking for financial backing to do a Broadway show called *Rudy!*"

Lozzi owned a management and public relations company and his letter said that he believed a major production based on Rudy's life and career would be a hit. The news excited us so much we danced around the red-tiled rotunda and called our director friend, Alex Grasshoff. "Bring Marilyn over. We're celebrating!" Rudy said. Ultimately, nothing came of Lozzi's idea.

Throughout his life, one of my husband's greatest joys was to take visitors through the archives, the long, long halls with floor-to-ceiling shelves brimming with scrapbooks and albums. Some people were persuaded to go on this often three-hour "tour" again and again but were too kind to tell Rudy he was repeating himself.

The BBC in London sent producer Rosemary Wilton and a crew over in 1980 and they spent two days doing the "grand tour" for a four-part series on Hollywood. She had heard of Rudy's archives and believed they would be invaluable for her research. We invited her to stay. Rudy's publicist, Chris Harris, taped the interview and said that my Vagabond Lover spoke so rapidly, recalled so many events, dates, names, and even times of day, Rosemary left with her head spinning.

We never saw the results of that intensive interview. But if it was produced and shown, I'm sure Rudy was front and center, along with his incredible collection of memorabilia.

"Mother, make sure you keep this. I'm going to be very famous one day," said a solemn, ten-year-old Rudy Vallée, handing over his school report card.

Thus began one of the most comprehensive and valuable archives ever amassed by an American entertainer. Rudy's collection, now at the Thousand Oaks Library in California, is a summing up of his life achievements. His scrapbooks, all 553 of them, are meticulously organized complete with indexes. They chronicle many of the era's high points, reflecting his great love of history.

My husband's massive archives are a reflection of the man: a pack rat who saved every document, press clipping, fan letter, telegram, postcard, memento, and photograph. Rudy's favorite shot among all the rare photographs he saved was an x-ray of his impacted wisdom tooth.

There are letters to and from every celebrity in Hollywood— Alan Ladd, Elizabeth Taylor, Katharine Hepburn, Billie Burke, Groucho Marx, Eddie Cantor, Buddy Atkinson, Johnny Carson, and some to the Darby Cleaners asking them to please keep their cleaning machine noise down. A letter from Paul Newman reads: "Yes, I would like the beer stein if you have a chance to send it to me."

Many of the most revealing clues to Rudy's complex and paradoxical character are found in his private correspondence. A liberal on environmental issues, an animal rights supporter, and adamantly opposed to censorship—he supported Hugh Hefner in a court case—Rudy's letters reveal that he nevertheless was a staunch conservative and campaigned for Republican presidential candidates. Yet his personal political views were, like the man, often at odds. Republican Rudy believed in labor unions and was a union supporter.

In my husband's "catacombs" were his trophies; awards; original music arrangements with Rudy's personal notations in the margins; radio scripts; music scores; orchestrations; audio, video, and eight-track cassettes; business and financial correspondence; and personal papers. "Whenever I visited," said Frank Bresee, "he'd pull out drawers and drawers stuffed with letters and notes, but he knew exactly where everything was."

The red, cloth-bound scrapbooks with Rudy's name gold-embossed on each spine were numbered, categorized, and cross-referenced.

Original wax phonographs were arrayed along one wall and opposite, hundreds of seventy-eight-speed phonograph records in storage albums.

The radio program scripts were organized by date in eighteen file drawers, while his audio tape copies of radio transcriptions occupied nine linear feet. The several book introductions he wrote for celebrities and musicians, book manuscripts, joke and routine books, and the dozens of notebooks of our tours together occupied the rest of the space.

Walter Scharf, now semiretired, was an occasional visitor. Rudy often told me he thought Walter was a genius at the piano and a brilliant composer. Rudy liked taking him down to the archives because patient Walter, who'd known Rudy since the 1930s, could reminisce about the early days with him. "Rudy and I would talk for an hour about a single piece of 1934 sheet music he'd take from his files," Walter said. "His memory was incredible."

The letters Rudy treasured from Presidents Hoover, Nixon, Kennedy, Reagan, and Bush were filed neatly away. At times Rudy complained. "I'm buried under an avalanche of papers, Ellie. What shall I do?"

"I'll sort it out for you, darling."

"Alright, but I don't want anyone touching anything."

"Of course not, dear." And off he'd go until he remembered to tell me about it again.

Rudy was a keen and vocal observer of the political scene. He carried on an active if sporadic correspondence with various presidents, senators, and representatives, expressing his views. Among his archives are letters to and from Lyndon B. Johnson regarding a proposed military bill; to John F. Kennedy and Robert F. Kennedy referencing the Popeil Brothers; and several between Rudy and George Bush, Ronald Reagan, and Richard Nixon. He also wrote to Mrs. Walter Mondale, urging her to tell her husband not to smile quite so often when on television.

At times Rudy offered to hit the campaign trail for someone he respected, as he did for Nixon and Reagan. "I realize," wrote Richard Nixon on January 19, 1961, thanking Rudy for campaigning for him, "how much easier it would be for someone in your position to avoid taking sides on controversial questions which might adversely affect the popularity which is so essential for continued success in your chosen profession . . ."

In a lengthy debate on the economy conducted by mail with Barry Goldwater in 1976, Rudy received this warning in a letter from the Arizona senator: "Within five years this country is going to be in very, very difficult straits. We could even have a bankrupt economy and a vastly changed government. We have to keep Carter from becoming president. I'm backing Ford."

Rudy's natural talent for debate—he often said he'd have studied law if he hadn't chosen music—was well tested when we campaigned for Richard Nixon. Rudy appeared opposite David Susskind on *The Merv Griffin Show* and told viewers in authoritative terms Nixon was the most qualified man for the presidency. Many credited Rudy for Dick's heavy voter turnout in Hollywood.

Rudy considered himself one of America's great patriots. In 1983 he telegraphed Senator Alan Cranston: "Please head congressional challenge unless Gromyko personally apologizes on TV camera for daring to even suggest that the U.S. deliberately arranged for the plane with sixty Americans to be shot down."

Cranston replied: "I, too, am deeply outraged and disgusted."

In 1980 George Bush wrote: "Dear Rudy, I welcome your support, even though it will doubtless cause some people to suspect a Yale conspiracy to seize the White House. Therefore, please discourage all speculation that I have already asked you to sing 'The Whiffenpoof Song' at my Inauguration. Looking forward to seeing you and thanking you in person." Another note read: "Thanks for your amusing letter and for the tape, which was the hit of the White House."

During the Watergate hearings, Rudy remained a firm supporter of his friend, Richard Nixon. In 1967 Dick wrote to Rudy: "Several friends have called me with reports of how you came to my defense on *The Merv Griffin Show*. I have asked my aide, Pat Buchanan, to write you a brief note with any help he can provide for your idea."

Rudy took pride in his loyalties and was appreciative years later when Tom Duggan commented in his column: "Rudy Vallée was a friend of Dick Nixon during Dick's darkest days." One of the last letters we received from Richard Nixon was a scrawled, handwritten note dated May 5, 1981, from the Nixon's apartment in New York: "Please let us know the next time you are back this way. We would enjoy a visit. With warm regards." The final communication came in 1986: "Dear Ellie, I was very distressed to hear about Rudy's operation. I would be delighted to do a television tape for your film on Rudy. John Taylor from my office will be in touch. Pat joins me in sending our very best wishes."

One morning, when we were in Valley Forge, we picked up

the newspaper and read: "Rudy Vallée Wants U.S. Senate Seat." *The New York Times* reported that Rudy wanted to "clean up the mess in the Pentagon." In June of that year we received a letter from Nixon, thanking Rudy for the comedy material he sent along to help Dick liven things up at the San Francisco Republican convention.

Rudy did consider running for office as Mayor of Los Angeles. He was intrigued by the idea and we mulled it around for a couple of months. We had banners and posters printed up to hang all over Silver Tip. Rudy had meetings with advisors, many of whom were fraternity brothers. They warned Rudy if he took office he would have to learn how to compromise, which was not one of Rudy's best characteristics. Finally, Rudy made his decision and came up with two good reasons to decline. "Ellie, I can't run against the incumbent mayor, he's a fraternity brother." Rudy was referring to Norris Poulson. "Besides, you know I never rise before noon. What would the administration say?"

That same week we attended a Christmas party at Abner and Marie England's. The Nixons were guests, too. We assured them Rudy was not going to run for mayor, governor, or even president, and we shared a good laugh.

The following year, 1966, we spent part of our free time campaigning on behalf of Ronald Reagan for governor of California. He wrote us a note of appreciation: "I have no words to express how deeply grateful I am for what you have done. If ever there was a team victory, this was it and I have some understanding of the price you were willing to pay to be on the team. . . . Nancy and I will have memories to treasure for a lifetime, thanks to you. . . . Best regards, Ronald Reagan."

When Rudy found it difficult to sleep, he'd get up in the middle of the night, pour himself a glass of sherry, and start pounding the typewriter. His desk occupied a large corner in the archives office. Floor-length windows gave him a view of the huge sandstone rockface from which the building was carved, and the office walls were lined with bookshelves. His L-shaped desk was completely covered with piles of papers, clippings, gadgets, souvenirs, and books. A large sign next to the typewriter admonished Rudy to "THINK."

He loved writing letters and often sent out as many as ten or twelve a day. Rudy considered himself a master analyst of human behavior and wrote his opinions to those he believed deserved them. Some of Rudy's letters became legendary. A literary purist, he felt compelled to correct other people's grammar, believing he was being helpful. He wrote with withering contempt to Walter Cronkite, Connie Chung, and other newscasters suggesting they change their prose and pronunciation. Connie replied: "If half our staff pronounced the capital of Iran 'Teheran' and the other half 'Tehran,' it would be very confusing . . ."

To NBC's Kelly Lange, he admonished: "Don't say 'people' when you really mean 'persons.'"

While corresponding about diction with Gerald and Esta Brown of Two Buttes, Colorado, Gerald analyzed Rudy's over-sized, looping handwriting. He said Rudy's large flourishes showed self-confidence; the high loops showed idealism; the plainness of the capital letters indicated his love of language; and the expanded lower loops showed imagination. All of this, in my opinion, was perfectly correct.

When Rudy replied to friends' letters, he invariably went off into reminiscences, straying from the subject as he recalled his early times together with the writer, or pointing out where his career led at the time. Right to the end, Rudy's memory was extraordinary. He remembered every detail of every day from the time he was two, complete with word-for-word conversations, and the exact places they occurred.

Occasionally my husband's remembrances revived the anger he felt at the time, even if it was fifty years ago, and he repeated the same fiery language he used then. Whether this was good therapy or not, all I can say is I knew very little of this correspondence. Otherwise there are some friends I could not have faced, had I known.

After Rudy died, several of his films were acquired by the University of California at Los Angeles and some of his memorabilia went to the University of Maine. But most of the four-ton collection was sold to the Thousand Oaks Library. Archivist Martin Getzler is still cataloging the vast Rudy Vallée Collection, ten years later.

THIRTEEN

Rudy's Voice Is Stilled

"Ellie, there's a box of tennis gear down here on the stairs. Where does it belong?"

"Up here, dear."

"I'll bring it up in a moment."

We'd just finished playing a match with Alex Grasshoff and other friends. I went upstairs to get dressed for a dinner at Chasen's to honor George Burns.

The next thing I heard was a scream. I ran out onto the terrace and looked down the stairs to see Rudy sprawled on the tiles. He'd tripped coming up the stairs, carrying the box. Rudy's head was bleeding. I helped him up, and Marilyn Grasshoff and I drove him directly to Cedars-Sinai Medical Center. All the way there, and even while the doctors sewed up his head injury, Rudy was telling jokes and singing snatches of songs.

Five days later we went to our own doctor, Dr. Gerald Labiner, to have the stitches removed. "Well, Rudy, your head's healing nicely," he said. "But you know, you're voice sounds strange. Let me take a look." After a slight pause, the Dr. Labiner said, "I'm sending you back to Cedars-Sinai for an x-ray of your throat."

Rudy was diagnosed with cancer of the esophagus. Our friend, Dr. Marvin Jensen, myself, and everyone we knew begged Rudy not to have surgery.

"The cancer could remain just as it is for many, many years," Marvin told Rudy. "If you have the operation, you could risk spreading the disease or having a stroke. The tumor is in the most difficult area to get at, behind the heart. Rudy, you're eighty-four years old. You've had a marvelous life. Enjoy the rest of it as you are."

Rudy had just performed at Queen's Cafe, a small, neighborhood Chinese restaurant on Melrose Avenue. He'd met the owners somewhere and promised them a show. He played the sax, told his jokes, and put on a slide show. It was, as it turned out, his final performance.

"Rudy, dearest, please, please don't have the operation," I begged. But he was insistent.

Dr. Jensen checked Rudy into the Pasadena hospital for a week of tests, putting his own limo and driver at my disposal as I went back and forth to see Rudy. I brought him books, home-cooked meals including "Ellie's Meat Loaf" and lamb stew, and ran his errands.

Then I had my own crisis. We had two youths working for us at Silver Tip. While I was busy with Rudy, they took off in his beloved station wagon.

During the testing, Rudy remembered he'd invited some guests home to see his one-man show. The hospital was not willing to discharge him, so he simply dressed, walked out, and took a cab home. That's my Rudy!

On February 11 we drove to Cedars-Sinai Medical Center for the operation. Before the surgery, he wanted to make out his will. We asked Joanne Kosrog and Timmie Masters to witness it. In a wavery script on a single sheet of his personal letterhead imprinted with a few bars of music from "My Time Is Your Time" at the top, Rudy wrote that I was to inherit his entire estate.

Actually, the will read more like a diary, filled with fascinating facts and colorful details that Rudy had uncovered about the doctors:

"This is my last testament and will. Tomorrow morning at

Cedars-Sinai Hospital, I am going to be taken down to the seventh floor intensive care room of this hospital, and at nine o'clock a team of three surgeons and two anesthesiologists will prepare me for the removal of a very small but cancerous tumor now lodged in the esophagus. This is a very difficult and long operation. This team is three of the best: two, father and son, are chest men, and Dr. Epstein will cut out the portion in which the small tumor is lodged. He has done the sewing of the end of the esophagus to the stomach valve six times. I have gone through so many tests, they are all optimistic of my survival . . ."

Rudy came through the thirteen-hour operation with flying colors. During the lengthy ordeal, my girlfriends Virginia Carey, Joanne Kosrog, Loralee Knotts, Stella Atkinson, Joy Claussen, Marilyn Grasshoff, Cathy Singer, Ruth Lamport, and Timmie Masters took turns staying with me.

A week later, still in his hospital bed, Rudy was inadvertently given a medication that he was allergic to, and he suffered a stroke.

My husband stayed at Cedars-Sinai for six months while the medical staff worked to rehabilitate him. Sometimes he didn't recognize me. It was terrible. But therapy helped.

Anxious to keep busy from his hospital bed, even at age eighty-four, Rudy dictated several letters to me. One of the first was to a friend from Yale, David Randolph Milsten, an attorney in Tulsa, who had written asking for Red Buttons' address. In reply Rudy wrote: "I have to get out and entertain. I'm hoping that about forty of my big record hits (these are priceless and I should sell at least two million of them if I get the right distribution and advertising from the right live company) will enable me to give Ellie a million dollars to assuage her worry if I die."

Wondering how I would manage to care for Rudy, I explored the idea of putting him in a Catholic home and invited two of the nuns to meet him. As they approached his hospital bed Rudy found his voice. Unfortunately, he hadn't forgotten a single swear word. "What the hell are they doing here? Godammit, get the hell out of here!" The nuns hurriedly left. They phoned me later.

"Mrs. Vallée, we'd love to take Rudy in, but his language would upset the priests and the other patients."

Finally, I was told Rudy was ready to leave the hospital. I could hardly wait for the big day. But I was in for one more shock before leaving the hospital. "I'm taking my husband, Rudy Vallée, home today. Is there a bill to be paid?" I asked at the nurse's reception desk.

"Oh sure, Mrs. Vallée. We have it all ready for you." I was handed a thick wad of papers. Searching for the grand total, I finally found it—for one million dollars—and promptly fainted. Fortunately, Rudy's medical insurance covered the entire bill.

Revived, I tucked the papers away, anxious to keep them from Rudy. I had hired Carl, a male therapist, to stay with us at Silver Tip. The two of us got Rudy dressed, out of the hospital, and into the ambulance for the ride home.

I was tremendously excited to finally have my darling husband back with me once again. And I anticipated how thrilled he'd be at seeing Silver Tip, and his friends and doggies. Marilyn had brought brightly colored balloons, and Iona Sturdza, from Romania, was among those who greeted him.

As Rudy was wheeled through the front door, the balloons began exploding, the dogs barked and jumped excitedly onto Rudy's lap, and the phonograph blared out "The Stein Song" at full blast. It was too much. Rudy clutched his chest and suffered a severe anxiety attack. Within an hour, he was back in the hospital.

Fortunately, Rudy's stay this time was a lot shorter, and I made sure his next homecoming would be a quiet one. I must admit I was very anxious. I had no idea how to take care of a sick person. When his mind was clear, Rudy was a perfect patient; when it wasn't, he could be difficult.

When he refused to let me or anyone else cut his hair, my friend, Monique Fisher, dressed up in a cute little miniskirt and put on a blond wig. We convinced Rudy she was a hair stylist. He let Monique give him a decent haircut. It was so sad I had to play little tricks like that.

After eleven days, Carl came to me. "Mrs. Vallée, can I have a day off?"

"Oh no," I said, panicked, "You can't leave me alone here. I need you. You can't take any days off at all." I must have sounded ridiculous to the poor man. I was so nervous about making a mistake with Rudy and sending him back to the hospital that I offered to pay Carl double his salary if he would give up days off.

Two months later Rudy and I received an invitation from Ronald Reagan to be his special guest at the unveiling of the refurbished Statue of Liberty during America's birthday celebrations. But we both knew Rudy would never leave Silver Tip again.

"Rudy? Are you awake, dear?" I walked quietly over to the wheelchair. Rudy sat next to the massive fieldstone fireplace where Hollywood's greatest stars once gathered. He slowly raised his head.

My husband now spent his time here, immobile, staring out at our panoramic view of Los Angeles and the film studios below where he'd starred in *I Remember Mama* and *The Palm Beach Story*.

During the last days of his life, Danny Newman and Bud Testa, his tennis buddies, helped me wheel Rudy to the estate's lower building to watch friends play tennis on the rooftop court. Other times I'd bring up a scrapbook from the archives, and we'd reminisce.

As evening fell on July 3, 1986, Rudy said nothing. The voice that had thrilled millions was momentarily silent. I didn't know that by the next day the voice would be silent forever. "I'll play some of your music, Rudy. Would you like to hear 'The Stein Song'? Or 'The Whiffenpoof Song'?" The slender fingers that had coaxed magic from his saxophone stroked the blue cashmere blanket I'd put around his shoulders.

"Where's my Waring blender?" he asked querulously.

His blender? I hadn't seen it in months. Maybe I'd thrown it out.

Rudy managed a weak smile. "Come on, Buttercup. Find the blender and we'll have a party." It was heartbreaking to see my brave husband still fighting fiercely to hold on to life.

Ever since I'd brought him home from the hospital for the second time, Rudy had tried to resume a normal life. Jack and Elaine LaLanne, Morey Amsterdam, Don Knotts, Stella and Buddy Atkinson, Beverley and Buddy Rogers, and many other longtime friends visited to cheer him up.

They sat patiently beside Rudy and watched his favorite videos, listened to his old radio shows, and talked over old times. Once an icon, an entertainer who crammed six careers into one, a celebrity among celebrities, rich in fame and women, he was finally nearing the end. I knew beyond any doubt that the Rudy Vallée name now belonged to a bygone era.

"Rudy, I'll find the blender," I said, tears blurring my eyes.

Toward noon we settled down in front of the television to watch the festivities in New York harbor in honor of America's birthday. "There's Ron," whispered Rudy, pointing to President Reagan. Rudy gripped my hand.

"Wouldn't it be fun to be there, Ellie? You know how I love a party!" As the last word left his lips, Rudy's head fell to the side. The husband I adored was gone.

Epilogue

fter Rudy's death, there was such an outpouring of affection, praise, and sympathy, I was moved beyond words. In a private telegram from the Reagans, addressed to "Silver Tip, 7430 Rue de Vallée, Hollywood," the president said he mourned the loss of "an American institution."

President Reagan issued a press statement released by White House spokesman Larry Speakes: "He was a dedicated patriot who interrupted his career to serve in the U.S. Coast Guard, and it was appropriate that Rudy's last moments were spent watching the illumination of the Statue of Liberty. The music of Rudy Vallée will be part of American culture for generations to come."

When Dorothy Lamour heard of Rudy's death, she said that she "remembered how good he was to me. He was very instrumental in any success I might have had in the business."

And from Jane Russell: "I'll miss that encyclopedia memory of his."

Alan Thicke wrote, "I will never forget the generosity, hospitality, and kindness you both showed me a few years ago." Sidney Sheldon commented: "He was quite wonderful in the part he played in *The Bachelor and the Bobbysoxer*. I wish I had known him better."

Frank Sinatra wrote he was shocked to hear of Rudy's death, adding: "I want you to know you have been in my prayers ever since." Marie Windsor and her husband, Jack Hupp, telegraphed: "We are so sorry you have lost your amazing and wonderful fellow. You helped him so much to enjoy a long and eventful life." Tiny Tim said: "Sincerest sympathy on the passing away of . . . the world's greatest crooner."

Civic offices throughout California closed in Rudy's memory and flags dropped to half-mast. The County of Los Angeles adjourned its Board of Supervisors meeting; the California Senate adjourned its session on July 7 in memory of Rudy Vallée. There were several other tributes to Rudy. I had a memorial service at St. Charles Catholic Church in North Hollywood, and Paul Caruso held a service at his home.

Monique Fisher and I carried my husband's ashes to Maine for burial next to his mother, father, and brother Billy in St. Hyacinth's Cemetery. The services were led by Monsignor Brian Keleher, Rudy's stepnephew, and the Coast Guard and U.S. Navy were represented. As I stood hand-in-hand with my sister-in-law, Dorothy Vallée, and her son, Bill Jr., listening to a lone bugler play the Sailor's Hymn, we were overcome with grief.

Rudy's devoted fan, Norman Ostrowski, and his wife, Rose, made the trip by cab all the way from Albany to Bangor to attend the memorial service. It cost them two hundred dollars and took seven and a half hours.

"He was the greatest," Norman said, wiping away tears. "I first listened to Rudy Vallée on a crystal radio set in 1929. I saw him in person at a concert in New Brunswick, Canada, in 1949." Norm finally met his idol in 1967. Rudy and I enjoyed our friendship with the Ostrowskis and often had them for a visit to Silver Tip.

At the end of the funeral service, a squad of Coast Guard riflemen fired a three-volley salute, then presented me with the American flag that had covered his ashes.

In the years since, there have been many tributes to Rudy Vallée. One he would have loved was a 1988 week-long event hosted by the University of Maine at its Museum of Maine. The schedule included screenings of seven of Rudy's most successful films, a series of lectures on Rudy Vallée's music titled, "The Making of an American Sound," and a presentation by Frank Bresee of Rudy's records, films, and television shows. The museum opened a Rudy Vallée wing with a ribbon-cutting by Rudy's nephew, Bill Jr.

Another compliment Rudy would have valued greatly was Don Freeman's column six days after Rudy's death: "I was interviewing Sinatra [who] said at one point, 'I learned enunciation by listening to Rudy Vallée. You have to remember that Rudy was a Yale man and I was a dese-dem-and-dose guy from New Jersey. I had a lot to learn.'" But the accolade Rudy wanted more than anything else eluded him: a television special on his lifetime of performing.

When Rudy died in 1986, he left only Silver Tip, the beloved pink castle in the Hollywood hills, and his precious memorabilia. I had to sell the house. It was heartbreaking. All those memories, that wonderful over-sized, romantic French bed.

Years before, Johnny Carson predicted, "One day I'm going to own this house, Rudy," but it didn't happen. We finally found a buyer. Talk show host Arsenio Hall bought the historic mansion. And promptly tore it down.

Today, there is a small pile of rubble where Silver Tip once proudly stood. The view is as glorious as ever over the canyons, down into the valleys, and across to the Pacific Ocean. The film studios sit below; the stone pillars marking the driveway stand silent sentinel. But there is nothing to indicate Rudy Vallée lived there. Not even on the name of the street.

Soon, I built a beautiful new, Spanish-style villa high on a mountaintop above Los Angeles and named it "Villa Eleanor," where I live with my little French poodle, Princess Valentine.

Creating a new picture gallery along the upstairs hall, I have filled it with personal photos of Rudy and all our friends and relatives. On my bedroom dresser are the pair of gold cufflinks I gave Rudy on the opening night of *How to Succeed*. Occasionally I come across one of the miniature flashlights or pens he gave away, engraved with "In appreciation, Rudy Vallée."

I keep busy with volunteer work for the Muscular Dystrophy Association and the Motion Picture Home. In 1992, the Joseph and Mary League was kind enough to vote me "Woman of the Year."

On January 13, 1995, during their international film festival, Palm Springs paid tribute to Rudy with a ceremony installing the Rudy Vallée Star on their sidewalk "Walk of Stars," adjacent to those for Alice Faye, Buddy Rogers, and Phil Harris. Rudy's star recognizes him in four categories: radio, stage, film, and television, one of only two singers—Frank Sinatra is the other—to be honored as an entertainer in all four disciplines of the performing arts.

During the dedication ceremony, a crowd of three hundred of Rudy's show business friends paid tribute—Tony Curtis, Buddy Rogers, Ginger Rogers, Paul Burke, Howard Keel, Kay Ballard, Paul Henning, Paul Caruso, Patrick McNee, Toni Holt, Joy Claussen, George Montgomery, Ruta Lee, the Grasshoffs, and many others.

I am carrying on Rudy's show business tradition. Currently, Fil Perell and I host a celebrity television talk show on Continental Cable in Los Angeles called "The V.I.P. Show," with announcer and coproducer Byron Clark. Some of the guests have included Los Angeles City Councilman John Ferraro, Oscar-winning producer Marty Pasetta and his wife Elise, and Elaine and Jack LaLanne, among others.

I also appear in plays and work as a volunteer. In 1992 I was elected president of Operation Children. In Los Angeles, I'm a member of the Muscular Dystrophy Association; The Footlighters; the Screen Smart Set for the Motion Picture Home; Lifelighters; Les Dames; and I'm very active in my sorority, Kappa Alpha Theta.

We all appreciated Rudy as a decent, honest, compassionate gentleman who was generous in heart and spirit. One of my favorite stories is when Ken Kosrog overheard Rudy on the telephone:

"Yes, you can buy my saxophone for $600," Rudy said to the caller. "Yes, that's right, $600," he repeated, and hung up the phone.

"Rudy, you can't sell your sax for just $600. It's worth a lot more than that. I'll give you $800 for it right now!"

"Thanks, Ken, but you won't play it, and that young boy from Wisconsin will."

Epilogue

There is more than just an entertainer's life in his legacy. He uplifted Americans during the Great Depression and had an influence on our country's music culture as few others of his era.

Rudy will live on in the annals of radio history as one of the brightest stars in show business. Gone but never forgotten.

Selected Discography

Rudy Vallée recorded approximately 650 songs, many of them with several different arrangements, for a variety of record companies: RCA Victor, Decca, Capitol, Columbia, Crown, Olympic, New World, Sunbeam, Viva, Box Office, United Artists, Unique, and Camden, among others. The following is a selection of some of Rudy's most popular songs:

"The Stein Song"

"The Whiffenpoof Song"

"Deep Night"

"My Time Is Your Time"

"The Vagabond Lover"

"As Time Goes By"

"Alouetta"

"Betty Coed"

"All the Things You Are"

"All Points West"

"Goodnight Sweetheart"

"Winchester Cathedral"

"Would You Like to Take a Walk?"

"You Oughta Be in Pictures"

"Doin' the Raccoon"

"Heigh-Ho, Everybody, Heigh-Ho"

"Vieni, Vieni"

"Sweetheart of all My Dreams"

"The Song I Love"

"Marie"

"Caressing You"

"You'll Do It Someday"

"Makin' Whoopee"

"Outside"

"If I Had You"

"Weary River"

"Lover Come Back to Me"

"A Little Kiss Each Morning"

"St. Louis Blues"

"If I Had a Girl Like You"

"Harbor Lights"

"How Deep Is the Ocean?"

"I Didn't Know What Time It Was"

"If You Were the Only Girl in the World"

"I'll Take Roma"

"Is It True What They Say about Dixie?"

"Besame Mucho"

"Kitty from Kansas City"

"Let's Do It"

"Let's Put Out the Light and Go to Sleep"

"Life Is Just a Bowl of Cherries"

"Mad Dogs and Englishmen"

"My Blue Heaven"

"Temptation"

"Nasty Man"

"A Pretty Girl Is Like a Melody"

"Beer Barrel Polka"

"Say It Isn't So"

"Star Dust"

"Strangers in the Night"

"These Foolish Things"

"The Way You Look Tonight"

"When Yuba Plays the Rumba on the Tuba"

"Who"

Filmography

The Vagabond Lover (1929)

Glorifying the American Girl (1930)

International House (1933)

George White's Scandals (1934)

Sweet Music (1935)

Gold Diggers in Paris (1938)

Second Fiddle (1939)

Too Many Blondes (1941)

Time Out for Rhythm (1941)

The Palm Beach Story (1942)

Happy Go Lucky (1943)

Man Alive (1945)

It's in the Bag (1945)

People Are Funny (1946)

The Fabulous Suzanne (1946)

Sin of Harold Diddlebock (1947)

The Bachelor and the Bobbysoxer (1947)

Unfaithfully Yours (1948)

So This Is New York (1948)

I Remember Mama (1948)

My Dear Secretary (1949)

Mother Is a Freshman (1949)

Father Was a Fullback (1949)

The Beautiful Blonde from Bashful Bend (1949)

Mad Wednesday (1950)

The Admiral Was a Lady (1950)

Ricochet Romance (1954)

Gentlemen Marry Brunettes (1955)

Jazz Ball (1956)

TV Variety, Vol. 10 (1958)

The Helen Morgan Story (1959)

On Broadway Tonight (1964)

How to Succeed in Business without Really Trying (1967)

The Night They Raided Minsky's (1968)

Live a Little, Love a Little (1968)

The Phynx (1970)

Slashed Dreams (1974)

Sunburst (1975)

Won Ton Ton, the Dog Who Saved Hollywood (1976)

Index